FREE Study Skills Videos, DVD Offer

Dear Customer,

Thank you for your purchase from Mometrix! We consider it an honor and a privilege that you have purchased our product and we want to ensure your satisfaction.

As part of our ongoing effort to meet the needs of test takers, we have developed a set of Study Skills Videos that we would like to give you for FREE. These videos cover our *best practices* for getting ready for your exam, from how to use our study materials to how to best prepare for the day of the test.

All that we ask is that you email us with feedback that would describe your experience so far with our product. Good, bad, or indifferent, we want to know what you think!

To get your FREE Study Skills Videos, you can use the **QR code** below, or send us an **email** at studyvideos@mometrix.com with *FREE VIDEOS* in the subject line and the following information in the body of the email:

- The name of the product you purchased.
- Your product rating on a scale of 1-5, with 5 being the highest rating.
- Your feedback. It can be long, short, or anything in between. We just want to know your impressions and experience so far with our product. (Good feedback might include how our study material met your needs and ways we might be able to make it even better. You could highlight features that you found helpful or features that you think we should add.)

If you have any questions or concerns, please don't hesitate to contact me directly.

Thanks again!

Sincerely,

Jay Willis
Vice President
jay.willis@mometrix.com
1-800-673-8175

Praxis II

Art: Content Knowledge (5134) Exam
Secrets Study Guide

Praxis II Test Review for the
Praxis II: Subject Assessments

Written and edited by Mometrix Test Prep

Printed in the United States of America

This paper meets the requirements of ANSI/NISO Z39.48-1992 (Permanence of Paper).

Mometrix offers volume discount pricing to institutions. For more information or a price quote, please contact our sales department at sales@mometrix.com or 888-248-1219.

Mometrix Media LLC is not affiliated with or endorsed by any official testing organization. All organizational and test names are trademarks of their respective owners.

Paperback
ISBN 13: 978-1-63094-244-1
ISBN 10: 1-63094-244-8

Ebook
ISBN 13: 978-1-5167-0273-2
ISBN 10: 1-5167-0273-5

DEAR FUTURE EXAM SUCCESS STORY

First of all, **THANK YOU** for purchasing Mometrix study materials!

Second, congratulations! You are one of the few determined test-takers who are committed to doing whatever it takes to excel on your exam. **You have come to the right place.** We developed these study materials with one goal in mind: to deliver you the information you need in a format that's concise and easy to use.

In addition to optimizing your guide for the content of the test, we've outlined our recommended steps for breaking down the preparation process into small, attainable goals so you can make sure you stay on track.

We've also analyzed the entire test-taking process, identifying the most common pitfalls and showing how you can overcome them and be ready for any curveball the test throws you.

Standardized testing is one of the biggest obstacles on your road to success, which only increases the importance of doing well in the high-pressure, high-stakes environment of test day. Your results on this test could have a significant impact on your future, and this guide provides the information and practical advice to help you achieve your full potential on test day.

Your success is our success

We would love to hear from you! If you would like to share the story of your exam success or if you have any questions or comments in regard to our products, please contact us at **800-673-8175** or **support@mometrix.com**.

Thanks again for your business and we wish you continued success!

Sincerely,
The Mometrix Test Preparation Team

> **Need more help? Check out our flashcards at:**
> **http://mometrixflashcards.com/PraxisII**

TABLE OF CONTENTS

Introduction

Thank you for purchasing this resource! You have made the choice to prepare yourself for a test that could have a huge impact on your future, and this guide is designed to help you be fully ready for test day. Obviously, it's important to have a solid understanding of the test material, but you also need to be prepared for the unique environment and stressors of the test, so that you can perform to the best of your abilities.

For this purpose, the first section that appears in this guide is the **Secret Keys**. We've devoted countless hours to meticulously researching what works and what doesn't, and we've boiled down our findings to the five most impactful steps you can take to improve your performance on the test. We start at the beginning with study planning and move through the preparation process, all the way to the testing strategies that will help you get the most out of what you know when you're finally sitting in front of the test.

We recommend that you start preparing for your test as far in advance as possible. However, if you've bought this guide as a last-minute study resource and only have a few days before your test, we recommend that you skip over the first two Secret Keys since they address a long-term study plan.

If you struggle with **test anxiety**, we strongly encourage you to check out our recommendations for how you can overcome it. Test anxiety is a formidable foe, but it can be beaten, and we want to make sure you have the tools you need to defeat it.

1

Secret Key #1 – Plan Big, Study Small

There's a lot riding on your performance. If you want to ace this test, you're going to need to keep your skills sharp and the material fresh in your mind. You need a plan that lets you review everything you need to know while still fitting in your schedule. We'll break this strategy down into three categories.

Information Organization

Start with the information you already have: the official test outline. From this, you can make a complete list of all the concepts you need to cover before the test. Organize these concepts into groups that can be studied together, and create a list of any related vocabulary you need to learn so you can brush up on any difficult terms. You'll want to keep this vocabulary list handy once you actually start studying since you may need to add to it along the way.

Time Management

Once you have your set of study concepts, decide how to spread them out over the time you have left before the test. Break your study plan into small, clear goals so you have a manageable task for each day and know exactly what you're doing. Then just focus on one small step at a time. When you manage your time this way, you don't need to spend hours at a time studying. Studying a small block of content for a short period each day helps you retain information better and avoid stressing over how much you have left to do. You can relax knowing that you have a plan to cover everything in time. In order for this strategy to be effective though, you have to start studying early and stick to your schedule. Avoid the exhaustion and futility that comes from last-minute cramming!

Study Environment

The environment you study in has a big impact on your learning. Studying in a coffee shop, while probably more enjoyable, is not likely to be as fruitful as studying in a quiet room. It's important to keep distractions to a minimum. You're only planning to study for a short block of time, so make the most of it. Don't pause to check your phone or get up to find a snack. It's also important to **avoid multitasking**. Research has consistently shown that multitasking will make your studying dramatically less effective. Your study area should also be comfortable and well-lit so you don't have the distraction of straining your eyes or sitting on an uncomfortable chair.

 The time of day you study is also important. You want to be rested and alert. Don't wait until just before bedtime. Study when you'll be most likely to comprehend and remember. Even better, if you know what time of day your test will be, set that time aside for study. That way your brain will be used to working on that subject at that specific time and you'll have a better chance of recalling information.

Finally, it can be helpful to team up with others who are studying for the same test. Your actual studying should be done in as isolated an environment as possible, but the work of organizing the information and setting up the study plan can be divided up. In between study sessions, you can discuss with your teammates the concepts that you're all studying and quiz each other on the details. Just be sure that your teammates are as serious about the test as you are. If you find that your study time is being replaced with social time, you might need to find a new team.

2

Secret Key #2 – Make Your Studying Count

You're devoting a lot of time and effort to preparing for this test, so you want to be absolutely certain it will pay off. This means doing more than just reading the content and hoping you can remember it on test day. It's important to make every minute of study count. There are two main areas you can focus on to make your studying count.

Retention

It doesn't matter how much time you study if you can't remember the material. You need to make sure you are retaining the concepts. To check your retention of the information you're learning, try recalling it at later times with minimal prompting. Try carrying around flashcards and glance at one or two from time to time or ask a friend who's also studying for the test to quiz you.

To enhance your retention, look for ways to put the information into practice so that you can apply it rather than simply recalling it. If you're using the information in practical ways, it will be much easier to remember. Similarly, it helps to solidify a concept in your mind if you're not only reading it to yourself but also explaining it to someone else. Ask a friend to let you teach them about a concept you're a little shaky on (or speak aloud to an imaginary audience if necessary). As you try to summarize, define, give examples, and answer your friend's questions, you'll understand the concepts better and they will stay with you longer. Finally, step back for a big picture view and ask yourself how each piece of information fits with the whole subject. When you link the different concepts together and see them working together as a whole, it's easier to remember the individual components.

Finally, practice showing your work on any multi-step problems, even if you're just studying. Writing out each step you take to solve a problem will help solidify the process in your mind, and you'll be more likely to remember it during the test.

Modality

Modality simply refers to the means or method by which you study. Choosing a study modality that fits your own individual learning style is crucial. No two people learn best in exactly the same way, so it's important to know your strengths and use them to your advantage.

For example, if you learn best by visualization, focus on visualizing a concept in your mind and draw an image or a diagram. Try color-coding your notes, illustrating them, or creating symbols that will trigger your mind to recall a learned concept. If you learn best by hearing or discussing information, find a study partner who learns the same way or read aloud to yourself. Think about how to put the information in your own words. Imagine that you are giving a lecture on the topic and record yourself so you can listen to it later.

For any learning style, flashcards can be helpful. Organize the information so you can take advantage of spare moments to review. Underline key words or phrases. Use different colors for different categories. Mnemonic devices (such as creating a short list in which every item starts with the same letter) can also help with retention. Find what works best for you and use it to store the information in your mind most effectively and easily.

3

Secret Key #3 – Practice the Right Way

Your success on test day depends not only on how many hours you put into preparing, but also on whether you prepared the right way. It's good to check along the way to see if your studying is paying off. One of the most effective ways to do this is by taking practice tests to evaluate your progress. Practice tests are useful because they show exactly where you need to improve. Every time you take a practice test, pay special attention to these three groups of questions:

- The questions you got wrong
- The questions you had to guess on, even if you guessed right
- The questions you found difficult or slow to work through

This will show you exactly what your weak areas are, and where you need to devote more study time. Ask yourself why each of these questions gave you trouble. Was it because you didn't understand the material? Was it because you didn't remember the vocabulary? Do you need more repetitions on this type of question to build speed and confidence? Dig into those questions and figure out how you can strengthen your weak areas as you go back to review the material.

 Additionally, many practice tests have a section explaining the answer choices. It can be tempting to read the explanation and think that you now have a good understanding of the concept. However, an explanation likely only covers part of the question's broader context. Even if the explanation makes perfect sense, **go back and investigate** every concept related to the question until you're positive you have a thorough understanding.

As you go along, keep in mind that the practice test is just that: practice. Memorizing these questions and answers will not be very helpful on the actual test because it is unlikely to have any of the same exact questions. If you only know the right answers to the sample questions, you won't be prepared for the real thing. **Study the concepts** until you understand them fully, and then you'll be able to answer any question that shows up on the test.

It's important to wait on the practice tests until you're ready. If you take a test on your first day of study, you may be overwhelmed by the amount of material covered and how much you need to learn. Work up to it gradually.

On test day, you'll need to be prepared for answering questions, managing your time, and using the test-taking strategies you've learned. It's a lot to balance, like a mental marathon that will have a big impact on your future. Like training for a marathon, you'll need to start slowly and work your way up. When test day arrives, you'll be ready.

Start with the strategies you've read in the first two Secret Keys—plan your course and study in the way that works best for you. If you have time, consider using multiple study resources to get different approaches to the same concepts. It can be helpful to see difficult concepts from more than one angle. Then find a good source for practice tests. Many times, the test website will suggest potential study resources or provide sample tests.

Practice Test Strategy

If you're able to find at least three practice tests, we recommend this strategy:

UNTIMED AND OPEN-BOOK PRACTICE

Take the first test with no time constraints and with your notes and study guide handy. Take your time and focus on applying the strategies you've learned.

TIMED AND OPEN-BOOK PRACTICE

Take the second practice test open-book as well, but set a timer and practice pacing yourself to finish in time.

TIMED AND CLOSED-BOOK PRACTICE

Take any other practice tests as if it were test day. Set a timer and put away your study materials. Sit at a table or desk in a quiet room, imagine yourself at the testing center, and answer questions as quickly and accurately as possible.

Keep repeating timed and closed-book tests on a regular basis until you run out of practice tests or it's time for the actual test. Your mind will be ready for the schedule and stress of test day, and you'll be able to focus on recalling the material you've learned.

Secret Key #4 – Pace Yourself

Once you're fully prepared for the material on the test, your biggest challenge on test day will be managing your time. Just knowing that the clock is ticking can make you panic even if you have plenty of time left. Work on pacing yourself so you can build confidence against the time constraints of the exam. Pacing is a difficult skill to master, especially in a high-pressure environment, so **practice is vital**.

Set time expectations for your pace based on how much time is available. For example, if a section has 60 questions and the time limit is 30 minutes, you know you have to average 30 seconds or less per question in order to answer them all. Although 30 seconds is the hard limit, set 25 seconds per question as your goal, so you reserve extra time to spend on harder questions. When you budget extra time for the harder questions, you no longer have any reason to stress when those questions take longer to answer.

Don't let this time expectation distract you from working through the test at a calm, steady pace, but keep it in mind so you don't spend too much time on any one question. Recognize that taking extra time on one question you don't understand may keep you from answering two that you do understand later in the test. If your time limit for a question is up and you're still not sure of the answer, mark it and move on, and come back to it later if the time and the test format allow. If the testing format doesn't allow you to return to earlier questions, just make an educated guess; then put it out of your mind and move on.

On the easier questions, be careful not to rush. It may seem wise to hurry through them so you have more time for the challenging ones, but it's not worth missing one if you know the concept and just didn't take the time to read the question fully. Work efficiently but make sure you understand the question and have looked at all of the answer choices, since more than one may seem right at first.

Even if you're paying attention to the time, you may find yourself a little behind at some point. You should speed up to get back on track, but do so wisely. Don't panic; just take a few seconds less on each question until you're caught up. Don't guess without thinking, but do look through the answer choices and eliminate any you know are wrong. If you can get down to two choices, it is often worthwhile to guess from those. Once you've chosen an answer, move on and don't dwell on any that you skipped or had to hurry through. If a question was taking too long, chances are it was one of the harder ones, so you weren't as likely to get it right anyway.

On the other hand, if you find yourself getting ahead of schedule, it may be beneficial to slow down a little. The more quickly you work, the more likely you are to make a careless mistake that will affect your score. You've budgeted time for each question, so don't be afraid to spend that time. Practice an efficient but careful pace to get the most out of the time you have.

Secret Key #5 – Have a Plan for Guessing

When you're taking the test, you may find yourself stuck on a question. Some of the answer choices seem better than others, but you don't see the one answer choice that is obviously correct. What do you do?

The scenario described above is very common, yet most test takers have not effectively prepared for it. Developing and practicing a plan for guessing may be one of the single most effective uses of your time as you get ready for the exam.

In developing your plan for guessing, there are three questions to address:

- When should you start the guessing process?
- How should you narrow down the choices?
- Which answer should you choose?

When to Start the Guessing Process

Unless your plan for guessing is to select C every time (which, despite its merits, is not what we recommend), you need to leave yourself enough time to apply your answer elimination strategies. Since you have a limited amount of time for each question, that means that if you're going to give yourself the best shot at guessing correctly, you have to decide quickly whether or not you will guess.

Of course, the best-case scenario is that you don't have to guess at all, so first, see if you can answer the question based on your knowledge of the subject and basic reasoning skills. Focus on the key words in the question and try to jog your memory of related topics. Give yourself a chance to bring the knowledge to mind, but once you realize that you don't have (or you can't access) the knowledge you need to answer the question, it's time to start the guessing process.

It's almost always better to start the guessing process too early than too late. It only takes a few seconds to remember something and answer the question from knowledge. Carefully eliminating wrong answer choices takes longer. Plus, going through the process of eliminating answer choices can actually help jog your memory.

Summary: Start the guessing process as soon as you decide that you can't answer the question based on your knowledge.

How to Narrow Down the Choices

The next chapter in this book (**Test-Taking Strategies**) includes a wide range of strategies for how to approach questions and how to look for answer choices to eliminate. You will definitely want to read those carefully, practice them, and figure out which ones work best for you. Here though, we're going to address a mindset rather than a particular strategy.

Your odds of guessing an answer correctly depend on how many options you are choosing from.

Number of options left	5	4	3	2	1
Odds of guessing correctly	20%	25%	33%	50%	100%

You can see from this chart just how valuable it is to be able to eliminate incorrect answers and make an educated guess, but there are two things that many test takers do that cause them to miss out on the benefits of guessing:

- Accidentally eliminating the correct answer
- Selecting an answer based on an impression

We'll look at the first one here, and the second one in the next section.

To avoid accidentally eliminating the correct answer, we recommend a thought exercise called **the $5 challenge**. In this challenge, you only eliminate an answer choice from contention if you are willing to bet $5 on it being wrong. Why $5? Five dollars is a small but not insignificant amount of money. It's an amount you could afford to lose but wouldn't want to throw away. And while losing

$5 once might not hurt too much, doing it twenty times will set you back $100. In the same way, each small decision you make—eliminating a choice here, guessing on a question there—won't by itself impact your score very much, but when you put them all together, they can make a big difference. By holding each answer choice elimination decision to a higher standard, you can reduce the risk of accidentally eliminating the correct answer.

The $5 challenge can also be applied in a positive sense: If you are willing to bet $5 that an answer choice *is* correct, go ahead and mark it as correct.

Summary: Only eliminate an answer choice if you are willing to bet $5 that it is wrong.

Which Answer to Choose

You're taking the test. You've run into a hard question and decided you'll have to guess. You've eliminated all the answer choices you're willing to bet $5 on. Now you have to pick an answer. Why do we even need to talk about this? Why can't you just pick whichever one you feel like when the time comes?

The answer to these questions is that if you don't come into the test with a plan, you'll rely on your impression to select an answer choice, and if you do that, you risk falling into a trap. The test writers know that everyone who takes their test will be guessing on some of the questions, so they intentionally write wrong answer choices to seem plausible. You still have to pick an answer though, and if the wrong answer choices are designed to look right, how can you ever be sure that you're not falling for their trap? The best solution we've found to this dilemma is to take the decision out of your hands entirely. Here is the process we recommend:

Once you've eliminated any choices that you are confident (willing to bet $5) are wrong, select the first remaining choice as your answer.

Whether you choose to select the first remaining choice, the second, or the last, the important thing is that you use some preselected standard. Using this approach guarantees that you will not be enticed into selecting an answer choice that looks right, because you are not basing your decision on how the answer choices look.

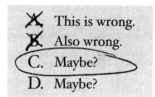

This is not meant to make you question your knowledge. Instead, it is to help you recognize the difference between your knowledge and your impressions. There's a huge difference between thinking an answer is right because of what you know, and thinking an answer is right because it looks or sounds like it should be right.

Summary: To ensure that your selection is appropriately random, make a predetermined selection from among all answer choices you have not eliminated.

Test-Taking Strategies

This section contains a list of test-taking strategies that you may find helpful as you work through the test. By taking what you know and applying logical thought, you can maximize your chances of answering any question correctly!

It is very important to realize that every question is different and every person is different: no single strategy will work on every question, and no single strategy will work for every person. That's why we've included all of them here, so you can try them out and determine which ones work best for different types of questions and which ones work best for you.

Question Strategies

⊘ READ CAREFULLY

Read the question and the answer choices carefully. Don't miss the question because you misread the terms. You have plenty of time to read each question thoroughly and make sure you understand what is being asked. Yet a happy medium must be attained, so don't waste too much time. You must read carefully and efficiently.

⊘ CONTEXTUAL CLUES

Look for contextual clues. If the question includes a word you are not familiar with, look at the immediate context for some indication of what the word might mean. Contextual clues can often give you all the information you need to decipher the meaning of an unfamiliar word. Even if you can't determine the meaning, you may be able to narrow down the possibilities enough to make a solid guess at the answer to the question.

⊘ PREFIXES

If you're having trouble with a word in the question or answer choices, try dissecting it. Take advantage of every clue that the word might include. Prefixes can be a huge help. Usually, they allow you to determine a basic meaning. *Pre-* means before, *post-* means after, *pro-* is positive, *de-* is negative. From prefixes, you can get an idea of the general meaning of the word and try to put it into context.

⊘ HEDGE WORDS

Watch out for critical hedge words, such as *likely, may, can, sometimes, often, almost, mostly, usually, generally, rarely,* and *sometimes.* Question writers insert these hedge phrases to cover every possibility. Often an answer choice will be wrong simply because it leaves no room for exception. Be on guard for answer choices that have definitive words such as *exactly* and *always.*

⊘ SWITCHBACK WORDS

Stay alert for *switchbacks.* These are the words and phrases frequently used to alert you to shifts in thought. The most common switchback words are *but, although,* and *however.* Others include *nevertheless, on the other hand, even though, while, in spite of, despite,* and *regardless of.* Switchback words are important to catch because they can change the direction of the question or an answer choice.

10

⊘ Face Value

When in doubt, use common sense. Accept the situation in the problem at face value. Don't read too much into it. These problems will not require you to make wild assumptions. If you have to go beyond creativity and warp time or space in order to have an answer choice fit the question, then you should move on and consider the other answer choices. These are normal problems rooted in reality. The applicable relationship or explanation may not be readily apparent, but it is there for you to figure out. Use your common sense to interpret anything that isn't clear.

Answer Choice Strategies

⊘ Answer Selection

The most thorough way to pick an answer choice is to identify and eliminate wrong answers until only one is left, then confirm it is the correct answer. Sometimes an answer choice may immediately seem right, but be careful. The test writers will usually put more than one reasonable answer choice on each question, so take a second to read all of them and make sure that the other choices are not equally obvious. As long as you have time left, it is better to read every answer choice than to pick the first one that looks right without checking the others.

⊘ Answer Choice Families

An answer choice family consists of two (in rare cases, three) answer choices that are very similar in construction and cannot all be true at the same time. If you see two answer choices that are direct opposites or parallels, one of them is usually the correct answer. For instance, if one answer choice says that quantity x increases and another either says that quantity x decreases (opposite) or says that quantity y increases (parallel), then those answer choices would fall into the same family. An answer choice that doesn't match the construction of the answer choice family is more likely to be incorrect. Most questions will not have answer choice families, but when they do appear, you should be prepared to recognize them.

⊘ Eliminate Answers

Eliminate answer choices as soon as you realize they are wrong, but make sure you consider all possibilities. If you are eliminating answer choices and realize that the last one you are left with is also wrong, don't panic. Start over and consider each choice again. There may be something you missed the first time that you will realize on the second pass.

⊘ Avoid Fact Traps

Don't be distracted by an answer choice that is factually true but doesn't answer the question. You are looking for the choice that answers the question. Stay focused on what the question is asking for so you don't accidentally pick an answer that is true but incorrect. Always go back to the question and make sure the answer choice you've selected actually answers the question and is not merely a true statement.

⊘ Extreme Statements

In general, you should avoid answers that put forth extreme actions as standard practice or proclaim controversial ideas as established fact. An answer choice that states the "process should be used in certain situations, if..." is much more likely to be correct than one that states the "process should be discontinued completely." The first is a calm rational statement and doesn't even make a definitive, uncompromising stance, using a hedge word *if* to provide wiggle room, whereas the second choice is far more extreme.

☑ BENCHMARK

As you read through the answer choices and you come across one that seems to answer the question well, mentally select that answer choice. This is not your final answer, but it's the one that will help you evaluate the other answer choices. The one that you selected is your benchmark or standard for judging each of the other answer choices. Every other answer choice must be compared to your benchmark. That choice is correct until proven otherwise by another answer choice beating it. If you find a better answer, then that one becomes your new benchmark. Once you've decided that no other choice answers the question as well as your benchmark, you have your final answer.

☑ PREDICT THE ANSWER

Before you even start looking at the answer choices, it is often best to try to predict the answer. When you come up with the answer on your own, it is easier to avoid distractions and traps because you will know exactly what to look for. The right answer choice is unlikely to be word-for-word what you came up with, but it should be a close match. Even if you are confident that you have the right answer, you should still take the time to read each option before moving on.

General Strategies

☑ TOUGH QUESTIONS

If you are stumped on a problem or it appears too hard or too difficult, don't waste time. Move on! Remember though, if you can quickly check for obviously incorrect answer choices, your chances of guessing correctly are greatly improved. Before you completely give up, at least try to knock out a couple of possible answers. Eliminate what you can and then guess at the remaining answer choices before moving on.

☑ CHECK YOUR WORK

Since you will probably not know every term listed and the answer to every question, it is important that you get credit for the ones that you do know. Don't miss any questions through careless mistakes. If at all possible, try to take a second to look back over your answer selection and make sure you've selected the correct answer choice and haven't made a costly careless mistake (such as marking an answer choice that you didn't mean to mark). This quick double check should more than pay for itself in caught mistakes for the time it costs.

☑ PACE YOURSELF

It's easy to be overwhelmed when you're looking at a page full of questions; your mind is confused and full of random thoughts, and the clock is ticking down faster than you would like. Calm down and maintain the pace that you have set for yourself. Especially as you get down to the last few minutes of the test, don't let the small numbers on the clock make you panic. As long as you are on track by monitoring your pace, you are guaranteed to have time for each question.

☑ DON'T RUSH

It is very easy to make errors when you are in a hurry. Maintaining a fast pace in answering questions is pointless if it makes you miss questions that you would have gotten right otherwise. Test writers like to include distracting information and wrong answers that seem right. Taking a little extra time to avoid careless mistakes can make all the difference in your test score. Find a pace that allows you to be confident in the answers that you select.

12

⏱ Keep Moving

Panicking will not help you pass the test, so do your best to stay calm and keep moving. Taking deep breaths and going through the answer elimination steps you practiced can help to break through a stress barrier and keep your pace.

Final Notes

The combination of a solid foundation of content knowledge and the confidence that comes from practicing your plan for applying that knowledge is the key to maximizing your performance on test day. As your foundation of content knowledge is built up and strengthened, you'll find that the strategies included in this chapter become more and more effective in helping you quickly sift through the distractions and traps of the test to isolate the correct answer.

Now that you're preparing to move forward into the test content chapters of this book, be sure to keep your goal in mind. As you read, think about how you will be able to apply this information on the test. If you've already seen sample questions for the test and you have an idea of the question format and style, try to come up with questions of your own that you can answer based on what you're reading. This will give you valuable practice applying your knowledge in the same ways you can expect to on test day.

Good luck and good studying!

14

Art Making

Elements and Principles of Art

THE ELEMENTS OF ART

The seven elements of art are **color, texture, shape, form, line, space, and value**. **Color** has three characteristics: hue (such as red, yellow, or green), intensity (how bright or dull the color is), and value (how light or dark the color is). Colors can be divided into primary, secondary, and tertiary on a color wheel, where the primary colors are red, yellow, and blue, and the secondary colors are the result of two primary colors mixed together (red and yellow make orange, red and blue make violet, and yellow and blue make green). The tertiary colors are those in between the primary and secondary colors, such as blue-green or red-orange.

- **Colors** opposite each other on the color wheel are considered complementary. Examples include red and green or blue and orange.
- **Texture** is how something feels, or appears to feel, and it can be real or implied. Examples of textures include smooth, rough, or bumpy. A real texture is one you can actually feel, whereas an implied texture is two-dimensional yet appears to have texture.
- **Shapes** are categorized as geometric or organic. Geometric shapes include named mathematical shapes such as circles, ovals, squares, and triangles. Organic shapes are asymmetrical and are often found in nature.
- **Form** is used in three-dimensional art such as sculpture, and it describes the shape of the artwork.
- A **line** is used to define a shape, and it is the path between two points. A line can be straight, curved, broken, implied, or free-form. Lines can be used to create movement or to lead the viewer's eye around the artwork.
- **Space** can refer to the foreground, middle ground, and background of an artwork. It can also refer to the positive and negative space created by the artist. Positive space is the subject of the artwork, and negative space is the area that surrounds it. An artist can create the illusion of three-dimensional space within an artwork.
- **Value** is the lightness or darkness of a color. An artist can use value to provide visual interest in an artwork, to create a mood, or to draw the viewer's eye to a certain focal point. Contrast is the difference in value or the difference in the lightness and darkness.

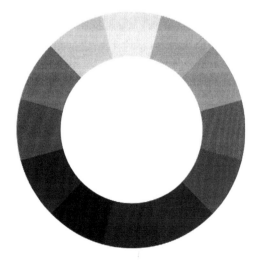

15

PRINCIPLES OF DESIGN

The principles of design include balance, contrast, movement, emphasis, pattern, rhythm, and unity. An artist can use multiple principles of design in their artwork, or they can focus primarily on one principle.

- **Balance** is how an artwork's visual weight is organized, and it can be symmetrical or asymmetrical. Symmetrical balance has the same weight on both sides, whereas asymmetrical balance is visually weighted more on one side. Asymmetrical balance gives the artwork more visual interest and leads the viewer's eye around the artwork.
- **Contrast** is when an artwork's elements are juxtaposed against each other to create interesting differences. This could include a difference in warm and cool colors or a difference between organic and geometric shapes.
- **Movement** is using the elements to lead the viewer throughout the piece. One example is a repetition of shapes that moves the viewer's eye through the artwork.
- **Emphasis** creates a focal point in the artwork by using a bold color, asymmetrical balance, or a strong contrast. Pattern and rhythm consist of a repetition of elements.
- **Pattern** is repeating elements in the same order, whereas **rhythm** is repeating elements without a specific order.
- **Unity** is harmony throughout the artwork created by elements working together. This can be achieved by a repetition of an element, similarity of elements, or even a rhythm of elements.

THE RELATIONSHIP BETWEEN ELEMENTS AND PRINCIPLES OF DESIGN

The elements of art are the building blocks of visual art, and the principles of design are ways to organize these elements of art. An artist can use multiple elements and principles in their artwork, or they can focus primarily on certain elements and principles. By using the principles of design to organize the elements of art, the artist can decide what the focal point of the artwork is and where they want to lead viewers' eyes. An artist can use the principles of design to arrange the elements of art in their artwork, and they can use the terminology of these elements and principles to explain their artistic decisions. They can also use them to analyze another artists' artwork. The elements of art and principles of design are both sets of established criteria that are used to objectively judge artwork rather than using personal preferences.

Many of the elements of art and principles of design can be found in two- and three-dimensional artwork. **Texture** can be real on a three-dimensional work, whereas it will be implied on a two-dimensional work. A marble statue might be smooth, whereas a steel sculpture could have a rough texture. **Space** in a two-dimensional work will be created by how the artist uses the elements and principles to arrange the artwork and even to create a foreground, middle ground, and background. **Space** in a sculpture or three-dimensional work is how the artist uses the space in three dimensions. In three-dimensional artwork, **form** has width, depth, and height. The form can be viewed either from all sides, which would make the sculpture in-the-round, or it can be viewed from one side, which is a relief work (built from a solid background). Form describes the shape of the artwork.

APPLICATIONS OF PRINCIPLES OF DESIGN
TWO-DIMENSIONAL ARTWORK

This painting, *Composition with Red, Yellow, and Blue* (1927), is by Dutch artist Piet Mondrian. It is a product of the de Stijl art movement, which began in Holland. He eliminated any representational forms in his artwork and pared it down to a few elements. The main elements of art used in this

16

painting are color, line, and shape. Mondrian used planes of pure color in this painting, separated by thick black lines. Here you see the primary colors — red, yellow, and blue — along with black and white. He used black lines to create geometric shapes throughout the canvas. The geometric shapes and the parallel and perpendicular lines give the work a solid and stable feel. Mondrian placed the planes of color in an asymmetrical way and balanced them with panes of white.

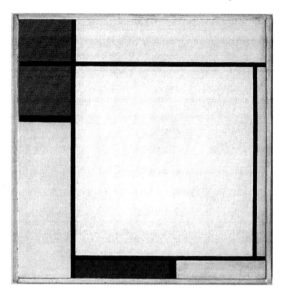

THREE-DIMENSIONAL ARTWORK

This sculpture is titled *Embrace IV*, by Emilia Glaser. The main elements evident in this sculpture are color, value, shape, line, and texture. The sculpture is mainly one color of red-orange, with a darker value of the color on part of the sculpture and a different color and value for the base. This use of warm color can invoke a feeling of happiness or excitement, and it can draw the viewer closer to the sculpture. The sculpture appears to be a combination of different shapes, and strong lines visually separate the borders of these shapes. The lines have mostly upward movement, giving the sculpture a strong, uplifting feel. The sculpture appears to have a rough and bumpy texture, which in this case would be real texture because it is a texture that could actually be felt.

THE STARRY NIGHT

This painting is called *The Starry Night* (1889) by Vincent van Gogh. The artist used several principles of design, including contrast, emphasis, balance, and movement. There is contrast in the values used throughout the painting — the darker blues and grays and the lighter whites and yellows. There is also a contrast of warm (yellow) and cool (blue) colors, in which the warm colors advance and the cool colors recede in the artwork. The bright yellow moon in the top right shows emphasis, being the largest portion of this light value and the brightest color in the painting. The large dark shape on the left of the painting is visually balanced by the smaller, bright moon and glow on the right. Van Gogh's brushstrokes look like wind blowing through the sky, and they provide movement in the painting, which leads the viewer's eye around the artwork.

SCREWARCH

This sculpture by Claes Oldenburg and Coosje van Bruggen is called *Screwarch* (1978–1984). It appears to be an oversized screw, bending to create an arch. The main principles of design evident in this sculpture are balance, pattern, contrast, and movement. The sculpture is asymmetrically balanced, being much visually heavier at the thicker end on the left. The threads of the screw show a repeating spiraling pattern, which follows the arch to the pointed end on the right. The larger, bulkier end of the screw is smooth and sharply contrasts with the rest of the screw, which tapers slowly to a point and has a spiraling pattern and texture. The sculpture shows movement with its arched form, leading the viewer's eye from the heavier end of the screw to the tapered point on the other end.

ORGANIC SHAPES

The elements of art and principles of design can all be found in nature, but it is likely that you will find more organic shapes than geometric. The natural environment contains many textures, such as rough bark, smooth petals, or gritty sand. Many colors and values can be found throughout landscapes, as well as a depth of space and varied forms of plants, trees, and rocks. Bright flowers contrast against dark leaves, providing a focal point or emphasis against the green. Wind creates movement in the natural world, and the repetition of plants or trees creates rhythm. The edges of objects in nature can create implied lines between each other, and lines can be found in the veins of a leaf. The repetition of greens throughout a spring scene or reds and oranges in a fall scene can create unity throughout the landscape.

COMPOSITION

Composition is how an artwork is organized, and the principles of design help an artist decide how to arrange the elements of art in their artwork. An artist can use the principles of design to decide what will stand out in their artwork and where they will lead the viewer's eyes. An artist could focus on the use of color as an element in their artwork but then use a pattern to repeat the colors in a certain order or use emphasis to draw attention to a certain color in a certain part of the artwork. They could create unity in the work by repeating a certain color throughout. An artist could focus on certain shapes in their artwork, but then they could use contrast by putting different shapes next to each other. They could use the shapes to create a rhythm by repeating them without a specific order. The artist could even focus on using lines in the artwork, but then they could use movement to guide the viewer's eyes around the artwork with the lines.

Drawing and Painting

ORIGINS OF DRAWING

Drawing is a medium that was first used on cave walls as early as 10,000 B.C., and then by the Egyptians starting in 3,000 B.C. In the Middle Ages, drawings were mostly used to prepare for paintings. In the Renaissance era, drawing became a more widely used art form. This is partly due to the availability of paper and the fact that drawing became the foundation for other art forms. Art students during the Renaissance were first taught to draw before painting and sculpting. Drawing was used to study and record nature and anatomy. The artists used pen and ink, as well as black and red charcoal. In the baroque period, drawings were more free-flowing and less exact than those in the Renaissance era. In the 1600s, Rembrandt used pen lines to create expressive drawings. In the 1800s, pencils were first manufactured, and they became a widely used drawing tool.

HISTORY AND USE OF DRAWING

Drawing was originally used to express ideas and scenes in cave paintings. As artists and materials became more refined, drawing was primarily used as a preliminary step before starting a painting. In the Middle Ages, drawings were mainly completed on animal skins, wood, wax, or slate. Artists would keep records of their sketches to use for artwork instead of working from live models. Some artists in the Middle Ages would complete finished drawings as illuminations for manuscripts.

During the Renaissance, when paper became more readily available, artists would learn to draw before painting or sculpting. Drawing was still considered more of a preliminary step before using other media. When large-scale paintings were created, such as in the Sistine Chapel, many preparatory drawings were created to use for the final paintings. In the 1500s in northern Europe, artists began creating drawings as finished works rather than as preparatory materials. Albrecht Dürer and Hans Holbein the Younger created detailed drawings that could stand alone as artworks. In the 1600s, Rembrandt created expressive drawings and Dutch artists took their sketchbooks into the fields to capture scenes to paint from later. Artists continued to create sketches prior to finished artworks, but drawing became an accepted medium for a final artwork.

HISTORIC DRAWING MEDIA

- **Charcoal** is an early drawing material made from slowly burned wood. Charcoal was used for cave drawings, when burnt sticks were rubbed on cave walls.
- **Red chalk** is made from iron oxide pigment and refined clay. It was popular in the 16th and 17th centuries, and Leonardo da Vinci used it for many sketches. **Black chalk** is carbonaceous shale, and it is softer than red chalk. It was used in 15th-century Italy for underdrawings for ink or metalpoint artwork. Albrecht Dürer and Anthony van Dyck used black chalk for portraits. **White chalk** is calcium carbonate or soapstone, and it is used for highlights on drawings.
- **Conté crayons** were developed in the early 1800s. They are made in red, black, and white. They are harder than chalk and produce smoother lines.
- **Graphite** is a form of carbon, and it was first discovered in the 1500s. It was later cut into strips and encased in wood for pencils.
- **Ink** is a liquid pigment that can be used with a pen or a brush. It was also commonly used for writing. **Pens** were first made with bird feathers (quills) and reeds, and later they were created with metal tips.

PENCILS AND CHARCOAL

Pencils are made from graphite encased in wood. They are available in a range of hardnesses, from 10H to 10B. A 10H pencil has the hardest lead, and it will stay the sharpest and leave the lightest

20

mark on the paper. A 10B pencil has the softest lead, and it will wear down quickly, leaving the darkest mark on the paper. In the middle are F and HB, which are a medium hardness and darkness.

Charcoal is a lightweight carbon that can be found in stick form or pencil form. Compressed charcoal is a hard charcoal stick, whereas vine charcoal is a thin, delicate stick. Charcoal also comes in different hardnesses, although it is usually just in the B (soft) range. A higher number before the B indicates a softer charcoal.

Charcoal and pencil can be used for sketching and drawing, but pencil will generally give the opportunity for greater detail, since there are harder graphites available. Charcoal is often used for large-gesture drawings and putting ideas onto a canvas prior to painting.

OTHER TOOLS FOR DRAWING

In addition to materials used to draw with, there are several tools used along with drawing media. A **tortillon** is a piece of paper wrapped up tightly, ending in a point, that can be used to blend pencil and charcoal drawings. A maulstick, or mahlstick, is a stick with a padded head used to rest and support your hand to keep it steady while drawing or painting. Various **erasers** are used for drawing: A kneaded rubber eraser is one that can be manipulated and rolled into smaller sizes to erase small areas, and it will not leave eraser crumbs behind. A gum eraser is yellowish and will crumble quickly. It is best for larger areas. A pink eraser is firmer and more precise, but it will still leave crumbs on the paper. A large brush can be used to gently brush the eraser bits off of the paper. A dry cleaning pad is a fabric bag filled with pieces of eraser that can be used to clean up fingerprints, smudges, and dust from larger areas of paper.

DRAWING SURFACES

A commonly used drawing surface used in the Middle Ages was **parchment**, which was created from animal skin. Paper was first created in A.D. 105 in China, but it wasn't widely used as a drawing material until it was produced more quickly and more inexpensively in the 1800s.

Paper comes in hot-pressed and cold-pressed surfaces. Hot-pressed paper will be smooth, whereas cold-pressed paper will have a texture. Sketch paper is thinner than drawing paper, which is made to be more permanent. Newsprint is the kind of thin paper that newspaper is printed on, and it is used for sketching. Illustration board is a thicker cardboard with a hot-pressed or cold-pressed white surface. Bristol board is thicker than drawing paper, and it also comes in hot- or cold-pressed. A smooth surface will allow for greater detail and better control of pencil marks, whereas a rough surface is better suited for looser drawing and sketching or for a drawing with a rough texture.

Paper considered archival will be labeled as acid-free, and it should not yellow and deteriorate over time. Acid-free paper should be used for finished drawings, whereas any paper, including sketch paper and newsprint, can be used for preliminary sketches.

CONTOUR AND BLIND CONTOUR

A **contour drawing** seeks to define the outline of an object, and it can contain as much or as little detail as the artist desires. This technique uses only lines to delineate the outer edges of the subject; it does not include any shading or other values in the drawing. For a contour drawing, the artist will study the subject and show the proportions and volume, rather than focusing on values or fine details. This type of drawing can be used to quickly capture a subject or scene.

A **blind contour** drawing is used by an artist to practice sketching and perception. To create a blind contour drawing, the artist will look directly at the subject and draw a contour without looking back at their paper. They may occasionally glance at the paper to reorient their drawing tool, but generally will keep their focus on the subject. Rather than being used to capture a subject or scene, this is typically reserved as a drawing exercise to help strengthen the artist's hand-eye coordination.

GESTURE AND PERSPECTIVE DRAWING

Gesture drawing is a technique used to quickly capture the action and form of a model or subject. A gesture drawing can be completed in as little as 30 to 60 seconds. The artist uses loose lines to simplify and capture the essence of the subject. These drawings are generally done to study and capture different poses of the human figure. Gesture drawings can help an artist choose a pose to use for a more detailed study of the figure.

Perspective drawing is a drawing technique that shows spatial relationships and the illusion of space on a flat surface. An artist can portray a three-dimensional scene on a two-dimensional drawing. One-point perspective shows the objects in the scene receding to one point in the horizon, as shown in the image. Two-point perspective has the scene receding into two points on the horizon. These points along the horizon where the objects disappear to in the distance are called vanishing points.

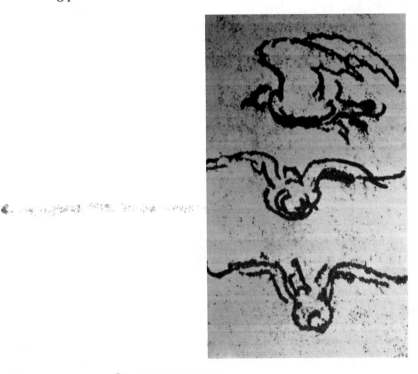

HATCHING AND CROSSHATCHING

Hatching is a technique that uses closely placed parallel lines to create shading and tones. Crosshatching is when hatching is used perpendicular to itself, creating heavier shades and tones. In this example from Albrecht Dürer, *The Penitent* (1510), he uses hatching heavily throughout the drawing. Notice how the lines are closer together to make darker values and how the lines follow the contours of the objects. On flat walls they are straight, and on the curtains, they follow the curves. Using the lines to emphasize the forms in the artwork helps to create a sense of volume for the viewer.

Dürer uses crosshatching in the heavier shaded areas of the drawing. In the darkest areas, the hatched patterns cross each other to create crosshatching. Again, the lines are closer together

22

where the values are the darkest. Although this example is a woodcut, these techniques are also used in the printmaking techniques of engraving and etching, as well as drawing.

SHADING

Shading adds depth and form to an artwork. An object with accurate shading can appear three-dimensional. To create this illusion with pencils, the artist needs to vary pressure, use pencils of appropriate hardnesses, and understand where the shadows and highlights should be placed. When light hits the object, it creates many different values. The area closest to the light source will have a highlight, which is the whitest part of the drawing. This can be created by leaving that part white or by erasing afterward. As the object gets farther from the light source, it will be gradually shaded darker. A smooth gradation can be accomplished with careful control of the pencil or by using a blending tool, or tortillon, to blend the graphite. If the object is on a light surface, that surface can create a reflection toward the bottom of the object. The object will also cast a shadow on the surface opposite the light source. Careful observation of the object, as well as the values and shadows, will help the artist create a realistic rendering.

CRITIQUING DRAWINGS

When critiquing a drawing as a finished artwork, you can describe, analyze, interpret, and judge it. Begin by describing the visual facts — what you see in the drawing. Is it representational? What kinds of shapes, lines, or textures do you see? Next, begin analyzing the artwork. Recognize the elements of art and how they are arranged (the principles of design). Do you see shapes arranged in a pattern? Where is the emphasis in the drawing? How are the lines used, and where do they lead your eye? Next, interpret the artwork, or use what you have learned so far to decide what the artist is trying to say. What is the mood of the artwork? What does the subject matter tell you? Why do you think the artist decided to portray it in this way? After completing these steps, you can begin to make your own judgement of the artwork. Did the artist successfully use the principles of design to organize the elements of art? Does the artist successfully convey the feelings, mood, and ideas they were aiming for? Do you see ways that the artwork can be improved?

Following these steps will give you a way to thoroughly and objectively critique a drawing and recognize the successes and failures within it.

CREATIVITY IN DRAWING AND SKETCHING

Drawing and sketching are commonly used to elicit creativity and **refine ideas**. A sketch pad and pencil or pen are easily portable and can be used to quickly jot down ideas or capture a form or scene to be added to a later artwork. Drawings can be completed quickly and started and stopped easily, unlike paintings, which require preparation, more materials, and drying time.

An artist can gather ideas in a sketch book and then look back at them later to think further and get more ideas from them. An artist can also combine their ideas and sketches into a bigger artwork. They can experiment with different pencils, line widths, and techniques to find the ones that work best for them or what will work best for a particular artwork. An artist can observe the world around them and draw what they see and then add those common items into imaginary scenes or draw from the imagination altogether to create new, inventive scenes. Through sketching and experimentation, an artist can prepare their ideas and techniques for a well-planned final artwork that will showcase their creativity.

OIL PAINTING

Oil painting was developed as a fine art painting medium in the 15th century in northern Europe, and Jan van Eyck is credited with being the first to use oil paint on wood panels. Toward the end of the 15th century, artists began painting on canvas instead of wood panels. The popularity of painting on canvas grew because it was cheaper, easier to transport, and easier to create larger artworks. The canvas was coated with a layer of animal glue and then a layer of lead white paint prior to painting.

~~Oil paint is made from a pigment suspended in a drying oil.~~ The master painters' apprentices were in charge of mixing and preparing the oil paints. In the late 18th century, oil paints started to be manufactured so they could be purchased.

The pigments and paints used today are more lightfast and durable than the oil paints used in the past. Many times, colors have faded or oxidized due to exposure to light and air, and older paintings do not look as they were intended. One example is Van Gogh's *Sunflowers* (1880s), in which he used a chrome yellow pigment that has turned brown over time.

WATERCOLOR

Watercolor has been used for cave paintings and manuscript illustrations, but it was first widely used as a fine art medium during the Renaissance. Albrecht Dürer was one of the earliest watercolor painters, as seen in *The Hare* (1502). During the baroque period, watercolors were used for sketching and cartoons. In addition to fine art, Renaissance artists used watercolors for botanical illustrations. In the 19th century, John Audubon used watercolors for his well-known bird illustrations.

Watercolor is created by adding pigment to a gum arabic binder. It can be found in a dry cake form, which needs to be wet with water, or in a tube. Watercolor brushes are generally soft and made with natural (sable, squirrel) or synthetic hairs, and they have a shorter handle than oil and acrylic brushes. Watercolors are transparent, meaning they can be layered upon each other and the color underneath and white paper will show through. The most common surface for watercolor painting is paper, which comes in hot-press (smooth) and cold-press (rough) finishes.

EGG TEMPERA

Egg tempera was a popular painting medium until after 1500, when oil painting became widely used instead. Traditional egg tempera paint is created by adding pigment to egg yolk, which is used as a water-soluble binder. White wine, vinegar, or water can be added in various proportions to keep the dried paint from cracking. When the yolk is exposed to air, it begins to dry, so the artist continually adds water to keep the consistency correct for painting.

Egg tempera paint dries very quickly, so it is applied in thin, transparent layers and usually with short brushstrokes. The technique of crosshatching can be used to layer the colors. Unlike oil paintings, tempera paints have survived over history in much the same condition as they were intended. In the 20th century, some artists began using tempera again, such as Andrew Wyeth, Thomas Hart Benton, and Jacob Lawrence.

Egg tempera is painted onto stiff surfaces such as wood panels or Masonite because a flexible surface will allow it to crack and flake off the support.

GOUACHE

Gouache is an opaque medium with characteristics similar to watercolor. It is traditionally created with gum arabic as the binder, but it also has a filler added to make the paint opaque. Like watercolor, dried gouache can be rewet and reworked. It dries to a matte finish, and it is usually used on watercolor paper or illustration board. With a smooth hot-press surface, an artist can create great detail with gouache. Gouache is commonly used for graphic arts including illustrations, comics, and posters. It has also been used in animation.

The term gouache was first used in France in the 18th century to refer to opaque watercolor, but the medium and techniques were used prior to this — as early as the 9th century in Persia.

26

Gouache is now manufactured as watercolor type and a newer acrylic type. The acrylic gouache is water resistant once it's dry, and it cannot be rewet. It differs from acrylic paint in that it dries to a matte finish and can be worked with for slightly longer.

COMMON PAINTING TOOLS

Paintbrushes used for oils and acrylics generally have a longer handle than do watercolor brushes. Watercolor brushes have soft natural or synthetic hairs, whereas acrylic and oil brushes have stiffer natural or synthetic hairs, including hog bristles. Whereas watercolors and acrylics are water soluble and the brushes can be cleaned with soap and water, oil brushes will need to be cleaned with a paint thinner solvent.

Drying oils, such as linseed and poppy oil, can be added to oil paints to decrease drying times and thin the consistency. There are many types of media for acrylic paints that will decrease the drying time or change the texture to thicker or thinner.

Primer is a base for painting, and it is commonly used with oil and acrylic painting. A commonly used primer is called gesso, which is essentially a water-based white paint mixture used to prepare the support.

For watercolors, a **masking fluid** will cover areas of the paper that are needed to stay white for highlights. After the watercolor painting is finished, the masking fluid can be removed, revealing the white paper.

All paints will benefit from the use of a **palette**. A palette can be a basic piece of wood or Masonite, or it can be a more involved structure with divots for each color. A palette is used to organize and mix colors for a painting. The selection of colors and organization is up to the individual artist.

OIL AND WATER-BASED PAINTS

With advances in **acrylic paints**, an artist can now get similar finished products to that of oil paints, but there are still differences in the media and processes. Oil paint allows for a much longer working time than acrylic. Oil paint will stay workable on the palette for four to eight hours, whereas acrylic paint can dry in less than an hour. A finished oil painting can take six months or more before it is considered dry. The oil paint on the canvas will stay workable to allow for more blending, whereas acrylic dries more quickly and does not lend itself to as much blending. Acrylics turn into a kind of plastic when they dry, so if they dry in the paintbrush, it can be difficult to impossible to clean the brush. Watercolors can be rewet and washed out of the brush at any time, and oil paints can be soaked and removed with paint thinners.

Acrylic can be used as a base for oil paintings, but it cannot be painted on top of oils. When painting with oils, it is important to remember the rule "fat over lean." this means the artist should build increasingly flexible layers on top of each other. The increased flexibility is accomplished by adding an oil medium to the paint and using less solvent.

PAINTING SURFACES

Wood has been used as a support for oil and acrylic painting for centuries. It is rigid and minimizes any flexing or cracking of the paint. Wood should be primed before painting on it to seal the surface and also to make it smoother. For the smoothest surface, layers of gesso can be applied, let dry, and sanded between applications.

Paper is used for watercolor or acrylic, but the oil from oil paints will break paper down, so it is not well suited for oil painting. Canvas has been the most popular surface for oil paints since the 17th century, and it is often used for acrylics, too. **Canvas boards** are now used, which are made from canvas stretched over rigid cardboard and preprimed.

Paper for watercolors, acrylics, and gouache is usually thick to accommodate the amount of paint and water used. Watercolor paper needs to be stretched so that it does not warp after use. Some watercolor pads come with glue around the edges to prevent this warping; otherwise, it will need to be taped to a surface on four sides, then wet and let dry to prepare the paper.

UNDERPAINTING AND GLAZING

Underpainting is a technique used for oil and acrylic painting to create a base for a finished painting. An artist can use the underpainting to lay out the highlights and shadows for their artwork. Underpainting can be used to layer and build up rich color, and it serves as a foundation to establish the tones throughout the artwork. An underpainting for oil can be done in acrylic so it will dry quickly or with thinned oil paint. A tonal underpainting is done with one color of paint, just to establish the layout and tones before beginning the painting.

Glazing is a technique used with oil paints to layer transparent colors over a dried opaque color. Each layer is allowed to dry before another transparent layer is painted on top. The colors interact and visually blend without being physically blended on the palette. Glazing can be used to create skin tones and other complex colors that would be difficult to create otherwise. Some colors are naturally more transparent than others, so the artist needs to know the qualities of the paint and whether to add a medium to increase the transparency.

DRY BRUSH AND SGRAFFITO

Dry brush is a technique used with water-based and oil-based paints. For acrylic and watercolor painting, the brush is loaded with paint after the water is squeezed or blotted out of it. With oil painting, the brush is loaded with paint after the oil or medium is squeezed or blotted from the brush. Dry brushing creates a scratchy-looking texture on the surface, and the brushstrokes will be evident. This can be used to add texture to a painting, including fur or grass, or it can be used for emphasis and contrast to a smoother area.

Sgraffito is a technique of scratching through a layer of paint to reveal the layer or surface underneath. Sgraffito can be accomplished with a palette knife, the handle end of a paintbrush, or even a stick. This can also be done with only one layer of paint, with the artist scratching through the wet paint and revealing the canvas underneath.

WET-ON-WET AND WASH

Wet-on-wet is a watercolor technique in which the artist paints onto already-wet paper. This will cause the colors to blend and bleed into each other. This technique takes practice because the wetness of the paper, the color already on the paper, the amount of water on the brush, and the color on the brush will all affect the final product. Experience will help the artist know what will happen when they add wet watercolor onto already-wet paper and how the colors will react with each other.

A wash is a technique of adding a large area of color to a watercolor painting. A flat wash is a large area of one color, and a graded wash goes from one color gradually to white or another color. It is easiest to control the wash on dry paper instead of already-wet paper. A large, flat watercolor brush is used to apply the mixture of paint and water. As paint is applied to the paper, it will begin drying; therefore, time is a critical factor to consider in order to achieve an even application of color.

PLEIN AIR AND ALLA PRIMA

Plein air is a painting technique that entails painting outdoors. This technique increased in popularity in the 1840s when paint became available in tubes, which is more convenient for travel. The box easel, or field easel, was developed around this time; it is a box that the artist can use to carry their painting materials, and it opens up into an easel. Claude Monet often painted en plein air (French for "outdoors"), using the natural light to capture scenes at specific times of the day. This can be done with any painting medium, including watercolors that can be found in small, portable boxes for this purpose.

Alla prima is a painting technique that entails painting wet oil paint onto wet oil layers that have not been allowed to dry. This can also be called direct painting or wet-on-wet. An alla prima painting can be completed in one sitting, unlike an oil painting with multiple layers of glazing, which requires time to dry between layers. Alla prima can create a spontaneous and fresh look in the artwork.

TROMPE-L'OEIL

Trompe l'oeil is a painting technique that means "to deceive the eye" in French. A trompe l'oeil painting is meant to depict objects in a realistic way to produce the optical illusion that the objects exist in three dimensions. This phrase was first used in the baroque period, but the actual technique was used earlier in Greek and Roman murals.

During the Renaissance, frescoed ceiling paintings were created that used foreshortening and realistic depictions to create the illusion of more space above the viewer. This was called di sotto in sù, which means "from below, upward" in Italian.

This painting from 1675 by Gysbrechts is an example of trompe l'oeil. The artist depicted objects piled and scattered on a wood surface, and he used realistic colors, proportions, and shadows to achieve a three-dimensional effect. Even the wood surface is carefully and realistically portrayed.

This technique requires a great deal of attention to detail as well as a deep understanding of color mixing and oil media by the artist.

ACRYLIC PAINT

Acrylic paint has only been in use since the 1940s, and it has provided an alternative to using oil paints. Acrylic paint has a much quicker drying time than oils, and the finished surface has a greater degree of flexibility, allowing it to be painted on more surfaces with fewer considerations than oils.

Acrylics do not require the use of solvents for thinning or cleaning up the paint. They are water soluble and clean up with water. As a water-based media, more media can be layered on top of acrylics than on oils, making it more versatile for collage art. Acrylics can be used on more surfaces and supports, including cardboard and paper, that are not suitable for oil paints because oil paints will break certain supports down. With a 15- to 20-minute drying time for each layer, acrylic layers can be completed more quickly than can those in an oil painting.

Acrylic paints were first developed for practical applications such as house painting, but when Andy Warhol began using acrylics in his paintings, including *Campbell's Soup Cans*, they gained more recognition as an artistic medium. Other notable artists who used acrylics are Robert Motherwell, Mark Rothko, and Roy Lichtenstein.

IMPASTO TECHNIQUE

Impasto is a painting technique in which the paint is laid onto the surface very thickly with a brush or palette knife. With this technique, the brushstrokes are usually very visible, and they can even become purposeful lines that lead the viewer's eye throughout the artwork. When using this technique, the artist can control how light hits and reflects off of the paint surface. It can make the painting appear three-dimensional, and it can also give the painting texture.

In Vincent van Gogh's painting *Wheatfield with Crows* (1890), he uses this technique, laying the paint on thickly with visible brushstrokes. The brushstrokes create lines throughout the painting, and the lines of the brown path lead the viewer's eye to the middle of the artwork. His use of brushstrokes also creates a sense of movement in his works. The dark blues and bold strokes in the sky suggest stormy and turbulent weather. The brushstrokes throughout the wheat field lean to the side and also suggest wind and storms.

PERSPECTIVE IN PAINT

Prior to the Renaissance, artists were aware of the varying sizes of elements related to being close or far away, but Renaissance artist Filippo Brunelleschi is credited with discovering geometric perspective in 1413. After this discovery, artists began to use vanishing points and horizon lines to compose their artwork. Decades after Brunelleschi's discovery, Leon Battista Alberti wrote a description of how to properly use perspective.

This image, *The Last Supper* by Leonardo da Vinci, shows the use of one-point perspective. This work was completed between 1495–1496. The lines in this painting converge to one vanishing point in the center of the painting. This serves to draw the focus to the central figure in the painting. Da Vinci's use of perspective masterfully showcases the relatively new technique, gives an architecturally correct feel to the room, and serves as a method of compositional emphasis in the artwork. Due to the discovery of perspective, artists were subsequently able to portray architecture and other scenes with greater accuracy.

31

HISTORICAL USE OF APPRENTICESHIP

An **apprentice** was someone who learned to be an artist by working under a master artist. In the medieval era, a painter was thought of as a **tradesman**, and their client would dictate what they would create. The master painter would use helpers, or apprentices, to complete the work. The apprenticeship system began in the medieval era, and it continued through the Renaissance, when a painter was considered an artist.

An apprentice would begin with menial tasks such as cleaning paintbrushes and grinding pigments for the master artist. A student would practice drawing by copying works, and then he or she could move on to painting. The apprentices would paint backgrounds and were trained to work in the style of the master artist. The master artist might only paint the figures or faces in an artwork, or the apprentices could complete the entire work in the master's style. The master's signature on a work did not indicate that they completed a certain amount of the work, but rather that it was up to their standards. After a certain amount of years as an apprentice, an apprentice could reach journeyman status and open their own shop.

TOOLS FOR PRINTMAKING

- A **brayer** is a hand tool used for printmaking to smooth out the ink and then roll it onto the printmaking surface for a relief print. It has a handle and a smooth rubber roller.
- A **burnisher** is a smooth metal tool that is used to smooth the surface of a metal intaglio printing plate. Lines are etched into the plate to hold ink, and the burnisher can polish the metal surface to reduce its ability to hold ink. The term burnisher could also refer to a flat disk used to press paper onto a surface to create a print.
- A **plate** is a copper or zinc sheet of metal used for intaglio printmaking. When using a plate, the lines are cut or etched into the surface, and these lines hold the ink, which is the opposite of a relief print in which the raised parts hold the ink.
- A **gouge** is used in relief printmaking to cut away the parts that will not hold ink. Gouges come in different sizes and shapes, including U-shaped and V-shaped, and they are used on surfaces such as linoleum or wood.

INTAGLIO AND LITHOGRAPHY

Intaglio is a printmaking technique in which the image is carved into a surface and the ink is held in those lines for printing. Lines are cut into a metal plate by a burin, which is a handheld metal tool, or by etching, which is a chemical process. For etching, the plate is first covered with an acid-resistant material and then the image is carved into that material to reveal the plate under it. The plate is dipped in acid, which bites only into the lines where the plate is exposed. The acid-resistant material is then removed, and ink is rubbed into the etched or carved lines and wiped off of the rest of the plate. The high pressure of a printing press pushes the paper into the inked grooves to produce the print. The image shown is an example of an etching.

For **lithography**, the artist uses a greasy medium such as a crayon or ink to produce an image on limestone or aluminum. The artist then puts a solution of nitric acid and gum arabic on the surface, and when a roller with oil-based ink is rolled over this, the ink will only stick to the greasy area. This is then run through a press with paper to produce the image.

RELIEF PRINTING AND SCREEN PRINTING

Relief printing is any method in which a raised surface is used to produce the image. Relief printing is commonly done with linoleum and wood, in which the parts that is not wanted to be printed are cut away by the artist with gouges. Letterpress is also an example of relief printing, in which the raised letters are printed onto paper. Ink is applied to the raised surface with a roller, and then paper is pressed onto the surface by hand or with a printing press, to transfer the image onto paper.

For **screen printing**, also called silk screening (as shown in the image), ink is pressed through a fine screen to produce the print. An image is created onto the screen through many different methods, including stencils or photo emulsion, and the parts of the screen that are left open are where the ink will go through to the surface. Ink is pushed through the screen evenly by a squeegee onto paper, cardboard, fabric, or any number of materials. Andy Warhol is famous for using the screen printing technique to produce multiple prints of the same image.

COLLOGRAPHY AND FROTTAGE

Collography is a printmaking technique in which materials of various textures are attached to a surface. The materials should all be of roughly the same height. Ink is then rolled onto the textured surfaces, and a print is produced on paper by pressing the paper by hand or with a printing press. Different textures and inking methods can produce different results for this technique.

Frottage is a printmaking technique in which the artist gets an impression of the surface of a material. For example, you could place various leaves on a surface, lay paper on top of them, and then carefully rub the side of a crayon onto the paper. The resulting image will show the textures and shapes of the leaves underneath. During the surrealist movement, Max Ernst would take rubbings from various surfaces and use these as a basis for his artworks.

MONOTYPE AND STAMPING

Whereas most printmaking techniques can produce multiple identical or similar prints, a **monotype** will only produce one print. The artwork is created on a nonabsorbent surface with oil- or water-based ink, and then it is transferred to paper with a printing press. In the process, most of the ink is transferred to the paper, so there is not enough left on the surface to produce another print. The print can then be embellished with ink, by drawing, or by other painting methods.

Stamping is another type of relief printmaking. A stamp can be made from rubber, wax, or other materials, including cardboard or even potatoes. The shape that will produce the image is cut into the material, with the negative space cut away. The shape is pressed into the ink and then pressed onto paper to create the image. A stamped image can be reproduced over and over.

LINOCUTS AND WOODCUTS

The process of creating a **linocut**, or linoleum cut, and a **woodcut** are similar. Both of these are relief printing methods, which involve cutting away pieces of the material to produce the image to be printed. For linocut and woodcut, gouges of various shapes and sizes are used to cut away the material. The cut-away areas will not carry ink, whereas the areas left behind will be inked. When the artist is finished cutting away the material, the surface is inked with a roller, and then it is run through a printing press to print the image onto paper. The image can be reproduced repeatedly.

Instead of using the printing press, an artist could use a burnisher to transfer the image to paper. A **burnisher**, or baren, is a disklike hand tool that is flat on the bottom and has a handle. The artist would put the paper on top of the inked surface and then rub the paper evenly with the burnisher to transfer the ink to the paper.

MEZZOTINT AND AQUATINT

Mezzotint is a printmaking technique in which the artist works from dark to light. The artist would work on a copper or steel plate and roughen parts of the plate for shading, while smoothing out other parts for the lighter areas. This would increase and reduce the areas' ability to hold ink. The technique was developed in the 17th century, and it could be used to create gradations in the printed work, rather than everything being black and white.

Aquatint is another way to create tonal effects in a print. Fine particles of acid-resistant powdered rosin are melted onto a metal plate, which is then dipped in acid. The acid eats away at the metal around the particles, creating an even, granular pattern that when inked and printed will give an effect similar to a watercolor wash. The darkness of these tones can be controlled by lengthening or shortening the time that the plate is exposed to the acid.

Sculpture, Ceramics, Fiber Art, and Jewelry

CERAMICS AS A MEDIUM

Throughout history, ceramics have been used for fine arts and for functional pieces. Around 24,000 B.C., humans began making small figures out of clay. In 9,000 or 10,000 B.C., the first functional pottery and bricks were made. Glazes were discovered in Egypt around 8,000 B.C. A potter's wheel was used in Central America around 3,000 B.C. In ancient Greece, decorative vases depicted daily life and religion and were later decorated with black figures and red figures. Porcelain was developed in China during the Han dynasty (206 B.C.–A.D. 220). Pottery now can be mass-manufactured, but many fine artworks and functional pieces are still created by hand.

Ceramics are items produced from clay, including fine artwork, sculptures, figurines, and functional items such as tiles, dishes, urns, and vases. The item is formed, and then it is heated to harden it. A glaze can be applied, and then the item is reheated to harden the glaze. An underglaze can be applied first as a painted decoration. They can be hand built, pressed into molds, or created using a wheel.

SCULPTURE AS A MEDIUM

Sculptures have been created throughout history from many media, and only the most durable have survived. They can be small figures, larger freestanding works, or reliefs attached to walls. The first known prehistoric sculptures are from the Stone Age, approximately 230,000 B.C., and they were made from basalt and quartz. Figures called Venuses (shaped as obese women, possibly related to fertility) have been found from the Stone Age and were made from materials such as bone and various stones. Mesolithic sculpture, from 10,000–4,000 B.C., included freestanding sculptures and bas-relief works. In the Neolithic period (4,000–2,000 B.C.), bronze statuettes were created. Classical Greek sculpture is some of the most well known, dating from 500–323 B.C., and these superbly crafted figures would only be surpassed by later Renaissance artists. The Renaissance (A.D. 1,400–1,600) was a "rebirth" of classical ideals, and the sculptors created figures with great realism. Michelangelo (Michelangelo di Lodovico Buonarroti Simoni) is considered as the greatest Renaissance sculptor. Traditional materials were used throughout history, including stone, wood, bone, and metal.

BAS-RELIEF VS HAUT-RELIEF

In terms of sculpture, a relief is a sculpture in which the sculptural elements are attached to a solid background. For the sculpture to appear raised from the background, the background elements are cut away, leaving the subject raised.

A bas relief is also called a low relief. The final sculpture has a shallow depth and is not raised far from the background. Coins are a good example of this. In this type of relief sculpture, elements are often distorted by being flattened.

A haut-relief is also called a high relief; this is when more than half of the sculptural form is projecting from the background. Heads and limbs might be completely detached from the background in this form of relief. Many ancient Greek relief sculptures used this technique. This image is an example of a high, or haut-relief sculpture. Although the figures are still attached to the background, they are mostly projecting from it, only being attached at their backs.

CLAYS

Clays can be classified as high fire and low fire. The three most commonly used types of clay are earthenware, stoneware, and porcelain. Earthenware was the earliest clay used, and it is fired to a temperature of less than 1,200°C. Terra cotta is a type of earthenware that is reddish brown in color. Earthenware is brown, orange, or red in its raw and fired state. Earthenware is more porous than stoneware or porcelain, and it is less durable.

Stoneware is a mid- to high-fire clay that ranges from light gray to brown when fired. Stoneware is nonporous, and it differs from porcelain in that it is more opaque.

Porcelain has a rich history in China, and items made with porcelain are often called china or fine china in some English-speaking countries. Porcelain is a high-fire clay that is made with kaolin, which makes the finished product pure white. Porcelain is fired to 1,800°C, and when it is fired, it is hard, nonporous, and translucent.

MATERIALS USED FOR SCULPTURE

Stone has been used for sculptures for centuries, and the artist must use the subtractive method — removing pieces of the stone to shape the sculpture. Marble has been a preferred material for traditional sculptors since ancient Greece, but artists also use granite, limestone, sandstone, and alabaster.

Wood has been used historically for carving, and many important sculptures in Africa, China, and Japan were carved from wood. It is lighter and much easier to carve than stone.

Glass can be cast in molds or heated in kilns and then blown or sculpted with hand tools. Larger scale glass sculptures are a modern development. Glass was believed to be discovered in Egypt around 8,000 B.C.

Clay has been used for thousands of years to form pottery. The first functional pottery vessels were created in 10,000 B.C. People were crafting human and animal figures from clay as early as 24,000 B.C. Many cultures have used pottery for fine arts and functional vessels. Clay is a natural material found in the earth, but artists prefer different types. Clay can now be bought commercially, or it can be mixed by the artist. TOOLS USED FOR SCULPTURE

Tools such as chisels, pitching tools, rasps, mallets, and rifflers are used to sculpt stone. A chisel is a piece of steel that is pointed at one end and flat on the other end. A pitching tool is a wedge-shaped chisel. The chisel or pitching tool can be positioned on the stone and hit on the flat end with a mallet to break away unwanted stone. Rasps are flat steel tools with a rough surface, which can be used to wear away excess stone. A riffler is a smaller rasp used for details. Sandpaper or emery (a type of stone) can be used to polish a stone sculpture.

For pottery, an artist uses tools such as cutters and rolling pins for hand building. Ribbon or loop tools are made from a flattened metal ribbon and are attached to a wooden handle. These are used to trim, carve, and hollow out shapes. A wire cutter is used to remove a pot from a potter's wheel. A caliper is an adjustable tool used to measure openings for making lids.

For wood sculpture, similar tools are used as those for stone sculptures: chisels, rasps, mallets, and sandpaper. Gouges are useful for digging into the wood, and knives are also used for carving.

ADDITIVE VS SUBTRACTIVE SCULPTURE TECHNIQUES

Subtractive sculpture is the oldest form of sculpture. This consists of removing material from a larger piece, such as marble, wood, or another material. Michelangelo was a master of this subtractive technique, also known as carving. Michelangelo would begin with a large block of marble, and then he would carve and chip away until he was satisfied with his sculpture. The original piece of material has to be big enough to accommodate the size and shape of the finished work of art.

The additive technique consists of adding material to create an artwork. A soft material, such as clay or plaster strips, is built up over an armature until the final form is achieved. This is also called modeling. With the additive technique, the sculpture can start small and be built larger.

Another additive sculpture technique is assembling. This technique became popular in the 1950s and 1960s. The artist creates a three-dimensional collage by gluing, welding, nailing, and otherwise joining objects — usually found objects. The final product is called an assemblage.

HAND BUILDING AND WHEEL THROWING

Hand building is working with clay without a pottery wheel. Three methods are slab building, pinch pot, and the coil method. For slab building, clay is rolled into sheets and cut into shapes. The shapes are cut out and then joined together. The artist would score the edges with a sharp clay tool and then add some slip (liquid clay) to join the edges securely.

A pinch pot is created by rolling a ball of clay and then inserting a thumb into the ball. The artist presses the sides out evenly with the thumb on the inside of the pot and the fingers on the outside, until the sides and bottom are of consistent width and are smooth.

For the coil method, the artist first makes a shallow pinch pot as the base. He or she then rolls long coils of clay and builds up the body of the bowl or pot in a spiral, scoring and adding slip as the object is built.

Wheel throwing consists of using a potter's wheel to throw clay objects. The artist will first get any air bubbles out of the clay by wedging (kneading) the item on a surface, and then he or she uses slip to create the object as the clay spins on the wheel.

MODERN VS TRADITIONAL SCULPTURE MATERIALS

Traditional sculpture materials include stone, wood, clay, and metal. Stone (including marble) sculptures have survived through the years better than other materials due to their durability. Most works created with wood have been lost to decay, insect damage, and fire. Sculptors in ancient Greece and during the Renaissance focused on depicting the human body, and many ancient sculptures depicted religious or political subjects.

Modern sculptors have moved away from traditional materials and subjects and focus more on assembling and found objects. Picasso changed the direction of sculpture when he began constructing sculptures from different objects, much like a sculptural collage, in the early 20th century. In the 1940s and 1950s, artists began creating abstract and surreal sculptures and experimenting with new materials. This includes Alexander Calder's mobiles and David Smith's stainless steel sculptures. By the 1960s, some artists began creating minimalist works and experimenting with steel and environmental installations. Modern artists have also created sound sculptures, light sculptures, street art sculptures, and kinetic sculptures.

THE STAGES OF CLAY

The stages of clay determine how fragile or workable it is and what can or should be done to it next. Clay that has partially dried but is not completely dry is **leather hard.** When a piece is leather hard, the artist can carve the piece or add decorative slip. Handles can be added, and the foot of a pot can be trimmed.

Bone dry refers to when the clay is completely dry. The clay will be a lighter color. The piece will be fragile; attaching and carving cannot be done at this stage.

Bisque is when the piece has been fired once in a kiln. Bisqueware can be glazed and fired again. At this stage, prior to being glazed, the clay is still porous. Prior to being fired, all unfired clay pieces are referred to as **greenware.**

Slip is a liquid clay mixture that can be used to join clay pieces together. Slip is a mix of clay and water, and it has a runny consistency.

SUMMARIZE THE USE AND SIGNIFICANCE OF CERAMICS IN CHINA.

Pottery was first made in China during the Paleolithic era, and it became the most well-known form of art in China. Porcelain, a type of ceramic, is so associated with China that porcelain wares are dubbed "china" or "fine china" in other countries.

Porcelain originated in China, and although proto-porcelain was made as early as 1,600 B.C., it developed into high-fire porcelain in the Han dynasty (206 B.C.–A.D. 220). Later during the Ming dynasty, they began exporting porcelain wares to Europe. During the Ming dynasty (A.D. 1368–1644), cobalt underglazing was perfected, leading to the production of the iconic blue and white vases from that period. The blue underglaze is painted onto the porcelain, and then a clear glaze is applied, and the piece is fired.

Contemporary artist Ai Weiwei blends modern ideas with historical Chinese materials. One of his performance art pieces involved dropping a Han dynasty urn. Another work involved creating 100 million porcelain sunflower seeds.

SCULPTURES FROM ANCIENT GREECE VS ROME

Sculpture in ancient Greece often depicted battles, mythology, and their rulers. Whereas earlier sculptures were made from limestone or bronze, the later larger sculptural works were made from marble or bronze. The classical period of Greek sculpture showed great skill in depicting human anatomy and natural poses. Sculptures were life-sized and realistic. Most bronze Greek sculptures have only survived as Roman copies. The Greeks used the lost-wax technique to create their metal sculptures.

Sculptures in ancient Rome focused more on portrait and less on the idealized human body. The sculptured figures were more rigid and less natural than the Greek sculptures. Their sculptures reflected the current styles and hairdos, and they could even be dated by historians based on these fashions. Romans sought to immortalize and capture a likeness of a person, whereas Greeks sought to idealize them. There are many original Roman sculptures, but there are also many Roman copies of Greek sculptures.

RENAISSANCE SCULPTURE SUBJECTS AND TECHNIQUES

The hallmarks of the early Renaissance were classical composition and realism. Artists portrayed their subjects with a naturalism of their clothing, proportions, and perspective. These Italian artists recalled the classical sculptures of ancient Greece, and their subjects and forms. Throughout the Renaissance, sculptors created religious and secular sculptures. Church interiors, palaces, and private homes were elaborately decorated. The Madonna and Child were a popular subject, as well as scenes from the life of Christ. During the High Renaissance, subjects broadened and diverged more away from religious themes to include mythology and other topics.

Lorenzo Ghiberti won a contest to create large bronze doors at the Florence Baptistery, and this is thought of as the beginning of Renaissance sculpture. Donato di Niccolò di Betto Bardi, better known as Donatello, is another well-known sculptor of the 15th century, second only to Michelangelo. Both created many large marble and bronze sculptures. Donatello's most well known work is his *David*, cast in bronze. Michelangelo is known for many sculptures including the *Pieta* and *David,* both marble. This image is of Michelangelo's *David.*

LOST-WAX CASTING TECHNIQUE

Lost-wax casting is a technique in which a metal copy of a sculpture is produced from an original sculpture. This technique was used as early as 3,700 B.C. To produce a sculpture with this method, a mold is first made of a clay sculpture. The inside of this mold is brushed with wax until the wax is the thickness of the intended metal sculpture. The mold is removed, and the shell of wax is filled with a heat-resistant material. Then a heat-resistant plaster covers the wax, and the assemblage is turned over and placed in an oven. The wax drains away through vents places in the shell; after the plaster mold has been filled with sand, bronze is poured into the void left by the wax. After the whole assemblage has cooled off, the plaster and center are both removed, and the artist can apply any finishing touches to the bronze sculpture.

FIBER ART AS A MEDIUM

The term fiber art was first used by curators after World War II. It described works relating to fabrics, and it includes embroidery, weaving, knitting, crocheting, and sewing. Fiber arts take into consideration the artist's skill and labor to create the work, as well as the materials used, and it focuses more on the aesthetics than on the usefulness of the item.

In the 1950s, fiber artists began weaving more nonfunctional artworks. Then in the 1960s and 1970s, artists began exploring different techniques including knotting, coiling, and pleating fibers. The feminist movement began using fibers as "high art" and celebrating needlework in the 1970s. From the 1980s to the present, fiber artists have created more conceptual work, influenced by postmodernism. They have focused on cultural issues including feminism, gender, politics, and social sciences. Judy Chicago first used the term feminist art and founded the first feminist art program in the United States. Her work *The Dinner Party* incorporated fiber arts and celebrated the position that needlework and fabric has had in the history of women.

FIBERS AND MATERIALS

A fiber is a threadlike piece or material created from threadlike pieces. This includes materials such as fabric, yarn, and embroidery thread. Fibers can be made of natural materials, such as cotton, wool from sheep, or silk from a silkworm, but they can also be made from synthetic materials such as acrylic used to make yarn.

Yarn can be bought premade, or it can be spun by the artist. To spin yarn, the artist starts with roving, which is wool that has been run through a mill to brush the fibers in the same direction but hasn't been spun into yarn yet. Yarn can be made with many materials, in many thicknesses and colors. Roving can also be used for felting, which is a process involving hot water and shrinking a wool piece down into a smaller, denser piece.

When using fabrics, the artist can use a sewing machine or sew by hand, but the artist needs to understand the properties of each material and how best to join them.

THE ACCEPTANCE OF FIBER ART

Textile and fiber work, including sewing, embroidery, knitting, and crocheting, have always been considered women's work and have been devalued for a long time. During the suffrage movement of the early 1900s, embroidery was highlighted as a fiber art medium for feminist protests. During the 1950s, artists began creating hanging and freestanding fiber works, but it wasn't until Judy Chicago's work that fiber arts really began to be accepted as an artistic medium. Artists took the perception of fiber as women's work and turned their works into fun and liberating works of art. Her most famous work, *The Dinner Party*, celebrates the accomplishments of 39 important women from history, setting a place at a table for each woman. The work, constructed as a long triangle, incorporates traditional needlepoint and embroidery among other materials. More than 400 people, mostly women, volunteered to assist with aspects of this artwork, and it is still known as the first major feminist artwork.

KNITTING, WEAVING, AND CROCHETING

Knitting consists of creating a series of interlocking loops using straight knitting needles that are pointed at one end. The knitter begins by casting on, or creating the first stitches on the needle. A variety of stitches are used; the main stitches are called knit and purl. The basic knitted pattern is called a stocking or stockinette pattern, and the right side looks like a pattern of V shapes.

For weaving, two sets of threads are interlocked in a perpendicular pattern. This can be done by hand or by machine. The lengthwise threads are called the warp and are held stationary on a loom while the other thread (weft) is passed back and forth between them.

Crocheting involves using a stick with a hook at the end, called a crochet hook, and creating stitches to interlock the yarn into a fabric or pattern. With crochet, each stitch is finished before starting the next, whereas in knitting, many stitches are kept open at the same time.

JEWELRY AS A MEDIUM

Prior to the discovery of precious metals, in prehistoric times humans used bone, shells, antlers, feathers, and pebbles to decorate their bodies. One of the oldest examples of traditional jewelry was discovered in a tomb in Sumer from 2,600 B.C. The findings included gold pins, amulets, earrings, and a headdress. Evidence was found of Sumerians using techniques such as welding, enameling, stonecutting, and filigree. The tomb of Tutankhamun in Egypt showed mastery of gold and jewelry techniques by the ancient Egyptians. Bracelets, amulets, pendants, earrings, and a large quantity of jewels were found in the tomb, showing a high degree of craftsmanship. Motifs used include the scarab, lotus flower, Horus, eye, serpent, and sphinx, among others. During the Bronze Age, the Minoans in Greece were stamping and cutting gold sheets into beads to form necklaces and decorate clothing. Jewelry making flourished during the Hellenistic period in Greece, and it was used to an even greater extent in ancient Rome. The gold ring became common in ancient Rome, and not just for noblemen. Rings and brooches became widely used in medieval Europe. With a rebirth of classicism, jewelry making reached new heights in the Renaissance era.

TOOLS AND SUPPLIES

Precious metals used for creating jewelry include gold and silver. They are both available in varying purities. 24 karat gold is 24 out of 24 parts gold, and it is also known as pure gold. Fine silver is 99.9% pure silver, whereas sterling silver is at least 92.5% pure silver. Other metals used include brass, which is an alloy of 70% copper and 30% zinc; copper, a bright reddish-orange element; and pewter, a silver-gray alloy of tin, antimony, and copper.

A soldering iron can be used for joining metal parts together. A jewelry artist will use a variety of pliers, saws, and cutters for working with metal, as well as a polisher to finish the piece. A mandrel is used to size and shape a ring; it is a tapered piece of metal that the ring fits onto. Clamps hold the piece steady for the artist to work on it. A loupe is a magnifier used to see the piece in detail. Calipers are used to measure the gauge (thickness) of materials.

ENAMELING

Enameling involves fusing powdered glass to a surface by heating it to between 750°C and 850°C. When fired, the glass powder melts and turns into a smooth, shiny coating. Enameling is often seen on metal jewelry, but it can also be used on glass and ceramics. It can be applied to gold, copper, silver, and aluminum. Commercially, it is often applied to stainless steel. After it is fired, it is durable and resistant to scratching. The finely ground glass used for enameling is called frit, and various minerals are added for coloring. Different colors of enamels can be mixed to create new colors, and enamel can be transparent, translucent, or opaque. Enameling was used in ancient Egypt for the creation of jewelry, as well as in ancient Greece, ancient Rome, and China. In ancient Rome, enamel was also used on glass.

This image is an example of enamel applied to a copper alloy disk, from between 1290 and 1310. It is a radial pattern with a rose window design.

SOLDERING AND FILIGREE

Soldering can be done on a clean ceramic tile or fire brick. The metal to be soldered should be clean and free of oil or grease. Flux is mixed with water and dabbed on the parts where the metal will be joined. The flux is a chemical used to promote soldering. Tiny pieces of solder are placed onto the fluxed seams of the metal with tweezers. A flame is applied, and the piece is heated evenly until the solder melts and the pieces join.

Filigree is a technique of forming metal threads to resemble a lace pattern. Making a filigree piece involves careful and skillful bending of wire. A filigreed metal piece can be simple or complex, consisting of many pieces carefully formed and combined. Before working with the wire and wrapping it, it should first be annealed. Annealing is a process of heating the metal, then cooling it slowly, so it is easier to work with for a specific technique. This silver ring contains a filigree pattern.

JEWELRY MAKING: ART AND CRAFT

Although art and craft are both thought of as ways to express creativity, the distinction lies in the purpose of the work produced. Crafts are created with an aesthetic and a functional purpose, whereas art is generally decorative but not functional. Based on this, jewelry's functional and decorative nature can be seen as both an art and a craft. Jewelry makers throughout time have used various techniques to create intricate and beautiful works that show superb craftsmanship as well as artistic inspiration. Jewelry making has followed artistic trends throughout major art eras, and the pieces have been used to adorn important leaders, politicians, and the common citizen. Jewelry making requires skill and understanding of the materials, but so does working with oil paints or sculpture materials. The line between art and craft has often been blurred, with artists creating decorative pieces with materials usually used for functional crafts.

Performance Art, Photography, Videography, and Digital and Print Media

THE EARLY CAMERA

The first **photograph** was taken by French inventor Nicéphore Niépce in 1827. In 1837, Louis Daguerre developed the first practical process to create photographs, which was called the daguerreotype. Daguerreotypes create an image on a silvered copper plate, and they require the subject to stay still from 15 to 30 minutes. Henry Fox Talbot next developed the calotype, or talbotype, process. The daguerreotype and the calotype both use two nested boxes as the body of the camera. The calotype used paper coated in silver iodide for the print.

Emulsion plates, or wet plates, using the collodion process followed. They needed much less exposure time than previous methods. Bellows were added to cameras at this time to aid in focusing the image. Ambrotype and tintype were two common emulsion plates. Ambrotype used a glass plate, whereas tintype used tin.

In 1888, George Eastman developed a film camera, and the first one was called the "Kodak." This camera did not require solid plates, and the cost was low enough for the average consumer. The first 35 mm camera was available in 1913, but the film was not affordable to average consumers until the 1940s.

DIGITAL PHOTOGRAPHY

Prior to the introduction of digital photography, the photographic process was slower and much more expensive. The number of shots was limited to the number available on each roll of film. Film had to be handled carefully and correctly, and then it was taken to a photo developing center, or it could be developed at home in a darkroom using special equipment. Until the pictures were developed, the photographer did not know how their pictures turned out. If the original prints and film are lost, the images can be lost forever.

With digital photography, the number of images is only limited by the storage space on the camera and the size of the digital image. Photographers can immediately review the images, delete unwanted images, and take more photographs until they are satisfied that they have a good shot. Digital photographs can be more easily edited and manipulated on a computer than photos developed in a darkroom. Digital photographs can be stored indefinitely on a digital device and printed inexpensively with online services or on a home printer.

PHOTOGRAPHY SUPPLIES

Although film cameras are still in limited use, **digital photography** has surpassed them as the medium of choice. Digital cameras range greatly from inexpensive cameras for casual use to high-priced cameras for professionals. Fewer dedicated low-end digital cameras are used now because the ability to take photographs is included in most smartphones.

The **resolution** of a digital camera is determined by its image sensor. A camera with a 1,000 × 1,000 pixel image sensor will take up to 1 megapixel photos. A digital camera can shoot up to 120 megapixels, whereas a smartphone will now shoot up to 12 megapixels. A digital camera can be compact and portable, or it can be larger with removable lenses. A digital single-lens reflex (DSLR) camera contains a mirror at a 45-degree angle to convey the image to the sensor. The DSLR camera will have a higher possible resolution than a compact camera, and it will usually have the option of multiple lenses for different purposes. This image is of a DSLR camera.

FILM PHOTOGRAPHY SUPPLIES

To shoot photographs with a film camera, the correct type of **film** is needed for the photographer's purposes. The most common size is 35 mm and speeds range from 100 to 3,200, with consumer film ranging up to 800. The speed of the film is determined by the International Standards Organization (ISO) scale, which dictates how much exposure the film needs to produce an image. Slower film will give better detail and color, but faster film can capture a subject in motion.

To develop the film, the camera back is opened, the film is removed in a completely dark room, and it is coiled into a reel as shown in the image. The reel is placed into the container, and a chemical process consisting of developer bath, stop bath, and fixer bath are introduced into the container. The film can then be exposed to light to be washed and dried.

After the film is developed, the images are printed onto photo paper in a darkroom lit with only a safelight, which will illuminate the room in a red or amber color. An enlarger is used to expose the film to the photo paper.

PARTS OF A CAMERA

The main part of a camera is called the **body**. The **viewfinder** is where the photographer looks through the back of the camera to compose the shot. Some digital cameras will have a liquid-crystal display (LCD) screen instead of a viewfinder. The shutter release button activates the shutter, and the amount of time that the shutter is left open is determined by the shutter speed. The lens is on the front of the camera, and it focuses and directs light into the camera. Lenses can either be fixed to the body, or they can be removable. The aperture of the camera controls the amount of light reaching the image sensor. It also determines how much of the image is in focus (depth of field). The aperture is expressed in f-stops. A film advance lever is found on a film camera, and it moves the film to the next frame. A flash can be built in or added to the camera; it adds light to the subject. A flash can be connected to the top of the camera on a socket called a hot shoe.

VIDEO ART

Video art began in the 1960s, and artists used mainly analog videotape as their medium into the 1990s. Nam June Paik is known as the pioneer of video art. The first instance of video art is when Paik used a Sony Portapak video recorder in 1965 to tape Pope Paul VI's procession in New York City, and then he played the tapes in another location. The availability of consumer video equipment such as the Portapak allowed artists to begin experimenting with this new medium. Artists experimented with the capabilities and limitations of the equipment by combining, layering, and distorting the signals. In the 1980s and 1990s, video editing software became more readily available and allowed video artists much greater flexibility and control over their work. With the advent of digital video technology, equipment has become increasingly compact and portable, as well as more easily available.

One of Paik's most famous works is *Electronic Superhighway* (1995), which includes a 51-channel video installation, along with neon lights. The scale and images represent the enormity of the United States as seen by this artist who came from Korea at only nine years old.

THE RULE OF THIRDS

The **rule of thirds** is a compositional technique used for not only photography, but also for other two-dimensional art forms. The rule of thirds involves dividing an image vertically and horizontally into three equal parts. This divides the image into nine equal parts. The subject or focal point of the image should then be placed at one of the intersections of these lines. Doing this creates tension and imbalance in the image, and it creates a more interesting composition than placing the subject or focal point squarely in the center of the photograph. This image illustrates the rule of thirds and the lines associated with it. In this image, the center of the nearest object is placed on the lower right intersection of lines and the tower in the background is aligned along the left vertical line. The horizon also falls along the lower horizontal line, rather than being placed in the center of the image.

APERTURE AND FOCAL LENGTH

A camera's **aperture** is the opening in the lens, and it is measured in f-stops. Moving from one f-stop to the next doubles or halves the size of the opening. A larger f-stop number means a smaller aperture. Adjusting the aperture will change the depth of field of your photograph, which is how much of the image is in focus. A shallow depth of field is a result of letting more light in or a larger aperture (a smaller f-stop). A shallow depth of field means that only a part of the image is in focus and the rest is blurry. A large depth of field results in most of the image being in focus, and this is done with a smaller aperture (larger f-stop).

The focal length of a camera lens determines the magnification of the image, and it is usually expressed in millimeters. The field of view and focal length are inversely proportional. A 24–35 mm lens will give a wider angle and capture more of a scene from the same distance as a 50 mm lens.

PHOTOGRAPHY USED TO DOCUMENT EVENTS

Early photographers attempted to record the events of war, but limitations of the process prevented them from recording movement and action. Instead, they photographed the still aspects, and they even recreated scenes to attempt to convey their impressions of the battles. During the Civil War, photographers staged scenes of battles to heighten the emotional effects of their images. They would even move and rearrange dead bodies. These images were used to convey the atrocities of war to the public.

During the Great Depression, the Farm Service Agency sent photographers out to document American life, especially rural America. These photographers, including Dorothea Lange, captured

47

images of life during this difficult time. These images serve as a reminder of this era, as well as documentation of how Americans persisted through their difficulties. One of the best-known images from this time is *Migrant Mother*, by Dorothea Lange. She skillfully captured the worry and fear on the face of a mother dealing with raising children during a time of extreme poverty.

ACCEPTANCE OF PHOTOGRAPHY AS AN ART FORM

Since the invention of the camera, photographers have struggled with acceptance in the art world. They questioned the role that photography would play in art and whether they should be confined to the aesthetics of other art forms or explore ideas and characteristics of the new medium. Photography has taken many forms, including photojournalism, but it has historically mostly been accepted as a craft.

In the early and mid-1900s, Alfred Stieglitz, Edward Steichen, and Ansel Adams were critical to advancing photography from a craft to the acceptance as a fine art. In Adams' case, his beautiful photographs of nature scenes were used not only as artistic expression, but also to promote the conservation of nature. His work *The Tetons and Snake River* is an example of this. It wasn't until after the 1950s that it was thought acceptable and unpretentious to frame a photograph for a show

or exhibition. Until the 1970s, the main genres of fine arts photography were portraits, landscapes, and nudes.

THE IMPACT OF THE CAMERA

After the invention of the camera in the early 1800s, people began using photographic techniques to attempt to capture reality in a more reliable way than they could by hand. People created millions of daguerreotypes to record images of their families, aware of their own mortality. Photographs were used to capture the atrocities of war, mundane life, and each other. Images of average people could be created as easily as images of important politicians. Action photos as well as posed scenes were created. Images captured in a photograph were more objective than those created by artists, taking out much of the imagination and artistic license, and giving a more reliable representation of the subject. By the mid-19th century, photography was becoming accepted as a powerful tool for communication. When the first mass-produced camera was created in 1901, photography became accessible to more people. With advances in equipment, photographers no longer needed to carry plates and chemicals to process their images.

CINDY SHERMAN

Cindy Sherman is a photographer whose work has been an inspiration for contemporary portrait photographers. She began her photography work in the 1970s. In her first self-portrait series, *Untitled Film Stills,* she plays the role of "everywoman," dressing up and characterizing herself in many different clichéd feminine roles including housewife and pinup girl. Sherman changed the perception of portrait photography to a depersonalized method of critiquing social issues. She used an antinarrative approach to photography, discarding notions of documentary realism and creating works that left unresolved ideas and emotions.

Sherman used her photography to examine assumptions and stereotypes, and her work is often associated with feminism. Her work has highlighted the objectification of women, as well as obsessions with youth and beauty. She explored identity and representation in new ways and opened the door for creative and conceptual photographic portraiture. In the 1980s, her work helped to drive photography into acceptance as high art.

ELECTRONIC ART AS A MEDIUM

Electronic art is an art form that uses electronic media, including digital art, video art, and interactive art. Digital art is created using a computer, and it started when artists began to

49

experiment with computers in the 1960s. As computers have become more affordable, digital art has grown as a medium.

Photoshop was first developed in 1987 at Industrial Light and Magic, a visual effects company, and it was later sold to Adobe. Many versions and related programs have followed, including a touchscreen version for tablets.

Nam June Paik is regarded as a pioneer in video art, which emerged as a medium in the late 1960s as video cameras became available to consumers. As time has passed, prices have dropped, and video cameras have become increasingly portable and more versatile.

Interactive art involves the viewer participating with the artwork. This could include the viewer walking into or onto the artwork, or even becoming part of the artwork. These works generally include some computer or motion sensor components. The earliest examples of interactive art date back to the 1920s.

DIGITAL ART: SUPPLIES

Supplies used for digital art include computers, tablets, video cameras, scanners, and digital cameras. The computer can be used to generate art, for example, with fractals or algorithms, in which data are put into the computer and the computer uses the data to create an image. The computer can also be the tool that the artist uses to create their artwork. The artist can use a mouse or a stylus to draw and edit images on the screen. This can also be done on the touchscreen of a tablet. The final product can be printed on papers of various thicknesses, colors, and surfaces. An inkjet printer blends colors smoothly and is cost effective. Laser and LED printers are more expensive and faster but are best with solid colors and black text.

Video cameras can be used to capture video, which can be edited on a computer to produce the final product. Another part of digital art includes using an electronic display in an art installation. The artist can include TV screens or projector screens to display their videos.

TECHNIQUES USED IN DIGITAL ART

To create digital art, the artist can use the computer to manipulate found images, images taken with a digital camera, or images scanned with a scanner. The computer can also be used to automatically generate images such as fractal or algorithm art. Once the artist has images in the computer, they can use editing software such as Photoshop to alter those images. Illustrator is another popular software used to create images, but it is used to create vector-based illustrations and text that can be enlarged or shrunk without losing quality. Photoshop is used to edit photographs and raster (pixel)-based artwork. If a raster-based artwork is enlarged too much, it loses quality and becomes pixelated.

To create artwork that includes an electronic display, the artist can use a projector and a screen to project a large video or can include TV or computer screens within their work to show their video art.

FILE FORMATS FOR DIGITAL ART

Common image file formats include JPG, GIF, TIFF, and PNG. JPG is the most commonly used image format, and it stands for Joint Photographic Experts Group. JPG images are highly compressed; this has the benefit of a small file, but the compression is lossy, meaning it sacrifices quality for a smaller size. A GIF file uses lossless compression, but it is limited in its display of colors. It is better for graphics than photographs. A TIFF file is lossless and is considered the best quality format for graphics work. It can be saved in red, green, blue (RGB) or cyan, magenta, yellow, and black

(CMYK). A PNG file will be smaller than a TIFF but larger than a JPG, and it is also lossless. It is the newest of these formats. A GIF or PNG file will support transparency or animation.

Videos are saved as Audio Video Interleave (AVI), Flash Video Format (FLV), Windows Media Video (WMV), Apple QuickTime Movie (MOV), or Moving Pictures Expert Group 4 (MP4) formats. AVI is one of the oldest video formats. FLV files are created with Adobe Flash. WMV was originally intended for streaming content online. MP4 is a newer format becoming popular for sharing videos online.

ADVANTAGES AND DISADVANTAGES OF DIGITAL ART

Digital art can be saved in an image or video format, and it can be shared and reproduced multiple times. A digital image can be printed, and this artwork can be shared with multiple people or shown in multiple locations. Many traditional art methods produce only one artwork, and if this artwork is damaged, there is not another copy saved elsewhere. Digital art can be created quickly, and it can be edited, erased, and changed until the artist is satisfied. As technology evolves, new techniques and possibilities emerge.

Because digital art can be reproduced and shared endlessly, it is not held in as high regard as other art forms. Digital art is thought to require less skill than other art forms, and because anyone can create digital art, it is thought of as a lesser art form. It does not require the knowledge of traditional art media or practice involved with drawing, painting, sculpture, and other media.

PERFORMANCE ART AS A MEDIUM

Performance art began in the early 20th century with the futurist, Russian constructivist, and Dada art movements. Performance art is a scripted or unscripted performance that is presented live in the context of fine arts. The performance is usually conceptual and not just for entertainment. The artist seeks to break away from the traditions of art and can even include audience participation if desired.

Performance art involves four components: the performer, time, space, and a relationship with the audience. It can be experienced live or through media, with no specific venue or length of time required. The artist might stick to a script or improvise as the performance goes on. Unlike the performing arts, performance art does not create a fictitious drama with a linear script. Performance art is often satirical or will make the viewer think about art in unconventional ways.

SITE-SPECIFIC ART AND INSTALLATION ART

Site-specific art is created to be displayed or erected in a certain location, and it loses meaning if it is removed from that location. The term was first used in the mid-1970s. Site-specific art includes sculptures, land art, or even a dance or performance created for and performed in a specific location. Christo and Jeanne-Claude are known for their large-scale, site-specific artworks including wrapped bridges and surrounded islands.

Installation art is a large-scale construction created with mixed media, for a specific location and length of time. An installation can take up an entire room and is sometimes referred to as an environment. The viewer can walk through the room to experience the art. An installation can also be smaller and be intended for the viewer to walk around. Installation art has been a major art form since the 1960s.

ENVIRONMENTAL ART

The **environmental art movement** began in the 1960s and consisted of site-specific sculptures. Environmental art can use part of the environment to create aesthetic artwork, or it can create a

51

statement on environmental, social, or political issues relating to the natural world. It can highlight and celebrate the artist's connection with the natural world, and it can use natural materials within the environment. The movement began in rural areas, but in the 1970s and 1980s, environmental art was also created in public and urban areas. It can be created to blend in with nature or highlight environmental issues, but sometimes environmental art actually damages the environment, like Robert Smithson's *Spiral Jetty*, shown here. The creation of this work permanently damaged the land it was created on, and it has been criticized for such. Another criticism of environmental art is the fact that it either has to be experienced on site or displayed as a photograph of the art, posing a challenge to gallery exhibitions.

A HAPPENING

A **happening** is a performance or event created in the context of fine art. Happenings include audience participation as a main component, and although some parts are planned by the artist, there is often also room for improvisation as well. Every time a happening was performed, it would be different due to the unplanned and improvised parts. This is in stark contrast to static, unchanging works of art, which provide the same experience to each viewer. Happenings exist as a fleeting moment, something that cannot be preserved and shown in a museum. A major difference between happenings and other types of art is that each happening is unique. They could be elaborate and large or intimate and small depending on the artist's intentions.

Allan Kaprow first used the term "happening" in 1957 to describe art events that he experienced at a picnic on George Segal's farm. Kaprow's 1959 work was titled *18 Happenings in 6 Parts*. A happening could include any combination of elements of dance, music, performance, poetry, and theater, as well as art creation.

ENVIRONMENTAL ART: MATERIALS.

Environmental art can incorporate materials from the natural environment, or it can introduce new and surprising materials into the natural environment. Some environmental art will include leaves, branches, rocks, moss, logs, vines, and other materials found in the local environment, changing the environment and emphasizing the local materials. Other environmental art will include nonnatural materials such as nylon fabric, spray paint, or metal.

This example by Robert Smithson, *Broken Circle and Spiral Hill*, was created in 1971 in the Netherlands. Smithson listed his materials as green water and white and yellow sand flats. Smithson used the local materials to create something different and recognizable as something not created by nature, but rather created with nature. Smithson had begun the "land art" movement, desiring to create art out in the open and not inside a studio. The life span of this type of artwork is finite, meant to be eventually reclaimed by nature.

PERFORMANCE ART: MATERIALS

Performance art involves the presence of the artist as the performer, the involvement of the audience, time, and a space for the performance. It includes the actions of the performer or performers as the artwork. The actual work requires live performance, but the artwork can reach a wider audience afterward by documentation through photography and videotaping. The documentation can affect how the viewer understands the work, and it can be different than experiencing the work firsthand.

In Marina Abramović's work *The Artist Is Present*" (2010), she sat silently at a wooden table, and people took turns sitting across from her, silently engaging her gaze. Abramović was experimenting with people's perception of expected time of a performance, stretching it out to eight hours a day for three months. She sought to push limits of the time of a performance piece, while engaging thousands of participants.

PERFORMANCE ART: TECHNIQUES

Performance art involves many techniques and materials, all depending on the artist and the messages that they are trying to convey. One example is Yoko Ono's *Cut Piece* (1964), in which she sat on a stage while viewers took turns cutting her clothing off of her with scissors. This was a commentary on voyeurism and a voyeur's participation and responsibility in objectifying women.

Another example is Chris Burden's *Shoot* (1971), which involved a friend shooting him in the arm while another friend documented the performance with a camera. This work touched on the second friend's desire to intervene, ideas of gun control, and even the Vietnam War.

For *Art/Life: One Year Performance* (*Rope Piece*), begun in 1983, Linda Montano and Tehching Hsieh were tied to each other by an eight-foot piece of rope for an entire year but did not touch each other. For this work, the rope represented people's struggle to connect to each other socially and physically.

ENVIRONMENTAL ART: TECHNIQUES

Environmental art seeks to challenge traditional notions of sculpture and bring sculptural elements to the natural environment. Some environmental art uses elements of the natural landscape to create the artwork, including sticks, sand, rocks, stones, and moss. The artwork is intended to disappear back into the landscape as time and weather affect the sculpture.

In the 1980s, artists began creating environmental art in public spaces, including vacant lots and other urban locations. Artists sought to bring their artwork closer to people, to engage them in the dialogue about art, the environment, and conservation. One artist planted cabbages in a pattern in an empty lot. Another made the particulates in the air visible for viewers. Yet another artist marked possible flood lines in at-risk cities that could result from climate change.

For environmental art to be shown in a gallery or museum, the artist must provide photographs, which do not give the full experience of the art.

The Evolution of Performance Art

Performance art has become accepted as an art medium in the past 30 years.

It differs from theater and performing art by its lack of a clear narrative. Inspired by the abstract expressionism movement, artists wanted to include the body's role in artmaking into the actual artwork. The act of creation, not just the final product, was seen as important, like Jackson Pollock's action paintings. His movements and process played a big role in the creation of his paintings. Performance art emphasizes the time and space in which art exists, as well as the actions of the artist. Artists sought new ways to express themselves, and museums have sought ways to display these works. In a way, this is opposite to the idea of performance art existing in a finite time and interacting with the viewers. New strategies of performance art have sought to create interactions between people who would not have interacted otherwise. Artists have even begun to reenact performance pieces from the past, attempting to recapture those experiences.

Environmental Art: Motivation

Environmental art, or land art, sprung partly from artists' desire to work outside of the studio and create artworks that could not be contained in a gallery or exhibit. Depending on the artist, it can be created to raise awareness of environmental issues such as erosion or conservation. It can explore humans' relationship with nature or the human-built world with the natural environment. It can capture how we are polluting the environment or how man is affecting the natural world. It can even highlight the artist's love of nature and the beauty of our world. Environmental art is created as site-specific artwork that will eventually be reclaimed by its surrounding environment, so its existence is usually short-lived. Photography is an important component of these works, capturing the scene for those who cannot view it in person before it is gone.

Christo and Jeanne-Claude

Christo and Jeanne-Claude are artists known for some of the largest and most ambitious site-specific artwork created. Whereas landscape art uses natural materials to create artwork, Christo and Jeanne-Claude used manufactured materials to contrast with the environment in which they created the artwork. Part of their process included negotiating with and gaining permits from the owners of the land or structure they wished to use. Each artwork created was large scale and required a lot of time and work to construct. They have insisted that the artwork was created for aesthetic value alone, and not for any deeper meanings. Some well-known artworks include wrapping the Pont-Neuf, the oldest bridge in France, in a sand-colored fabric, and surrounding several Miami islands in a bright pink fabric. *The Umbrellas* involved placing more than 1,000 umbrellas in Japan and the United States at the same time. In their project *The Gates*, installed in Central Park in New York City in 2005, visitors could walk through and around these 7,503 fabric gates throughout the park, which changed the look of the familiar landscape.

EARTH ART

Earth art, or Earthworks, is a genre of art that seeks to use materials taken directly from nature. This is a subgenre of environmental art, but it focuses on the use of local and natural materials to create sculptural forms. Artists would use water, stones, gravel, soil, and sticks, paying homage to the specific site by using local materials. Earth art shares some characteristics with minimalism, using a simplicity of form to express ideas. Earth art highlights the beauty and aesthetics of the natural world while rejecting the traditions of art creation and exhibition. Earth art can be categorized as invasive or noninvasive, with invasive Earth art making significant alterations to the environment. Noninvasive Earth art is thought of as being more respectful to the environment, preserving the integrity of the landscape. Because Earth art is site-specific, it is not accessible to the average viewer, cannot be displayed as is in a museum, and cannot be bought and sold.

Material Handling, Storage, and Safety

MECHANICAL AND CHEMICAL HAZARDS

When handling materials and tools, one must be aware of the potential safety hazards involved. Hazards can affect the people involved in the process, people in the area, or even tools and the environment. **Mechanical hazards** are safety concerns surrounding the tools and materials that can cause direct physical harm when the appropriate precautions are not followed. Examples include straining a muscle by lifting too much weight or receiving cuts from something sharp or abrasive. Other results of mechanical hazards include breaks, cuts, crush injuries, and burns. **Chemical hazards** are safety concerns mainly dealing with reactive or toxic substances. These can include explosive, flammable, acidic, corrosive, and toxic or poisonous materials. Where mechanical hazards are usually immediately apparent, chemical hazards can be less obvious and can cause serious short and long-term health effects.

STORAGE OF MATERIALS AND EQUIPMENT

Materials must be stored in a way that protects both the supplies and the users. Improperly stored materials can go bad or become a safety hazard. Principles of **proper storage** include ensuring proper labeling, including dating of materials to ensure they are not expired, keeping materials out of excessive humidity or moisture and sunlight, proper sealing of containers, and ensuring there is adequate ventilation. Some materials should not be stored together as they can produce dangerous chemical reactions. **Material storage cabinets** should be lockable and inaccessible to children and should ideally be made of a durable, corrosive-resistant, and heat-resistant material, such as painted metal to help prevent deterioration over time and to reduce risk in the event of a fire. **Ventilation** is particularly important when it comes to storing volatile materials that off-gas. Without proper ventilation, flammable, combustible, or toxic fumes can build up to produce unexpected reactions. Objects in storage should also be organized in a way which minimizes **physical risk**. For instance, items should never be stored in precarious positions and sharp objects should not be loose but should be in well-labeled containers.

MATERIAL HANDLING AND PROTECTIVE EQUIPMENT

When handling materials, one must be sure to use the appropriate protective equipment. Generally protective equipment refers to personal protective equipment (PPE), which generally means clothing used to protect the body. Common PPE includes the following:

- **Gloves** – Various types and uses ranging from protecting the hands from material exposure to protection from sharp, abrasive, hot, or cold objects.

- **Eye protection** – Generally recommended for any time a material might be introduced into the air or flung by a process.
- **Aprons or smocks** – Protects the body from exposure to materials that can cause abrasions, stains, burns, etc. Generally recommended when handling liquids.
- **Closed-toe shoes** – Necessary when handling chemicals, sharp objects, or heavy objects that could harm the feet if dropped.
- **Helmets** – Used primarily in construction where heavy materials are hoisted.
- **Hearing protection** – Necessary to protect against loud or sustained noises.
- **Respirator or Dust Masks** – Protects against fumes and dust exposure. The type of filtration needs to be sufficient for the materials in use.

The equipment used for protection, including PPE must be **sufficient** to handle the specific materials in use, such as using the appropriate type of gloves and apron to protect against the hazards on hand. For instance, workers' gloves may protect against minor abrasions, but they do not resist the penetration of chemicals. Likewise, the PPE must not be so restrictive that it actually causes greater risk. For instance, spinning tools are unsafe to use with most gloves as the gloves can be pulled into the machinery, creating a greater potential for injury.

SAFETY IN THE IMMEDIATE AREA

When working with materials or tools, the area must be secured in such a way that all people entering the area will be **aware** and **protected** from **immediate hazards**. Active work zones should be obvious and not have too much foot traffic. PPE such as hearing protection may limit the awareness of people working near one another, so a clear line of sight is important to maintain. All people in the immediate area should have clear access to first aid and other emergency response devices, such as fire alarms, wash stations, and fire extinguishers. Flammables, toxic materials, and aerosols should be used away from other people and require adequate ventilation. Ventilation requires access to fresh, clean air, and not just airflow alone. Blowing a fan in a closed area while using volatile chemicals can actually increase the buildup of harmful or dangerous chemicals and lead to a worse outcome than a closed room with no ventilation.

DISPOSAL OF MATERIALS

When disposing of materials, it is always important to follow federal, state, and local laws to prevent unnecessary environmental damage or risk to others. Many materials should not be placed in the general waste due to chemical or physical hazards associated. Likewise, chemicals should never be poured down sinks as solvents and volatile chemicals can either eat at the infrastructure or cause buildup of harmful gases that could be toxic, flammable, corrosive, or explosive. Many of these types of chemicals can be taken to a designated facility, or even recycled. Other materials, such as glue, concrete, paint, or adhesives should simply be set aside to continue curing until they become solids and are safe to dispose of in the trash. This can prevent unnecessary and harmful spills of liquids that are challenging or impossible to clean up.

SDS (SAFETY DATA SHEETS)

Safety Data Sheets (SDS, formerly Material Safety Data Sheets, MSDS) provide information on the physical and chemical properties of a substance as well as potential health and environmental concerns. OSHA requires that all chemicals be labeled appropriately and that SDS be readily available in the workplace. The hazard communication standard also requires employees to be trained, and for the employer to maintain records of the training given. The format for SDS includes sixteen sections. The required sections are as follows:

> **I:**Identification
> **II:**Hazard Identification

III: Composition/Information on Ingredients
IV: First Aid Measures
V:Firefighting Measures
VI: Accidental Release Measures
VII: Handling/Storage Requirements
VIII: Physical/Chemical Properties
IX: Exposure Controls/Personal Protection
X:Stability/Reactivity
XI: Toxicological Information
XII: Ecological Information
XIII: Disposal Considerations
XIV: Transportation Information
XV: Regulatory Information
XVI: Other Information

CHEMICALLY PROTECTIVE CLOTHING

SDS often recommend the usage of chemical protective clothing (CPC). Protective eye goggles with splash guards and air vents should be used when handling chemicals. Face shields should be used when working with large quantities of a substance and are most effective when used in conjunction with safety goggles. If the mode of possible hazard is through contact and/or absorption on skin, appropriate gloves should be worn. Gloves are chosen based upon their permeability to and reactivity with the chemical in use. Personal respiratory equipment may be indicated if fume hoods do not provide adequate ventilation of fumes or airborne particulates. Body protection depends on the level of protection needed and ranges from rubberized aprons to full suits that are evaluated for their permeability and leak protection. Closed-toed protective shoes should always be used when working with chemicals.

REQUIREMENTS FOR LABELS

The term *label* under the Globally Harmonized System (GHS) of Classification and Labeling of Chemicals refers to the label on the container. Under GHS, it's required to contain certain elements; these requirements apply whether the label is affixed by the manufacturer or whether the chemical is placed into a smaller, secondary container in the workplace. The label must include the identification of the chemical, the manufacturer's name and contact information, the applicable GHS pictograms, the applicable signal words (either *danger* or *warning*, as applicable), and precautionary statements (measures to reduce risk from exposure to the chemical).

PICTOGRAMS

The pictograms used in the GHS system are simple pictures used to convey hazards posed by the chemical. They are meant to be universally understandable by people with diverse language and reading fluencies. They are as follows:

Health Hazard	*Flammable*	*Sensitizer/ Irritant*

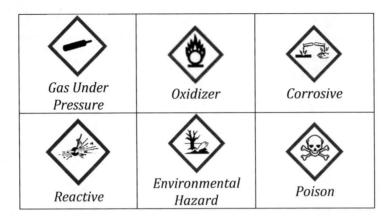

SIGNAL WORDS

Under the GHS hazard communication and safety data sheet system, the term **signal word** is used to describe one word that summarizes the degree of danger posed by the substances. There are only two signal words: *danger* and *warning*. The word **danger** is used for more hazardous substances that present immediate hazards such as flammability, reactivity, poison, and so on. The word **warning** is used for lesser hazards such as irritants, environmental hazards, and less toxic substances. The signal word is used on the label to provide a quick and easily understandable indication of the degree of hazard posed by the substance.

Historical and Theoretical Foundations of Art

Impact of Art on Society

THEMES

Themes are universal ideas explored and represented in artwork. One popular recurring example is identity. Identity includes the characteristics and behaviors that put an individual in a certain group. Some of the factors for identity include race, religion, culture, and language.

Photographer Cindy Sherman explored identity by photographing herself in different roles and costumes, essentially erasing her own identity and taking on the identity of other people. In doing this, she focused on the stereotypes of these female roles, addressing feminism, youth, aging, and obsession with status, ultimately questioning identity.

Kara Walker, an artist working with silhouettes, explores ideas of identity through race and gender. She portrays racism and historic scenes of slavery, getting past the romanticized notions of the past and exploring its reality. Her silhouettes simplify forms and focus on the topic at hand. She seeks to get past misconceptions and portray the true nature and identities behind tough subjects.

FINE ART VS APPLIED ART

Fine art is art with no purpose other than being aesthetically pleasing. This includes drawing, painting, sculpture, and other media. **Applied art** is art that serves a purpose. Applied arts are useful objects with artistic design applied to their creation. This includes graphic design, interior design, fashion design, decorative arts, and architecture. Graphic design and illustration are also categorized as commercial arts, which fall under applied art. Decorative arts is the creation of jewelry, metalwork, ceramics, embroidery, carpets, furniture, and more. Sometimes applied arts are used in fine art works, so the line between fine arts and applied arts can be blurred, depending on the creator and their intent. In the 1960s, artists such as Andy Warhol began to blur the division between the two, which had been clear in previous years. Warhol used commercial art techniques to mass-produce works that were considered fine art.

REALISM

The **realism movement** began in France in the 1850s, and it attempted to document people and ordinary life faithfully, rather than avoiding unpleasant subjects or romanticizing them. Realist artists depicted laborers and ordinary people engaged in everyday life activities, realistically documenting and preserving life and culture at that time.

This example by Gustave Courbet is called *The Grain Sifters* (1855). It shows a mundane scene of workers sifting grain, using dark and natural colors to portray the scene realistically. Courbet led the realism movement in France. The realism movement challenged the narratives and depictions of history paintings, which was an academic style with posed action scenes. Realism artists documented manual labor and the plight of everyday people, using dark, serious tones to show serious-looking people. Realism artists were not interested in depicting history or anything that they did not personally see or experience; they were only documenting the present-day struggles of the common man.

EMOTIONS AND IDEAS

Emotions and ideas can be expressed through artwork in many ways, including the imagery, subject matter, or colors used. Frida Kahlo is a Mexican artist who used the subject matter and imagery in her artwork to express her physical and emotional pain and frustration. Throughout her life, Kahlo experienced abuse as well as a near-fatal bus accident that caused many physical problems. She began to paint self-portraits and explore ideas related to her pain and injuries, including emotional pain from her divorce from artist Diego Rivera. In her paintings, she often depicted her physical problems as well as open wounds to portray her pain. She sometimes included imagery of roots, to symbolize growth and a feeling of being trapped. Kahlo would also depict issues of childbirth and miscarriage, to communicate her frustration over her own failed pregnancies. She would often mix reality with elements of fantasy and paint scenes relating to pain and death. She used self-portraits to communicate her emotions and ideas relating to her pain as well as to explore her identity.

POLITICAL IDEAS

Artists can use their artwork to support or criticize **political ideas**. Political protest is an often-used theme in artwork. The imagery in artwork can show the devastation caused by political decisions and the harm they can cause to innocent people. Pablo Picasso's *Guernica* (1937) is one of the best-known antiwar paintings in history. Picasso created this to depict the violence, chaos, and suffering of war. Picasso focused on how war affected innocent civilians, and he depicted this in his work, showing the pain and suffering inflicted by the Spanish Civil War. The imagery and title reflect the bombing of the town Guernica by German and Italian war planes. *Guernica* was painted in black, white, and gray, and it depicts a woman holding a dead child, a wounded horse, and a woman with her arms raised in horror, among other imagery. The woman's hand suggests the shape of an airplane. The color scheme allows the viewer to concentrate on the imagery without being distracted by other colors. To many, this painting has become a symbol of the devastation and horrors of war.

SOCIAL IDEAS

Artists will often reflect the social climate surrounding them through the subjects that they portray in their artwork. They can choose to portray marginalized populations, bringing social issues to the attention of a larger population. Romare Bearden is an African-American artist known for capturing the social and cultural climate of African-American neighborhoods in his collages. During the civil rights movement in the 1960s, he began to use cut paper and magazine clippings to portray the culture and community in African-American neighborhoods and to celebrate themes such as jazz music, the rural South, blues musicians, religion, and spirituality. He focused on unity and cooperation within the African-American community.

Another example of art reflecting society and culture is the social realism movement. Social realism artists sought to highlight the "forgotten" members of society, such as the poor, immigrants, and racial minorities. During the 1920s and 1930s, these artists portrayed the common worker as the backbone of society, and their artwork showed political corruption, materialism, joblessness, and poverty, among other social and political issues at the time. This example by Ben Shahn is a mural called *The Meaning of Social Security*, and it is an attempt to depict Franklin D. Roosevelt's speech on the upcoming social security legislation and the ambitions of the New Deal programs.

WOMEN'S EMERGING ROLE

During the medieval era, women would work with men to create manuscript illuminations and embroideries. During the Renaissance, though, some women artists gained international reputations, thanks to shifts in culture such as humanism. Humanism emphasized the value of all people. During the baroque period, women began depicting women as strong figures, and they also began painting still-life artworks. In the 18th century, women began to be accepted as students by famous artists and two women founded the Royal Academy of Arts in London. In the 19th century, women began to gain access to formal art education and more women began to exhibit their artwork. Photography was an accessible medium for women, with no formal training or traditions to constrict their creativity. In the 20th century, particularly the 1960s onward, feminism played a role in increasing the focus on women artists as well as their presence in formal training and prominent exhibitions. In 1985, the anonymous female artist group the Guerrilla Girls spoke out about gender inequalities, especially in the art world.

REFLECTING THE CURRENT ECONOMY

Artists can use their artwork to show how the economy is affecting certain populations and bring this awareness to a wider audience. One example of this is the visual depiction of the economic ruin caused by the Dust Bowl. In the 1930s, dust storms swept through the American West and wiped out many farms and ranches. The land was ravaged by drought and rolling clouds of dust. Farmers lost everything and had no way to make a living. The Dust Bowl, as it was called, was reflected in the artwork of the time. The artists who depicted this event attempted to show how it affected farmers and the economy. Thomas Hart Benton's lithograph *Prodigal Son* from 1939 shows the desolate and wasted land as well as the farmer mourning it. The farmer is meant not to represent one single man, but all farmers who were affected by this tragic event. Benton approached the topic symbolically, showing the ruined land and home, animal carcass, and the man who will have to move on from his land.

Another artist who depicted the Dust Bowl was Alexandre Hogue. Whereas Benton saw this event as something happening to passive victims, Hogue saw it as something created by man's effect on nature. Hogue showed the slashes and furrows made in the land and the ruined green plains.

INFLUENCE ON POPULAR CULTURE

Pop art served as both an art movement and a cultural movement. Pop art used images and objects from popular culture and blurred the line between "high art" and mass-produced cultural objects. This movement elevated common items to fine art, rather than sticking to traditional art themes. Andy Warhol took mundane Campbell's soup cans and Brillo boxes, creating repeated images and objects based on them, and showing them as artwork. Many pop artists, including Andy Warhol and James Rosenquist, began as commercial artists.

Warhol began to mass-produce his artwork, much like the products he was depicting were also mass-produced. In doing this, he equated artwork to a commodity that can be bought and sold, just like these products. Warhol would use bright colors, high contrast, and multiple prints of the same image, as if you were seeing the product repeated on a store shelf. The repetition, bright colors, and contrast of pop art are still used today in advertisements, perpetuating the link between art and culture.

TECHNOLOGY AND ART

Technology is used in conjunction with art in many different ways. Some artists use technology within their art, such as video artists. Others use computers, digital cameras, and scanners to create art, such as electronic artists or graphic designers. This art can be printed repeatedly, and multiple copies can be shown or sold. For those who do not use a form of technology to create their art, they might use it to compose a scene. An artist can use digital photography to capture images to work on, or he or she could use computer software to compose the artwork before drawing or painting it. An artist might draw or paint from life with no assistance from technology, but then he or she may use technology to document the work and put it online on a website for others to view. Technology can also be used to keep records of work or to submit artwork to art competitions across the world.

Art through History and Other Cultures

AFRICAN ART

African art includes painting, sculpture, pottery, masks, textiles, body decoration, jewelry, and rock art. Some African art is aesthetic, some is political or ideological, and some is used for rituals. Characteristics of African art include stylized realism, emphasis on sculpture, geometric forms, and an emphasis on the human figure. African artists will tend to visually abstract, or stylize, figures rather than represent them in a naturalistic way. Sculpture is a preferred art form rather than working in two dimensions. African artists use geometric forms and symmetry, with repeated geometric shapes throughout an artwork. This example of a mask is symmetrical and includes geometric shapes. The human figure has often been a main subject for African art, depicted in masks, paintings, and sculptures. Human figures tend to show youthful characteristics because of an emphasis on health and physical strength as well as youth.

CONTEXT AND PURPOSE

Some African art was created for religious purposes. In addition to regional religions, Christianity and other religions have been practiced there. Some art objects were created for display on an altar or shrine. Other artworks could be used to present sacrificial offerings, to commemorate leaders, or to contact spiritual ancestors. African art objects could also be used to connect with spirits through religious rites or by a religious specialist. These spirits could be summoned for healing or for communicating with ancestors.

Masks were used in performances and rituals with the participation of musicians, dancers, and the audience. When the masked dancer put on the mask, they took on the role of a powerful spiritual being. Many African societies have names for their masks, and these names include the dance, the meaning of the mask, and the spirits associated with the mask.

ASIAN ART

Eastern art does not follow the same aesthetics of the elements and principles as Western art. Asian art does not have a hierarchy of fine arts versus crafts; rather, the skill of craftsmanship is valued, and all types of arts and crafts will be exhibited simultaneously. The crafts of creating porcelain or textiles, for example, have a long and respected history in Asia. Calligraphy, or the art of writing, is also a valued art form, and it has included many different scripts from different times and cultures.

Eastern art focuses more on landscapes and spiritual ideas, rather than representational subjects or realism. It will often be shown on more of a flat plane, instead of showing traditional perspective that is used in Western art. Some common forms of traditional Asian art include silk painting, woodblock printing, and batik, as well as painting with ink on rice paper.

CONTEXT AND PURPOSE

Buddhism has had a great influence on Asian art. Mandalas, which are geometric artworks representing the universe, and Buddha statues are examples of this influence. Asian art has sought to depict man's understanding of natural forces and to understand the pattern of nature. The creation of artwork, including calligraphy, could refresh the spirit of the artist. Portraits would attempt to highlight the subject's moral character rather than just faithfully depict the subject. Art showed inspirational themes, and it often stayed away from subjects such as war, violence, death, and nudes. All objects in nature were seen as "alive," and rather than depicting nature realistically, Asian artists would try to capture the inner essence of these things. The artwork is full of symbolism, such as a dragon representing an emperor, or a pine tree symbolizing endurance. In the 1800s, Asian artists began to experiment with Western artistic traditions but turned back to Eastern traditions and began combining Eastern and Western ideas.

MIDDLE EASTERN ART

Middle Eastern or Islamic art includes artwork created by countries in the Middle Eastern region by Muslim and non-Muslim artists. This includes architecture, mosaics, calligraphy, manuscript illumination, metalworking, textiles, and more. Religion is the most important aspect of Islamic art, and the artwork will often include patterns that could be repeated into infinity. This concept is important to Muslims, contrasting the experience of infinity with man's finite existence on earth and disregarding this temporary presence. Another important concept is the dissolution of matter, which can be achieved by applying patterns and decoration to surfaces. Floral patterns were often used for patterns and decorations, and they could be highly intricate and ornate. Calligraphy was integrated into artwork and decorations as an important element, and the inscription is often a quote from the Qur'an.

This image is an example of a repeated infinite pattern as well as dissolution of matter by covering it with a pattern.

ABORIGINAL ART

Early Aboriginal art from Australia included rock paintings (shown) and carvings now found throughout the country, and many are protected in national parks. The rock art is thought to be for decoration or ceremonial purposes. Indigenous art is still created today in Australia and has become popular again since the 1970s.

The European colonization of Australia had a large impact on its artwork. Since the 1700s, Europeans began depicting Australian scenes, landscapes, and natural history illustrations. They attempted to capture the difference in lighting and scenery from the European landscape to the Australian landscape. The Victorian gold rush of the 1850s prompted wealthy landowners and merchants to commission landscape paintings. A distinctly Australian style of painting arose in the late 1800s, focusing on idealized landscapes and plein air painting. The main themes included working and conquering the land, the Australian outback, and the rural pioneer.

LATIN AMERICAN ART

Latin American art, from Central and South America, begins with the indigenous people. The first art objects were utilitarian, but eventually they began to produce artwork that represented the values and religions of the different regions. When South America was colonized by Europe, the art forms began to merge and blend. Latin American art is a blend of three cultures: Native American, African, and European. Prior to colonization, many Native Americans lived in Latin America, but then European settlers arrived and brought African slaves. During colonial times, art was usually religious, and it resembled traditional European artwork.

In the 1800s, artists began to develop their own regional styles that departed from European styles and traditions. One important artistic movement is muralism, which began in the 1920s. Hundreds of murals were painted in public places, with social and political messages, ideas of identity, and a unifying theme.

EUROPEAN ART

European artwork began with prehistoric rock painting and carving, and it has developed over the centuries through many different artistic movements. Beginning in the middle ages, art would be commissioned by a patron, usually by the church or state. This artwork mainly showed historic, biblical, and religious scenes and religious and political leaders. Secular artwork included landscapes and still lifes. Academies trained artists in methods, materials, and anatomy; attempted to elevate art from a craft to fine art; and began to exhibit artwork. Art was created in workshops by master artists and their apprentices. As the importance of the church and royalty declined, the subject matter changed. The industrial revolution brought changes in technology that included premade, portable paints. Artists became independent and could use their own creativity. Because the academies resisted these changes, innovative artists became avant-garde while academic art stuck to traditions.

NORTH AMERICAN ART

Prior to colonization, traditional Native American art dominated North America. **Early colonial** art was based on European traditions, and artists mainly painted portraits and landscapes. In the 18th century, artists such as Benjamin West, John Singleton Copley, and Gilbert Stuart became some of the first significant American painters. Starting in 1820, the Hudson River School produced romantic landscape painting artists. The American Revolution brought a demand for patriotic artwork, and artists began to document rural America. Prominent 19th-century painters created portraits and painted a wide range of subjects including pioneers, soldiers, and sailors. American impressionism flourished in the 19th century, and in the 20th century, European art continued to impact America. This influence gave rise to the abstract art scene. Many art genres have risen in North America since the beginning of the 20th century, including pop art, minimalism, and photorealism.

PREHISTORIC ART

Prehistoric art is art that was produced in preliterate times, prior to writing or recordkeeping. The first known art is from the Paleolithic era, and it consisted of petroglyphs, cave paintings, and sculptures and carvings in bone. Humans were making art to express ideas and to represent their beliefs and surroundings visually. One of the earliest representational artworks from prehistory is the *Venus of Willendorf* (shown), from roughly 28,000 BC

In China and Japan, prehistoric pottery has been found, as well as bronze figures. In Europe, cave paintings were found in Lascaux and Chauvet, France, and in parts of Spain. Aboriginal painted rock art has been found in Australia, and engravings and paintings on stone and walls have been found in African caves. A large percentage of known prehistoric art is attributed to hunters and foragers. Repeated motifs include animals, humans, tools, maps, and symbols. Portable objects, such as rocks and bones, and stationary surfaces such as cave walls, were used for art creation.

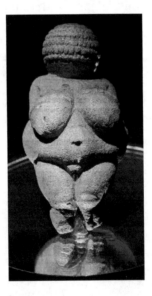

CHARACTERISTICS AND PURPOSE

Whereas some think that cave art was purely decorative, others think it was created for other reasons. Some of the cave walls used were remote and inaccessible, so it is thought that they were used for religious ceremonies or to summon better hunting conditions. Animals and other figures were generally depicted from a simplified side view. Artists painted and drew animals, hunting scenes, landscapes, maps, and many different symbols.

Petroglyphs have also been found, which are prehistoric rock carvings created by removing parts of the rock. Some show real subjects, whereas others are abstract. They might have been used to convey information or for religious purposes. Some might even be a form of prewriting, or a way to map the stars.

The Venus figurines from prehistory are women with exaggerated features, and they are thought to be fertility idols, good luck statues, or a symbol of a mother goddess. The *Venus of Willendorf* is one of the earliest examples of a female nude.

MATERIALS

Paleolithic artists used five main colors: black, white, yellow, red, and brown, as shown in this example from the Lascaux cave art in France. Color pigments were used for body and face decoration long before creating artwork. Some would mix earth or charcoal with animal fat for blacks and browns, and many paintings like this most likely vanished over time. Later rock art that has been discovered used materials such as iron oxide, kaolin, hematite, and manganese. Crayons were developed from solid pieces of pigment, and brushes were formed from animal hairs. Artists would also apply paint with their fingers or a pad made from lichen or moss.

Later in the Stone Age, artists used ochre for yellows, browns, and reds and used manganese or charcoal for black. White was ground calcite or kaolin. The artist would grind the pigment into a powder and mix it with water, blood, animal fat, juice, or other materials to help the pigment stick to cave walls or other surfaces.

EGYPTIAN ART

Painting, sculpture, and jewelry were created in ancient Egypt from 3,000 BC to 30 AD. Most of the art from this time was found in monuments and tombs. The artwork is mostly formal, and it follows their own guidelines for depicting figures. The stone statues are rigid and formal, whereas wood figures are more expressive. Ancient Egyptians' two-dimensional art is a combination of people, animals, and symbols. The organization of this artwork depends on the context: For more formal, organized scenes, they are sorted with the more important figures at the top. For a chaotic scene, such as a battle, this organization is not used.

The art we are most familiar with was found in the tombs of wealthy leaders; however, items of lesser quality are found in the burial sites of people of lower status. Statues were used as a conduit for people to interact with their gods. A ka statue is a statue intended as the resting place for a person's life force. Certain conventions were used for the creation of these, such as the sky god Horus always being represented with a falcon head. This consistency gave the figures a timeless quality.

CHARACTERISTICS AND PURPOSE

Much of the artwork created in ancient Egypt was not meant to be seen; rather, it was mostly created for tombs, and it emphasized life after death. Tombs in ancient Egypt were packed with furniture and food, as well as art and jewelry. The more important and wealthy the person, the more precious artifacts were found in their tomb. These items were meant for the person in their afterlife.

Egyptians used a hierarchy of scale to depict people, leaders, and gods: The larger the figure, the more important they were. Kings and deities might be shown on the same scale. Another common element of Egyptian artwork was hieroglyphs, or images that were symbols for sounds and words. These were the writing system of ancient Egypt, and they often accompanied the artwork.

Two-dimensional scenes were organized in registers, or parallel lines that separated scenes and served as ground lines. People were depicted with a simultaneous profile view and front view.

MATERIALS

Ancient Egyptians used soft stones such as limestone, sandstone, and calcite for sculpture. Copper chisels and stone tools could be used on these softer stones, and ancient Egyptians used copper alloys on harder stones such as quartzite, basalt and granite. Most statues were painted, as evidenced by traces of paint left on them. For wood carving and sculpting, a variety of native woods was used, including acacia, fig, fir, and cedar.

For metalwork, Egyptians used copper, bronze, gold, and silver. Many metal statues were melted down, and the materials were reused. They were able to cut stones for jewelry with precision. They used many stones in jewelry including lapis lazuli, feldspar, jasper, amethyst, and quartz.

The pigments used for painting came from local minerals. They used carbon for black, gypsum for white, iron oxide for reds and yellows, azurite and malachite for blues and greens, and orpiment for bright yellow. Paints were applied directly, or they were layered to create other effects.

RENAISSANCE ART

The **Renaissance** was a revival of classical learning during the 14th, 15th, and 16th centuries in Europe. Renaissance artists sought to capture the value of the individual and the beauty of the natural world. This revival of drawing, painting, sculpture, and architecture was partly driven by humanism, which is a philosophy that attached importance and worth to the individual.

Increased prosperity led to an increase in commissioned artwork from wealthy patrons (especially the Medici family). At the same time, the church was conflicted on spiritual and secular issues, which helped the spread of humanism. The church was also a big patron of the arts, and it spent a great deal on art and architecture at the time. In addition to the wealth of Italy, Italy also contained a lot of Roman architecture and artifacts, which contributed to the beginning of the Renaissance in this area.

CHARACTERISTICS AND PURPOSE

The ideas of humanism brought greater attention to detail and greater realism, as well as a focus on virtue. Artists began to use linear perspective foreshortening, bringing a natural realism to faces and figures. Sculptures, drawings, and paintings showed increased knowledge of anatomy. Most painters began to use oil paint rather than tempera at this time, which contributed to this realism.

Christianity was still the main subject of artwork at this time, reflected in the paintings and sculptures of many prominent artists including Michelangelo, Leonardo da Vinci, and Raphael. Stories from mythology were depicted, too, to promote the idea of humanism. During the Renaissance, artists were creating artwork for patrons and their status was raised to a level above craftsman. Because of the Renaissance movement, Western art developed from the ideals of classical artwork.

Altarpieces were commissioned often, and these would be the focal point of the space they occupied. Frescoes were often created in churches and in private buildings. This painting method was time consuming, with a prominent example being Michelangelo's Sistine Chapel ceiling (shown). Patrons also commissioned portraits of themselves and artworks for their homes.

MATERIALS

Frescoes, that is, murals painted onto plaster walls, were painted during the Renaissance period. The pigments were mixed with water and applied to wet plaster, and once the plaster dried, the pigments were visible on the wall. This was a time-consuming process, but it was used for large works of art including the Sistine Chapel ceiling.

Artists also painted with oil paints, which became available in the 15th century. The slow drying time allowed artists to blend and paint with greater realism and detail than before. More colors were available, and the transparency allowed artists to use glazing techniques, layering transparent colors for greater depth and richness. Artists during this time also still painted on wood panels or rigid supports with tempera.

For sculpting, the most common material was marble. Michelangelo's famous sculptures, including *David*, *Moses*, and other notable works, were carved from marble.

BAROQUE ART

Baroque art dominated Europe in the 17th and 18th centuries. The style was propagated by the Catholic Church, often in the form of monumental works of public art. This style was meant to counter the rationality and simplicity of the Renaissance style and inspire a sense of awe. Many baroque artworks illustrated Catholic ideas, within biblical or mythological depictions. Architecture, painting, and sculpture all reflected these ideals successfully. Baroque sculpture also used a dramatic sense of movement, contrasting with the comparatively still and calm Renaissance sculptures.

Baroque paintings would often include allegories, which are stories with hidden meaning and messages. The educated viewer was expected to recognize and understand symbols and hidden meanings in the artwork.

The *Trevi Fountain in Rome* (1732, shown) is an example of the overly ornate baroque style in sculpture. Some of the major artists of this time include Rembrandt, Caravaggio, and Peter Paul Rubens.

CHARACTERISTICS AND PURPOSE

The **baroque** art style is characterized by exaggerated motion and attention to detail. The scenes are created to enhance a sense of drama and grandeur. The chiaroscuro technique is often used in baroque art. This is the use of strongly contrasting tones of light and dark, usually in a dramatic,

high-contrast scene. Another technique used is tenebrism, which consists of keeping an area black, while a portion of the subject is brightly illuminated, as shown in this painting from 1636.

To set their artwork apart from the Renaissance artworks, artists departed from tranquil scenes and expressions of that time and instead showed intense emotion and movement in their work. Instead of the even lighting of Renaissance artwork, they used more dramatic lighting and they used asymmetry to enhance the sense of instability and movement. Clothing would be moving by wind or the motion of the person instead of draped and resting motionlessly.

GREEK AND ROMAN ART

The great classical art period began in Greece, and this art later greatly influenced Roman artwork. Romans borrowed many elements of their religion from Greece, and they also borrowed art and architectural styles. Ancient Greeks used art to express noble ideas and emotions. They wanted to highlight the great accomplishments of man and honor their gods through their artwork. Sculptures included nude athletes in realistic poses, as shown, as well as gods and goddesses. The artwork was mostly sponsored by the government and made for the public to see, and it was a great source of pride for the people. Art from ancient Greece includes stone and wood statues and pottery in red figure and black figure styles. They also painted on panels and pottery.

Ancient Romans used their artwork more for aesthetics and decoration, rather than for lofty ideals like the Greeks. In Rome, art lost its spiritual quality and was used more to adorn homes. They did copy the Greek statues of gods and goddesses, but they also created skillful and realistic portrait sculptures. In addition to sculptures, they created paintings and mosaics for homes, showing scenes of daily life.

MATERIALS

The Greeks and the Romans used marble and bronze for sculptures. Roman artists used encaustic (pigment mixed with hot wax) and tempera for painting scenes on panels, and they created fresco paintings on architectural surfaces. For mosaics, Romans used small cut pieces of glass, tile, pottery stone, and shells. The pieces were called tesserae, and they were stuck to the surface with mortar.

The ancient Greeks also created wood sculptures in their early period, although few of these have survived. The preferred sculpture materials were marble and limestone, as well as cast bronze. They created figurines from terra cotta and bronze. The Greeks also painted on panels with encaustic and wax, and they painted their sculptures as well as parts of their temples. Most of the paintings that have survived are on pottery. Their pottery had a high iron oxide content, giving it a red color. This example is of the Greek red figure pottery.

MEDIEVAL ART

The period of medieval art spans more than 1,000 years, from the fall of the Roman empire to the Renaissance period. Subjects explored during this time include mythology, Christian themes, and biblical stories. The medieval period can be separated into Byzantine, Romanesque, and Gothic. Byzantine art was from the Eastern Empire called Byzantium, and it was highly stylized. Byzantine art favored symbolism over realism, and the subject matter included imperial and religious subjects. This example of Byzantine painting shows religious subject matter.

Romanesque art included massive churches built with stone arches, similar to Roman architecture. Romanesque painters created frescoes and used encaustic on panels. Gothic art began in Paris and spread throughout Europe. Its greatest contribution was the cathedral and elaborate architecture with complicated decoration. Painting during the Gothic period included animated figures and expressions, painted small in relation to their backgrounds.

THE MANNERISM STYLE

The **mannerism** style of art and architecture emerged as a reaction to the high Renaissance. From the end of the Renaissance in the 1520s to the beginning of baroque art in 1590, mannerism focused more on style and technique than the meaning of the subject. Mannerism arose partly from new scientific discovery that man was not the center of the universe, but, rather, the earth revolves around the sun. At the same time, the Reformation movement highlighted a need for church reforms, bringing turmoil and religious uncertainty.

Mannerist artists reflected this uncertainty, attempting to solve artistic problems by changing proportions and portraying people in new and strange ways. These included elongated limbs, small heads, and dramatic, unnatural, contrived poses. Departing from the linear perspective and depth used in Renaissance art, mannerists flattened the composition and arranged the figures on a flat plane, as shown. Mannerism artists experimented with form, portraying emotions, and bright and unusual colors.

EL GRECO AND TINTORETTO

El Greco, a nickname meaning "the Greek," painted in the mannerist style, using elongated and strange proportions and portraying strong, dramatic emotions. The poses are strained and unnatural, heightening the emotion conveyed by the subjects. Rather than using accurate lighting, the lighting in his works seem to come from within the figures or from an unseen source. In his later works, he elongated figures even more, especially on altarpiece works. This work from 1600 shows his odd use of lighting and forced, strained poses that illustrate the mannerist style.

Tintoretto, another mannerist painter, created monumental religious works and emphasized the mystical nature of religion. He also used elongated forms and forced poses, but his works show a mastery of lighting along with a better idea of spatial depth. He sought for viewers to experience the divine through his religious depictions. Through lighting and composition, he created a supernatural atmosphere, portraying scenes not from this world.

THE RENAISSANCE ART PERIOD

The **Renaissance** period of art was a rebirth of interest in classical learning and arts. Artists looked to the past for inspiration, while innovating and producing some of the best-known art in history. Artists used naturalism, attempting to portray figures realistically rather than exaggerating or stylizing them. Renaissance artists studied anatomy and perspective, as well as light and shadow, to use them accurately in their artwork. They took ideas from the mythology of classical civilizations and used them as a starting point to create their own monumental works.

During the Renaissance, the ambition of classical civilizations was rediscovered, boundaries were pushed, and artists innovated to capture the beauty of humanity. The Greek idea of humanism was used to celebrate the accomplishments of man. Renaissance artists saw the classical period as the height of humanity and attempted to recreate and build upon this movement.

LEONARDO DA VINCI, MICHELANGELO, AND RAPHAEL

Leonardo da Vinci, Michelangelo, and Raphael are a few of the best-known artists of the Renaissance period. Leonardo was a "Renaissance man," with knowledge of math, astronomy, architecture, art, inventing, literature, anatomy, and more. His well-known works include the *Mona Lisa* and *The Last Supper*. He pioneered a technique called sfumato, which uses subtle gradations to create a smoky look.

Michelangelo showed a mastery of anatomy in his artworks. His best-known works are his *David* statue and his painting of the Sistine Chapel ceiling. Unlike many artists, he achieved fame as an artist during his lifetime. He was accomplished in art, sculpture, and architecture, and he inspired the artist Raphael.

Raphael is known for his skillful composition, as well as his serene depictions of the greatness of human nature. One of his best-known works is the *School of Athens*, a monumental work from 1509–1500 depicting many ancient Greek philosophers (shown). This artwork also shows a mastery of perspective, as well as natural poses and lighting.

NEOCLASSICISM

Neoclassicism occurred during the late 18th and early 19th centuries. This movement in art and architecture was an attempt to revive the classical Greek style and depart from the highly ornate baroque style. It also came about partly from the discovery of Roman ruins at Pompeii and Herculaneum. Neoclassical artwork was serious, stoic, and heroic. Artists portrayed moral narratives of ethical superiority, returning to classical subjects and motifs from Greek and Roman art. This art is characterized by somber colors, shallow space, balance, clarity, and restraint. Artists sought to show smooth paint surfaces with no brushstrokes visible in their artwork.

This movement coincided with the Age of Enlightenment, or Age of Reason, which was an intellectual and philosophical movement focused on reason as the main source of authority. These ideas were also reflected in the art at the time, as artists moved from ornate and frivolous art to more serious, classical subjects. Neoclassical artists had few surviving Greek paintings to model their work after, but they had many more examples of sculpture to follow for their work.

JACQUES-LOUIS DAVID AND JEAN-AUGUSTE-DOMINIQUE INGRES.

One significant artist of the neoclassical style is Jacques-Louis David. His painting *Oath of the Horatii* is a prime example of the neoclassical movement. This painting (shown) tells a story from classical times, from a Roman legend in which the Horatii brothers take an oath to defend Rome. In this carefully organized composition, three arches with columns span the background, whereas all the figures and action are pushed into the foreground as if creating a sculptural relief.

Jean-Auguste-Dominique Ingres was a student of David, and he also created works in the neoclassical style. Unlike David, he began to favor more sensuous subjects and became known for portraits. His work *Oedipus and the Sphinx* (1808) was completed while Ingres worked in Rome. This scene is from the Greek myth of Oedipus, when Oedipus was guessing the riddle of the Sphinx. Ingres won the prestigious Prix de Rome for this painting. Keeping with classical standards, Oedipus is depicted as a beautiful and ideal young man.

ROMANTICISM

The **romanticism** movement began in 1770 and encompassed art, literature, music, and culture. The term romantic refers not to love, but to intense emotion. This movement emphasized emotion and individualism, and it was a reaction against the rationalism of neoclassicism. Romantic artists often illustrated literary themes. They emphasized and depicted emotions such as terror, awe, and apprehension, and they attempted to capture the beauty and sublime feel of nature. This painting by Thomas Cole from 1836, *The Course of Empire: Destruction*, embodies the focus on nature and destruction in a romantic artwork.

This style first manifested in landscape painting, and artists challenged the previously low status of landscape art by painting monumental works. History painters also created large works, portraying disaster, divine wrath, and natural catastrophe. Artists portrayed vast spaces with people dwarfed in comparison, mystical landscapes, and nature's triumph over man. No traditional religious art came from this period, but artists continued to portray small villages and the wilderness, despite the increase of urban spaces.

EUGÈNE DELACROIX, THEODORE GERICAULT, THOMAS COLE

Several significant artists worked in the romanticist style. Eugène Delacroix was at the forefront of the French school of romantic artwork. In *Liberty Leading the People*, he depicted the female figure of Liberty leading the French Revolution of 1830. It is a history painting, showing a violent, dramatic, catastrophic scene.

Theodore Gericault was another French romantic artist. His work *The Raft of the Medusa* is a significant romantic painting. This work is larger than life size, and it shows the aftermath of the wreck of a French naval frigate, with people escaping on a makeshift raft. It shows men dying and struggling to survive against nature, with strong emotions and an unfolding drama.

Thomas Cole was an American painter who portrayed the American wilderness in the romantic style. One of his well-known works is called *The Oxbow*, which shows a bend in the Connecticut

River, in a valley after a thunderstorm. There is a juxtaposition of broken trees, violent cliffs, and dark rain clouds beside blue skies and a tranquil bend in the river.

REALISM

The **realism** movement began in France in the 1850s, as a rejection of the ideas of romanticism. Rather than exaggerated scenes and heightened emotions, realism sought to portray ordinary scenes with accuracy and truth. The artists attempted to show people from all walks of life and social classes accurately and not smooth over or avoid unpleasant subjects. Realist artists did not portray people heroically or sentimentally; instead, they wanted to treat all subjects with equal seriousness. The advent of the camera helped to increase the desire to show subjects realistically.

The realism movement is thought to be the first modern art movement, because the artists rejected traditions and expanded the definition of what is considered art. They examined the political, cultural, and economic structure of society, and they used earthy tones to show what was happening in all parts of society. Realist artists painted real-life events, workers, street life, cafés, peasants, and nightclubs, rather than grand landscapes or posed scenes with extreme emotions.

GUSTAVE COURBET, JEAN-FRANCOIS MILLET, AND HONORÉ DAUMIER

The main realist artists in France were Gustave Courbet, Jean-Francois Millet, and Honoré Daumier. Courbet would paint ordinary scenes on vast canvases that were normally used for history paintings. Two of his well-known works include *The Stonebreakers* (shown) and *A Burial at Ornans*. *The Stonebreakers* was painted in 1849, and it shows ordinary workers in his native region of France. He uses natural color and lighting to portray his subjects.

In the United States, Thomas Eakins and Winslow Homer were significant realism painters. Winslow Homer began as a commercial illustrator, but then he was inspired by Courbet, Millet, and Daumier and began to paint ordinary subjects in America. Eakins painted his friends and local people in outdoor sports, including his work *Max Schmitt in a Single Scull, from 1871. His most well-*

known work is *The Gross Clinic*, which showed a scene from a surgical operation, and this was received unfavorably by critics due to its subject matter.

IMPRESSIONISM

The **impressionism** movement began in the late 1800s as artists in Paris began to practice plein air painting together. The artists included Claude Monet and Pierre-Auguste Renoir. Impressionists departed from a faithful depiction of a scene, and instead they attempted to capture their impression of it, or the momentary effect of lighting on the scene. Artists used small brushstrokes and pure color. They tried to capture the optical effects of light, and the differences that weather and sun position create in a scene.

The recent invention and availability of paint in a tube helped spur on this movement. Artists were able to paint outside more easily and capture scenes as they saw them. The emphasis in the painting was as much on the artist's perception of the scene as it was on the scene itself. The painting by Claude Monet, *Haystack. End of Summer. Morning.* from 1891, shows how Monet used color and brushstrokes to capture the lighting of a summer morning on the haystack.

CLAUDE MONET, EDGAR DEGAS, MARY CASSATT, AND AUGUSTE RENOIR

Claude Monet is the most well-known impressionist painter, and some of his subjects include cathedrals, haystacks, landscapes, water lilies, and his garden in Giverny, France. The paintings of his garden included a Japanese footbridge that spanned over water lilies. His paintings became increasingly abstract in later years due to his failing eyesight.

Edgar Degas was an impressionist painter best known for his paintings of ballerinas and dancers. He captured his impression of dance lessons and performances, showing the movement of the moment with visible brushstrokes. This example from 1873–1876, *The Dance Class*, shows a dance class being instructed by the man in the center. He did not capture outside light like other impressionists, but he still captured fleeting moments in time.

Mary Cassatt was the best-known female impressionist painter, and she often painted domestic scenes with a child and mother as the subjects. Cassatt was invited to exhibit with the impressionists by Degas, and she began to be influenced by their work.

Auguste Renoir captured stunning landscapes and beautiful portraits in the impressionist style. The visible brushstrokes, soft edges, and pure colors follow the patterns of impressionist painters, and he shows a masterful understanding of how light affects his subjects.

POSTIMPRESSIONISM

Postimpressionism was a French art movement from 1886 to 1905 that followed impressionism and preceded fauvism. Postimpressionism sought to explore the emotional response of the artist and depart from the naturalism of impressionism. These artists still used bold and pure colors as well as real-life subject matter, but they also leaned toward more geometric shapes, distorted forms, exaggerated or arbitrary colors, and sometimes heavy outlines.

Neoimpressionist Georges Seurat departed from the spontaneous nature of impressionism for a more planned approach that included the optical blending of spots of color. This is now known as pointillism, but it falls under the postimpressionist movement. Paul Signac carried on Seurat's ideas; he helped Seurat develop the pointillism style.

This work by Henri de Toulouse-Lautrec from 1889, titled *Monsieur Fourcade*, shows several major ideas of postimpressionism. Although the artworks and artists of this period are fairly varied, this work does show the bold, arbitrary colors and outlines used in postimpressionist artwork.

VINCENT VAN GOGH, PAUL GAUGUIN, AND PAUL CÉZANNE

Vincent van Gogh, a prominent Dutch postimpressionist artist, exhibited many of the ideas of this movement. He used bold colors, sometimes arbitrarily or in odd ways, as well as bold lines to express his emotion through his paintings. In this 1890 painting, *Portrait of Dr. Gachet*, van Gogh expresses emotion through the pose, facial expression, and colors. Bold colors and brushstrokes, along with heavy outlines, are visible in this artwork.

Paul Gauguin used bold and unusual colors, sometimes in flat planes and flattened spaces. This French artist's work includes many paintings of landscapes and people of French Polynesia, where he lived for 10 years.

Paul Cézanne was another French postimpressionist painter, and he is known as the father of postimpressionism. His exploration of geometric shapes and bold colors prompted Picasso and others to eventually experiment with multiple views of forms. He sought to reduce nature to geometric shapes and find new ways of modeling space and volume.

FAUVISM AND EXPRESSIONISM

The **fauvism** movement, from about 1905 to 1908, followed the postimpressionism movement and included some similar ideas. Fauvism emphasized strong and unusual colors, using color to express mood without being representational of actual colors. Fauvism also emphasized the flatness of the canvas, and it valued individual expression over naturalistic representation. The leaders of the fauvism movement were Henri Matisse and André Derain.

Expressionism began in Germany at the beginning of the 20th century, and it spanned from roughly 1905 to 1920. Artists of this movement used strong colors and distorted forms to express their feelings in their artwork. Artwork came from within the artist, rather than being copied from what they observed. They used swirling and exaggerated brushstrokes and sought to evoke emotional responses to their works. Edvard Munch's *The Scream* (1893) is an example of the

Expressionist style, with its unusual, nonrepresentational colors, distorted form, and desire to express a strong feeling of despair or agony.

FAUVIST AND EXPRESSIONIST ARTISTS

Henri Matisse was a fauvist artist who pioneered the movement. He applied large, flat areas of color to his paintings and worked with bright colors directly from the tubes to convey emotions. He is also considered a leader in defining the 20th-century modern art movement. One of his best-known works of this period is called *Woman with a Hat* (1905). He used unusual colors, including green on the woman's face.

Expressionism began with works of artists such as Vincent van Gogh and Edvard Munch, and then in 1905, German artists formed a group called Die Brücke that began the main wave of expressionism. This group included artists Erich Heckel, Fritz Bleyl, and Karl Schmidt-Rottluff, and they were later joined by Otto Müller, Emil Nolde, and Max Pechstein. Wassily Kandinsky was a notable Russian expressionist painter, and he went on to work in abstract art.

CUBISM AND FUTURISM

Cubism is an early-20th-century art movement in which several viewpoints are shown simultaneously, and simple geometric shapes or interlocking planes are used to construct a scene. Cubism began in 1907 and ended around 1915. Pablo Picasso and Georges Braque pioneered this movement, influenced partly by the three-dimensional representations in works by Paul Cézanne. Cubist artists would analyze a form, break it apart, and reassemble it visually in a more abstracted format.

Futurism, an early-20th-century movement that began in Italy in 1909, emphasized movement, technology, speed, and violence. The artwork included objects such as cars, airplanes, and industrial elements. Like cubists, these artists expressed dynamic elements in artwork. They also praised originality, admired technology over nature, and sought to convey movement through space. Futurist artists praised war and valued nationalism, and they would depict urban scenes such as riots and construction in the city.

PABLO PICASSO, MARCEL DUCHAMP, GIACOMO BALLA

Pablo Picasso is one of the most recognizable names of cubism. His cubist works include flat planes of color, distorted forms, geometric shapes, and reassembled faces with both eyes on one side of a profile.

Marcel Duchamp's work spanned both the cubist and futurist movements. His work, *Nude Descending a Staircase, No. 2*, from 1912, shows a dynamic scene of repeated abstracted and geometric forms of a nude descending from left to right in the painting. The repetition and form convey movement and rhythm.

Giacomo Balla's *Dynamism of a Dog on a Leash* from 1912 embodies some of the tenets of the futurist movement. The painting shows the feet of a woman, plus a leash and a walking dog, and through the repetition of the feet, leash, and tail, Balla shows the dynamic movement of the woman and the dog. The dynamic elements show almost a blur of movement, conveying speed and direction.

CONSTRUCTIVISM AND DE STIJL

The constructivism movement began as a Russian abstract style of art and architecture that started in the 1910s. This movement consisted of constructing dynamic three-dimensional forms from objects such as plastic, wood, glass, or iron. This movement began with Vladimir Tatlin, who was influenced by Picasso's cubist constructions and wanted to "construct" art with dynamic components. Tatlin began to make abstracted still lifes out of scrap materials.

De Stijl is Dutch for "the style," and this Dutch art movement that started in 1917 is also known as neoplasticism. This art movement promoted the reduction of artwork into geometric shapes, lines, and primary colors. Artists attempted to turn this style into a universal form of expression, departing from individual expression. Piet Mondrian is the most recognizable de Stijl artist. Neoplasticism refers to the style and ideas developed by this artist, promoting a new, abstract form of artwork for modern times. This is an example of Mondrian's work, showing his use of black lines, geometric shapes, and primary colors.

VLADIMIR TATLIN, PIET MONDRIAN

The **constructivism** movement began with artist Vladimir Tatlin in 1913. Tatlin was a Soviet architect and painter, and he constructed three-dimensional "counter-reliefs" of wood and metal.

His intention was to question the traditions of art. His main constructivist work was the *Monument to the Third International* (*Tatlin's Tower*), which joined the dynamic components of technology with the aesthetics of machines. This construction included searchlights and projection screens, and it was criticized for being a combination of functional items and art. This tower sparked an exchange of ideas between Russia and Germany on the ideas of revolutionizing art.

The main artist from the de Stijl movement is Dutch painter Piet Mondrian. He sought to create pure abstractions with horizontal and vertical lines, as well as primary colors. He wanted to reduce his artwork to the most basic elements, using them to represent the essence of the energy and forces of nature. The pure abstraction and minimal palette was meant to express an ideal and universal harmony in the art world. His idea of neoplasticism, which guided his work, relied on color, line, and form to express universal ideas.

DADA AND SURREALISM

The **Dada** art movement began around 1915 in Zurich, New York, Germany, and Paris. The movement came about as a reaction of disgust and revolt to the horrors of World War I, and the movement was also antibourgeois. They sought to depart from traditional values of art and create a new kind of art. It is considered antiart, challenging the definition and conventions of art. Dada techniques include readymades, which involves presenting a premade object as art, and the photomontage, using scissors and glue to assemble images from images printed in the press.

Surrealism began in the 1920s in France, and the movement included paintings of strange, dreamlike, and unnerving scenes with realistic accuracy. Surrealism sought to express unconscious thoughts and resolve contradictions between reality and dreams. This movement eventually affected literature, music, and film in many countries as well. This art movement drew heavily on Freudian theories of sexuality, fantasy, dreams, and irrationality.

MARCEL DUCHAMP, SALVADOR DALI, AND RENÉ MAGRITTE

As part of the Dada movement, Marcel Duchamp began creating artwork called "readymades," made from items that were already created and he just declared them to be art. One well-known example is his 1917 *Fountain*, which is an already-made urinal that he signed as R. Mutt. Another Duchamp artwork from 1919, *L.H.O.O.Q.*, shows the departure from and irreverence toward traditional artwork. He took a postcard depicting the Mona Lisa and drew a moustache and face on the portrait, then labeled it *L.H.O.O.Q.* With this artwork, he challenged artistic conventions of the past, and the value of traditional artwork.

Salvador Dali, a well-known surrealist artist, created his best-known work, *The Persistence of Memory, in 1931. The painting depicts melted pocket watches* on a dreamlike landscape.

René Magritte, a Belgian surrealist artist, created thought-provoking artwork by juxtaposing ordinary objects in unusual ways. In *The Treachery of Images* (1928–1929) he depicts a pipe with the words, in French, "This is not a pipe." The viewer is faced with the challenge of reconciling these words with the fact that this is a representation of a pipe, not an actual pipe.

ABSTRACT EXPRESSIONISM

Abstract expressionism refers to an art style from the 1940s and 1950s. The artists grouped under this style sought total freedom of expression through their artwork. They shared an outlook, rather than a specific style, and this is thought to be the first truly American art movement. Abstract expressionism is also called the New York School, because the movement was centered in New York. Its influence extended into the 1970s. Abstract expressionist artists were influenced by the surrealist idea of expressing the subconsciousness in artwork. Abstract expressionism includes color field painting and action painting, and mixes of these two, among other techniques.

Color field painting uses solid areas, or fields of color, on a large scale that extend to the edges of the canvas. The extension to the edges suggests the colors continuing to infinity, and the large scale helps to envelop the viewer in the colors. Action painting includes dribbling, splashing, and dripping paint onto a canvas using gestures and movements, while emphasizing the unconscious.

ARTISTS OF ABSTRACT EXPRESSIONISM

Jackson Pollock is known for his action paintings, or splatter paintings. The term "action painting" was coined to describe Pollock's methods of applying paint to a canvas. Pollock considered this technique to be a way to harness the capabilities of his unconscious, which expressed itself onto the canvas. He saw the drips and splatters not as random paint, but as a balance of chaos and control.

Mark Rothko, Barnett Newman, and Clyfford Still were all color field painters of the abstract expressionist movement. They were looking to get away from form and representation in artwork, and they did away with the figure/ground convention by turning the figure and ground into one. The color seemed to extend beyond the edges of the painting and was the focus of the artwork.

Helen Frankenthaler used a mix of techniques and invented the "soak-stain" technique, which involved creating large color washes by pouring thinned paint onto a canvas. She used Pollock's technique of pouring paint but also used elements of color field painting by incorporating large areas of pure color.

POP ART

Pop art was a British and American movement in the 1960s that used items from popular culture and incorporated them into artwork. This was partly inspired by the readymades of Dadaism. The artists of this movement went against the disengagement of abstract expressionism and celebrated popular culture and consumer items. They used bright, flat colors from advertising and imagery from comic books as well. As a response to and departure from abstract expressionism, pop art used hard edges instead of painterly techniques and impersonal, everyday reality instead of personal symbolism.

Some of the significant artists of the pop art movement used commercial imagery such as Campbell's Soup cans, imagery directly from comic books, and even a direct representation of the American flag. They were inspired by everyday objects and mass consumerism, and they combined objects, text, and images to create new meaning in their artwork.

ANDY WARHOL, ROY LICHTENSTEIN, AND JASPER JOHNS

Andy Warhol was a commercial artist who became a significant pop artist. He created video art, installations, performance art, and paintings, and in 1961 he began producing pop art paintings, including the iconic *Campbell's Soup Cans*. He also painted portraits of many celebrities in bright and vivid colors.

Roy Lichtenstein was a pop artist who is known for his comic book imagery. He altered images from comic books, added different text, and painted them on a large scale. He used Benday dots, the dots produced by mechanical means in printing, to create these images. One of his well-known works is *Drowning Girl* (1963), which depicts a comic image of a drowning girl and her boyfriend in a boat, along with text.

88

Jasper Johns was a pop artist known for his American imagery, especially the American flag. His *Three Flags* (1958) is a painting of three American flags layered upon each other. *Flag*, from 1954–1955, is a faithful reproduction of an American flag using encaustic.

POSTMODERNISM

Postmodernism is a mid- to late-20th-century art movement that departed from modernism. Since the beginning of the 20th century, modernism had led art practice and theory and had promoted the ideas of progress, reason, and idealism. Postmodern artists would not recognize the authority of previous art movements, and this movement was skeptical and antiauthoritarian. This "anything goes" style cast aside all rules of style and included elements of confrontation, tongue-in-cheek humor, and ludicrousness. Postmodernist artists built on the ideas of previous movements such as pop art and feminist art, but they questioned the ideas and subjectivity, authorship, and originality in previous art movements. This movement also questioned the commodification of art production.

Postmodernism is a cross-disciplinary term with philosophical origins, and it was highly influenced by French philosopher Jacques Lacan. Lacan added a contemporary intellectual significance to the ideas of Freud, and he suggested that the unconscious is just as complex and sophisticated as the conscious mind.

SIGMAR POLKE, AND GERHARD RICHTER

Sigmar Polke, a German artist whose artwork pioneered a postmodern approach, departed from coherence in his art as well as the idea that art comes from the artist's personality. In his 12 canvases collectively called *The Fifties* (1963–1969), he portrays a combination of cynicism and nostalgia while commenting on German culture. The grouping of paintings goes against the concept of stylistic coherence because he used different styles throughout the works.

Gerhard Richter's photo paintings of the 1960s combined photography with painting. In doing this, he combined high and low art into one technique. Richter would project a photograph onto a canvas, then paint it in neutral shades of gray, leaving out the black and white tones. He then used a dry brush to soften the edges, degrading the image to give a blurry effect. He assigned neutral titles to his works. This method of mechanical reproduction took any artist style out of the equation, as well as any emotion expressed through the artwork.

FEMINIST ART

Feminist art began in the late 1960s as female artists sought to revise the history of a male-dominated art world and bring attention to the contributions of female artists. They sought to abolish stereotypes as well as challenge and influence cultural attitudes. Prior to feminism, female artists did not get the same publicity or status that their male counterparts did, and the art world was dominated by male artists. Feminist artists began to embrace and use materials in their works that were tied to their gender, such as textiles and embroidery. They also used newer styles such as video, body, and performance art that did not have such a long history as a male-dominated style. These newer types of media allowed these artists to deliver more direct and personal messages to their viewers. Whereas some feminist artists explored the objectification of women in media, or ideas of domesticity, others focused on the absence of recognition of female artists throughout history.

BARBARA KRUGER, CINDY SHERMAN, AND FAITH RINGGOLD.

Barbara Kruger uses mass communication and advertising techniques, pairing black-and-white photos with Helvetica or Futura text, to explore identity and gender issues. The text and slogans she uses challenge the viewer, and her phrases often include pronouns such as I, you, we, or they. She often appropriates images from magazines and adds text to frame the images in a new context to make the viewer think. This image shows her artwork *Belief + Doubt* from 2012 and its iconic and recognizable style of text.

Cindy Sherman is a feminist artist who is known for her self-portraits. She used makeup, wigs, and props to transform herself to represent various female stereotypes in her photographs. Her artworks question ideas of authenticity and identity.

Faith Ringgold is an African-American feminist artist who worked in themes of racial and gender identity and equality. She told stories through quilts, and she recognized a need for equality in the art world. Ringgold would often insist that 50% of the artists included in prominent art shows should be women.

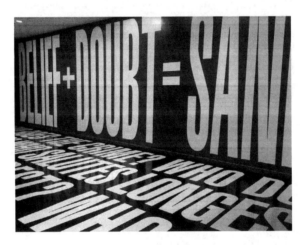

ARMORY SHOW

The Armory Show was the first major exhibition of modern art in America. This show is also called the International Exhibition of Modern Art, and it was held in New York City's 69th Regiment Armory building in 1913. The art exhibited here was influential to American art because of the inclusion of modern art by European and American painters and sculptors. Prior to this, Americans were used to seeing realistic art, but this show exposed them to cubist, impressionist, and fauvist artworks. Marcel Duchamp's *Nude Descending a Staircase* was included in this show. This collection of more than 1,300 artworks shocked many, and it was ridiculed and declared insane and immoral by many. The inclusion of these works in this successful art show served as a catalyst for many artists to rethink their styles and experiment with new ways of creating art.

THE DEGENERATE ART EXHIBITION

The Degenerate Art Exhibition was in held in Munich by Adolf Ziegler and the Nazi party in 1937. The Nazis had removed more than 20,000 artworks from state museums that had been deemed too modern or progressive. Works by foreign artists were also confiscated, including Pablo Picasso, Piet Mondrian, and Wassily Kandinsky, but these works were not exhibited. 740 of these confiscated works were shown in the Degenerate Art Exhibition to defame the artists and show the public the decay of culture. These works were thought to lack artistic skill or insult the German culture. The works were shown in the exhibition without frames and were accompanied by derogatory words or slogans. The art was divided into categories including "An Insult to German Womanhood," and "Nature as Seen by Sick Minds." More than two million visitors attended this show, and some works were destroyed after the show ended. Many other works were sold on the international market and found new homes in museums abroad.

THE GUERRILLA GIRLS

The Guerrilla Girls group formed in 1985 to speak out against sexism and racism in the art world. These women wear gorilla masks to hide their identities while they speak out against powerful institutions. They also hide their identities by using pseudonyms, taking the names of deceased female artists. They have used posters, billboards, and books, as well as public appearances, to disseminate their messages. This group has gained attention for their protest art, and their first well-known poster asked, "Do women have to be naked to get into the Met. Museum?" The image on the poster was a copy of Ingres' *La Grande Odalisque*, with a gorilla head over the woman's face. This poster was in reference to the number of nude women exhibited in the museum and the lack of female artists represented. The Guerrilla Girls have repeatedly brought attention to issues of inequity through their clean designs and jarring images.

MINIMALISM ART

The **minimalism movement** is characterized by an extreme form of abstract art. In the 1960s, artists began to reduce artwork to its barest form, not wishing it to represent anything. They used geometric shapes and challenged the previous conventions of creating and viewing artwork. Minimalist artists wanted their artwork to exist simply as its own form and material, not as a representational form. Minimalist artwork shows traits of simplicity, harmony, and purity.

Although minimalist art can be two-dimensional, it is often three-dimensional, using simple, sometimes repeated, geometric shapes. Early abstract ideas, as well as the constructivist ideas of reducing artwork to its simplest and most essential form, inspired minimalist artists. This example from 1991 by Solomon "Sol" LeWitt is called *Open Cubes*, and it shows white repeated geometric forms. These forms exist only as themselves and are not meant to be representational. The viewer should only accept the artwork as its purest form of geometry and simplicity.

STREET ART

Street art began with graffiti, but these artists have eventually shown their work in public areas and in galleries and museums in the 1970s and 1980s. Street art initially consisted of politically charged protest slogans and graphics illegally painted in public areas. Graffiti usually refers to vandalism, and street art was initially tied to hip-hop culture and lower income areas. In the 1970s, Jean-Michel Basquiat began spray painting his form of artwork in Manhattan. Later in the 1980s, Keith Haring was creating his distinctive artwork on the subway lines in New York City, and his well-known style of outlines and vivid colors, as shown, has persisted as popular artwork even now.

Banksy is another well-known street artist, although his identity is unknown. Banksy spray paints stencils designs onto walls and buildings throughout major cities, and those works have been turned into prints, t-shirts, and more. Street artist Shepard Fairey created the iconic Andre the

Giant stencil which can be seen in many locations, and he went on to make the well-known Barack Obama graphic in red, white, and blue.

THE HARLEM RENAISSANCE ART MOVEMENT

Between 1920 and 1930, a new wave of artistic creativity poured out from a group of African American artists in Harlem, a neighborhood in the borough of Manhattan in New York City. This movement became known as the Harlem Renaissance, and its influence continued through and past the 1930s. This area of New York became a center of African-American immigrants, and the movement sparked a racial pride that challenged racism and stereotypes. The artwork of this time had aims to uplift African-Americans' spirits and the race as a whole. Some of the common themes represented in the artwork were racism, the effects of slavery, folk traditions, and how to convey the experience of black life or black neighborhoods.

Jacob Lawrence was the first well-known African-American artist, and his Migration series showed the migration of blacks from the rural South to the urban North.

Aaron Douglas was an artist who painted murals on buildings and created illustrations for the covers of black publications. In this work, *Aspiration* from 1936, Douglas shows the progression from slavery to the freedom of the industrialized North.

ASHCAN SCHOOL

The Ashcan School describes a group of American realist painters who decided to portray urban life of New York in an unidealized fashion. This was not an organized movement; rather, it was a collective desire to portray modern life in a new way. This group believed that poor and working-class people were a worthy artistic subject matter, and they sought to portray these people in an authentic way. They used a dark palette, a sketchy quality, and visible brushwork to show scenes of everyday modern life in New York City, with subjects including street kids, alcoholics, subways, crowded tenements, and theaters. These artists challenged refined and idealized artwork, moving away from American impressionism and the more polished academic realism. After the Armory Show in 1913, as well as the advent of cubism and fauvism, the work of the Ashcan School no longer seemed as radical as it initially did.

THE HUDSON RIVER SCHOOL

The Hudson River School was an American art movement in the mid-19th century that included landscape painters intent on painting in a romantic style. The paintings of this movement depict the Hudson River Valley and areas surrounding it. The themes reflected in these artworks are exploration, discovery, and settlement. These landscapes are detailed and somewhat idealized, often showing a juxtaposition and harmony of settlers or agriculture with nature. They were also showing their belief in nature as a revelation of God.

This movement was the first native art movement in America. Thomas Cole is credited as the founder, and the movement spanned two generations of painters. The second generation was not as tied to a geographical location as the first, but rather followed the style. Albert Bierstadt was a notable artist of this second generation. This painting by Bierstadt, *A River Landscape, Westphalia* (1855), shows the accord of man with the beauty and grandness of nature.

FOLK ART AND OUTSIDER ART

Folk art is the art of peasants or a native culture. Folk art is generally characterized by simple or naive subject matter, and it is utilitarian or decorative in purpose. Folk art is not influenced by art movements or styles, and it will not include the work of professional artists. This type of art shares and expresses the values of a community as well as their cultural identity. Pottery, jewelry, paintings, sculpture, needlework, and costumes can all be folk art.

Outsider art is artwork created by untrained artists who learned their craft and methods on their own. These artists are not part of an artistic establishment and can include the mentally ill or even rural artists outside of urban areas. Outsider art is sometimes called "naive art." An increased interest in outsider art is in line with the general rejection of traditional values and methods of art by modernist artists.

WARHOL'S FACTORY

The Factory refers to Andy Warhol's studio in New York City. This location became a hangout for artists and celebrities, and it was known for its raucous parties. Warhol decorated this location with aluminum foil, mirrors, and silver paint, and it was also called the Silver Factory. The Factory later occupied two other locations. Warhol's time at this Factory location was referred to as the Silver Era.

In addition to the artistic experimentation and musical performances at The Factory, an assembly-line production of artwork also occurred. Warhol questioned the idea of artist and art production by mass-producing artwork with his silkscreen method and having a group of helpers create his work for him. These helpers became known as "Warhol Superstars," and they included musicians, free thinkers, drag queens, socialites, and celebrities, among others. He paralleled and reflected the concept of mass consumerism and mass-produced commercial objects by creating his own artwork in this way.

OP ART

The **op art movement** of the 1960s used geometric forms to create visual effects and optical illusions. Op art is abstract and nonrepresentational, and many works were created in just black and white. Viewers often were given the feeling of movement, vibration, hidden images, or swelling within the artwork. Op artists consider how our vision works and how the planes of the figure and the ground can work with or against each other. Op artists also work with colors and how they can function together to produce different effects on the viewer's eye. As an early op artist, Bridget Riley worked in black and white and later began working in color op art. Josef Albers is another well-known op artist who worked in color, and he would nest geometric shapes of contrasting colors within each other, making visual effects of the shapes receding and advancing against each other.

ART DECO MOVEMENT

The **art deco movement**, taking its name from the Exposition Internationale des Arts Décoratifs et Industriels Modernes held in Paris in 1925, began in Paris with architecture and decorative arts in the 1920s. It later became a major style in the 1930s throughout America and Western Europe. The art deco style is characterized by streamlined forms, symmetry, geometric shapes, smooth lines, and bright vibrant colors. This movement was influenced by the geometric forms of cubism, the industrial components of futurism and constructivism, and the bright colors of fauvism. The style was used during the roaring twenties as well as the Great Depression of the 1930s. Art deco was used to improve the style of mass-produced objects, and it was also used for posters and some fine arts. This poster from 1925 is an example of the art deco style, with hard lines, streamlined forms, and geometric shapes with vibrant colors. The style was meant to be pleasing to the eye.

ART NOUVEAU

Art nouveau sought to distance itself from historical styles, as well as challenge the hierarchy of fine arts over decorative arts. Art nouveau was a decorative style that focused on linear contours and outlines, and it used muted, limited colors such as blues, greens, yellows, and browns. Art nouveau artists wanted to revive good craftsmanship, lift the status of crafts, and skillfully create modern designs that did not rely on past design. This international style was popular between 1890 and 1910, and it was applied to art, architecture, as well as everyday objects such as furniture, lamps, and jewelry.

One prominent art nouveau artist was Alphonse Mucha, a Moravian artist who created many illustrations, posters, paintings, and other designs. This example shows his signature style, which was considered outdated by the time of his death. His designs often showed beautiful women surrounded by a symmetrical, flowing, floral and ornate design and muted colors.

CLASSICAL ARCHITECTURE

Classical architecture includes buildings that employs the principles and aesthetics of Greek and Roman architecture. This style includes a post and beam system with columns bearing the load. The pediment (shown) is the triangular part of a building above the columns. It might include elaborate sculptures within. Greek architects used the golden mean, or golden ratio, to create their ideal proportions for some of their buildings.

Columns were units of measurement in human scale, and several styles, orders, were developed over time. Caryatids functioned as columns in Greek architecture, but they were stone carvings of females used as support pillars. Greek architecture often used marble and stone, but the discovery of concrete in Rome enabled the construction of arches, domes, and vaults, as used in the Pantheon. Whereas Greek temples were invariably oriented east to west, Romans would orient their temples in respect to the other surrounding buildings.

96

GREEK AND ROMAN COLUMN ORDERS

Ancient Greek architecture has three distinct column orders. These styles are distinguished by their proportions and their unique characteristics. The Doric order is the simplest design, with a flat and unadorned design for the top and bottom of the column. This order is four to eight times its diameter. The Ionic order consists of spiral scrolls, or twin volutes, at the tops of the columns. This column's height is nine times its bottom diameter. The Corinthian order is much more ornate, as shown, with floral designs. This column is taller, at 10 times its diameter.

The Romans adopted all of these column styles, and they later added two of their own. Their Tuscan order is very plain, and it is a simplified version of the Doric order. The composite order is a blend of the Ionic and Corinthian orders, using the scrolls of the Ionic order and the floral motifs of the Corinthian order.

BYZANTINE ARCHITECTURE

Byzantine architecture is the architecture of the Byzantine, or later Roman Empire. This style was highly influenced by Greek and Roman architecture. Buildings became more complex, geometrically; in addition to stone, bricks and plaster were used in some instances. Mosaics were used in place of carved stone decorations, and many domes were used at this time. The architects used pendentives to support a circular dome over a square space, or they used an elliptical dome over a rectangular space. Prior to this, domes were used over circular spaces. Most of the surviving examples of Byzantine architecture are sacred in nature.

The greatest surviving example of Byzantine architecture is the Hagia Sophia in Constantinople (shown). A huge dome was constructed over a square space. The interior of the church included colored marble and other stones, and the vaults and domes were covered with elaborate mosaics.

ROMANESQUE ARCHITECTURE

Romanesque architecture is a style of medieval Europe beginning around the 11th century. This style is characterized by semicircular arches for doors and windows, and barrel or groin vaults. Many castles and churches were built in this style. Romanesque churches had large, thick walls and piers with few windows, a large tower where the nave and transept cross, and smaller towers at the western end of the church. An arcade, or row of columns, was constructed in the center of larger churches, separating the nave from the aisles. These buildings, both secular and sacred, give a feeling of solidity and strength by their massive size, thick walls, and masonry construction. Instead of relying on columns for support as in Greek and Roman architecture, this style, like the Byzantine style, relies more on walls. This example shows the few small arched windows that exemplify the Romanesque style.

GOTHIC ARCHITECTURE

The **Gothic architecture** style in Europe spanned from the mid-12th to the 16th century. Architects sought to solve problems created by simple, dark, damp buildings from previous styles and instead create light, airy, beautiful structures. Gothic architecture is characterized by grand tall designs with upward visual movement. New building techniques allowed builders to create taller towers. The flying buttress is a defining element of this style, and it helped to allow these new heights. The pointed arch is another characteristic of medieval architecture, along with the advent of vaulted ceilings and gargoyles. Gargoyles serve a practical purpose as a drainage spout, but they also serve as decorations with evil or menacing features. The medieval style is known for being ornate, as seen in this example of the Amiens Cathedral in France. Beauty and aesthetic considerations are shown in the designs for these highly decorative buildings.

BALUSTRADE, PEDIMENT, AND FLYING BUTTRESS

A **balustrade** is a series of pillars, or balusters, that support a rail to form a low wall or barrier. This could also be used for an ornamental parapet or balcony.

A **pediment** is the triangular gable used in classical Greek temples, as well as Renaissance and neoclassical architecture. It is found under the roof of the building and above the entablature. This would usually be on top of a portico or columns. The triangular area within the pediment is called a tympanum, and this was usually decorated with relief sculptures.

A **flying buttress** (shown) is a masonry support that transmits the thrust of a vault or a roof into the outer support. This is usually an inclined bar on a partial arch that extends, or flies out, from the wall and carries the weight of the vault or roof. This architectural element developed in Gothic architecture, from prior hidden supports in previous styles. This helped architects create the high ceilings characteristic of Gothic-style churches.

SPIRE, FACADE, CARYATID, AND ENTABLATURE

A **spire** is a tapering structure that comes to a point at the top of a building. These are often found on skyscrapers and church towers. A spire can function as a symbol of the power of religion, giving a sense of strength and reaching toward heaven.

The architectural term **facade** comes from a French word meaning "face." The facade of a building is its front or face, and this is often the most important design aspect when planning a building.

A **caryatid** is a stone carving of a female figure, draped in clothing, used to support an entablature. This caryatid, as shown, was used in place of a column in a Greek building. The entablature is the upper section of a classical order, and this is divided into the architrave, frieze, and cornice. The architrave is the lowest section of the entablature, which rests on the columns. The frieze is the middle section, in which relief sculpture might be found. The cornice is the crowning molding that will be found directly under the pediment.

100

BASILICA, APSE, NAVE, AND TRANSEPT

A **basilica** was originally a type of Roman building, but this later became the basis for the design of the Christian church. In ancient Rome, a basilica was a public building in which courts were held, and other public functions were held there as well. The basilica would be centrally located in town, near the main forum. It is a rectangular building divided by rows of columns, or colonnades, into three aisles. The center aisle is called the nave. The nave runs from the entrance or vestibule of the church to the apse. The apse, or chancel, is the vaulted semicircular structure at the end of the center aisle. This is where the altar would be located. The transept is part of the church that lies across the main body and forms the cross shape. In this illustration, it is just before the apse.

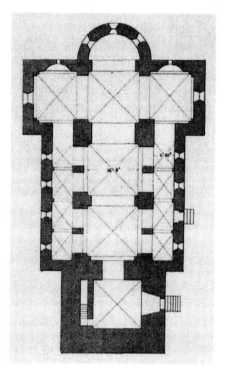

OBELISK, OCULUS, PILASTER, AND ROTUNDA

An **obelisk** is a tall, four-sided structure that is freestanding and tapers to a pyramidal point. These were often found at the entrances to Egyptian temples, and they continue to be used in Western architecture. One well-known example is the Washington Monument in Washington, D.C.

Oculus is the Latin word for "eye." In architecture, it is a circular opening in the center of a dome, and it is a feature in Roman, Byzantine, or neoclassical buildings. An oculus can also be found in a wall. The oculus in the Roman Pantheon is open and allows rain in, which leaves the building through drains in the floor.

A pilaster (shown) is a flat, upright architectural element that projects from a wall, giving the appearance of a column inset in the wall. A pilaster only functions as decoration, not as support.

A rotunda is a building that is round inside and out and is topped with a dome. A rotunda can also be a large interior space topped with a dome.

RENAISSANCE ARCHITECTURE

Renaissance architecture occurred in Europe between the 14th and 17th centuries. This style followed Gothic architecture, and it was followed by the baroque style. The Renaissance style emphasized proportion, geometry, and symmetry, and it included orderly composition of the columns and pilasters they used. These architects used semicircular arches, as well as hemispherical domes. The building plans are square and symmetrical, and facades are symmetrical as well. Church facades would usually be topped by a pediment, as shown in this example of St. Peter's Basilica. Renaissance architecture used the Greek and Roman orders of columns, either as structural objects or as purely decorative pilasters. The dome was used often as a large external feature or as a structural internal dome. Doors would have square lintels, and openings without doors would have arches with a decorative keystone. The keystone is the top center stone in an arch that carries the load of the arch structure. Moldings and decorative details were created with great attention to detail because they found it critical to master the techniques of the ancient Romans.

BAROQUE ARCHITECTURE

Baroque architecture originated in Italy in the late 16th century, and it was prevalent in areas including Germany and South America until the 18th century. The baroque style is characterized by complex architectural plans often based on an oval design, with broader naves in an oval shape. Other characteristics include purposely fragmented elements, dramatic lighting and contrast, large frescoes on the ceiling, trompe l'oeil paintings, sumptuous colors and decorations, pear-shaped domes, and marble or faux finishing in the interior. The interior might also include bronze gilding, sculpted angels, and twisting columns. Baroque architects sought to explore new forms and styles as well as methods of lighting. They were using this architectural style to express the wealth and power of the Catholic Church during the time of the Counter-Reformation, a movement in response to the Protestant Reformation.

ROCOCO ARCHITECTURE

The **rococo** style of architecture began in Paris in the early 18th century. It then spread throughout France and other countries. The rococo style first developed in interior design and decorative arts; then it expanded to architecture and other arts. This architectural style is characterized by pastel colors, serpentine lines, and excessive, elaborate ornamentation. The exterior of a rococo building will be simple, and the interior is filled with ornament and decoration, with the intent to wow the viewer. Floor plans of churches were complex, sometimes with interlocking oval shapes, and the stairways of palaces became ornate, central focuses. This style was meant to be highly theatrical and have something for a visitor to see at every turn. One example of rococo architecture is St. Andrew's Church in Kiev, Ukraine (shown). This facade shows a simplicity with a pastel blue and some ornamentation, but in keeping with the style, the interior is much grander and more elaborate.

NEOCLASSICAL ARCHITECTURE

Classical architecture of ancient Greece and Rome was revived later with neoclassical architecture in the mid-18th century. This style began as a reaction to the excessive ornamentation of the rococo style. This international movement was characterized by a return to the clarity, restraint, and balance, as well as subjects and motifs, of classical styles. Neoclassical architecture used columns, especially the Doric order, and it showed a desire for blank walls rather than decorations. The roof would be flat, sometimes with a pediment, and the facade would be flat and long, with a wall of columns across. No domes or towers were used in this style. Examples of this style include the National Mall and the Lincoln Memorial (shown) in Washington, D.C. The Lincoln Memorial exemplifies the long, flat facade with a row of columns and the flat roof used in this style of architecture.

ART NOUVEAU ARCHITECTURE

The **art nouveau style of architecture** was popular in the United States and Europe beginning in the 1880s, and it declined around 1910. Architects using this style sought to express modern ideas and use nontraditional forms in their buildings. This is sometimes referred to as the first modern architectural style. It is characterized by curved, graceful lines and decorations influenced by nature including leaves, vines, peacocks, and dragonflies. Ironwork and glass were used as sculptural elements as architects tried to embrace what was then possible because of the industrial revolution. These buildings also might contain mosaics, stained glass, and Japanese motifs. The architectural detail was often colorful and decorative, helping bring in the new, modern era.

This example, the Casa Batlló in Barcelona Spain, was remodeled and redesigned by Antoni Gaudi in 1904. It has the irregular shapes and flowing stone sculptural work that is characteristic of the art nouveau style. The facade is decorated with a mosaic made from broken tiles, and the roof is arched and rounded.

BEAUX ARTS ARCHITECTURE

The **beaux arts architectural style** was taught from the 1830s to the end of the 19th century at the École des Beaux-Arts in Paris. From there, it strongly influenced architecture in the United States. Beaux arts architecture drew from Greek and Roman styling and included arched and pedimented doors, arched windows, flat roofs, columns, and symmetry. Beaux arts may also include sculptural details as well as classical details such pilasters, garlands, and balustrades. Interiors often have grand stairways and marble floors, with arched doorways and large rooms. Government buildings may have domes and high, vaulted ceilings.

The San Francisco Opera House (shown) built in 1932 is an example of the beaux arts style in the United States. The bottom floor is rusticated, with rough-cut stones. The top floor features columns and archways, as well as a low-pitched roof.

NEO-GOTHIC ARCHITECTURE

Neo-Gothic architecture, also known as Gothic Revival or Victorian Gothic, is a style that occurred in the late 18th century in England. The use of this style increased in the early 19th century as architects sought to revive the Gothic architecture style. This style follows the original Gothic architectural style, with pointed arches for doors and windows; steeply pitched roofs; decorative ornamental patterns; spires; leaded glass, quatrefoil, or clover-shaped windows; pinnacles; grouped chimneys; stone carvings of gargoyles, leaves, and birds; and sometimes patterned brick or multicolored stone. A Gothic Revival building will emphasize vertical elements, leading the eye up to the sky. The style was often used in church architecture and also in the construction of colleges.

This example is the Salt Lake Temple in Utah, and it exhibits many of the Gothic architecture characteristics, including the emphasis on vertical elements. The spires are also reminiscent of the Gothic style.

ART DECO ARCHITECTURE

The **art deco style of architecture** began in Paris in 1903. This style was applied to apartment buildings and public structures, but rarely to private homes. Art deco architecture used rectangular, block-like forms, arranged geometrically, with these elements broken up by ornamental and curved decorative motifs. This style was sleek and linear, with a modern feel. Buildings were embellished with repetitive designs, such as chevrons or geometric shapes, and these decorations might be machine made rather than hand-crafted. Art deco emphasized the horizontal rather than the vertical, and for practicality, a simple geometric box-shaped building could be embellished in this style to create a modern fashionable design on a budget. Materials used in art deco architecture are smooth stone, terra-cotta, stucco, steel, aluminum, and glass blocks.

The Chrysler Building, built in New York City in 1928, is an example of this architectural style. It includes ornaments protruding from the corners, as well as contrasting brickwork and emphasis on horizontal elements.

BAUHAUS ARCHITECTURE

Bauhaus architecture developed from the Bauhaus School of Art and Design in Germany beginning in 1927. The Bauhaus School sought to connect art with design and technology. The director of this school was Walter Gropius, who was a German architect known as a pioneer of modern architecture. The architectural style is simple and straightforward, following the Bauhaus minimalist and industrial aesthetic. Bauhaus architects sought unadorned functionality rather than aesthetics, and they often used a limited palette of neutral colors. This style favored function over form, Gropius designed door handles that became a well-known component of Bauhaus architecture and design.

The Bauhaus Building in Dessau, Germany (shown), built in 1926, is attributed to Gropius and embodies the Bauhaus style. The building is simple, with a clean design, geometric styling, and it uses a limited palette other than the red doors. This building is an example of Bauhaus architecture valuing function over aesthetics.

THE PRAIRIE SCHOOL MOVEMENT

The Prairie School was a style of architecture prevalent in the Midwestern United States in the late 19th and early 20th centuries. Most architects associated with this movement were employed by Frank Lloyd Wright or Louis Sullivan, but Sullivan himself is not considered an architect of this style. The Prairie School style was used on some public buildings, but it is mostly known for home design. Common features include an emphasis on horizontal lines, overhanging eaves, low pitched or flat roofs, an open floor plan, clean lines, strings of windows in a row, built-in cabinetry, and the use of natural materials such as stone and wood. Wright favored geometric shapes as decorative designs in his buildings, whereas some other Prairie School architects used floral and circular geometric decorations. This example, Wright's Frederick C. Robie House in Chicago, Illinois, shows the clean lines, horizontal emphasis, overhanging eaves, and emphasis on geometric shapes prevalent in this style.

SKYSCRAPERS

Architect Louis Sullivan is known as the "father of skyscrapers" and is considered the originator of the modern skyscraper. The name skyscraper was first used in the 1880s as the first skyscrapers were built in the United States. Originally this referred to buildings containing 10 or 20 stories, but later it came to describe buildings higher than 40 or 50 stories tall. After the first safe passenger elevator was created in 1857 and a need for more business space arose in cities, it became desirable to build buildings more vertically than horizontally. The refinement of the steel process in the 1860s also allowed for taller buildings to be constructed. These buildings had a steel skeleton rather than load-bearing walls, and this steel construction allowed these skyscrapers to rise to greater heights. This load-bearing steel frame was developed by architect William Jenney. Sullivan's Wainwright Building (shown), built in 1891, was the first building with a steel frame and vertical bands to emphasize its height. It is considered the first skyscraper.

THE INTERNATIONAL STYLE OF ARCHITECTURE

The **international style of architecture** developed after World War I in the 1920s and 1930s, and it emphasized modern design. This was the dominant style of architecture until the 1970s, and it was influenced by the de Stijl and Bauhaus movements. This style is characterized by industrial materials, linear, geometric forms, an absence of ornamentation. Glass, steel, and reinforced concrete were the main building materials. The style grew from a desire to get away from eclectic and mixed architectural styles and decorations, the development of new construction technologies, and a growing need for office buildings and other industrial structures. These architects took advantage of the inexpensive mass-produced iron and steel, and sheathed the buildings in glass, creating a new, modern look for the era. Prominent architects of this style include Walter Gropius,

Ludwig Mies van der Rohe, Le Corbusier, and Philip Johnson. A notable example (shown) is van der Rohe's Seagram Building in New York, built in 1958.

GROTESQUE, PLINTH, KEYSTONE, AND STRINGCOURSE

- A **grotesque** is a carved mythical creature that is used for decoration on a building. Grotesques look similar to gargoyles, but gargoyles have a functional purpose as a water spout that carries water away from the side of a building.
- A **plinth** is the square slab at the bottom of a column. This term can also refer to a flat block at the base of a door, or a projecting course of brick or stone at the base of a wall.
- A **keystone** is the wedge-shaped stone at the top of an arch. This stone locks the arch pieces in place; it is the last piece placed in the arch to give stability to the structure.
- A **stringcourse** is a projecting horizontal course, or band, of bricks or stonework on a building. It can be thin and undecorated or larger and ornate. This stringcourse, above the window, runs along the building horizontally and has a decorative pattern.

THE PRINCIPLE OF FORM

The principle form follows function is associated with modernist architecture and design. It suggests that the design of a building should be led by its function, or purpose. This quote is attributed to American architect Louis Sullivan, who is known as the "father of skyscrapers," as well as America's first modern architect. Sullivan saw the purpose of the building as determining the form, reflecting the activities that will happen inside, instead beginning with a design and fitting the function to it. This became a maxim of modernist architects in the 1930s, who thought that decorative elements were inessential and should not be used in the design of modern buildings. Sullivan, however, continued to use some decorative art nouveau and Celtic elements in his design, including green ironwork that became a recognizable hallmark of his work. Sullivan was a mentor of Frank Lloyd Wright, who later altered the saying to "form and function are one."

Visual Perception Skills and Knowledge

PRIOR KNOWLEDGE AND PERCEPTION

A person's prior knowledge can affect how they perceive things visually. Prior knowledge carries expectations and biases based on what a person knows and has experienced. We combine what we see with what we already know, and we use this information to make assumptions when viewing new stimuli. We use our knowledge and experience to interpret familiar scenes and to provide a basis for unfamiliar scenes. For example, if a person encountered a familiar street sign, but part of the text on the sign was missing or obscured, based on prior knowledge of the color, shape, and visible text, the person would still perceive the sign as meaning what they expected, such as "YIELD" or "STOP." Without this prior knowledge, someone would not know how to interpret the sign with the missing text or might interpret it erroneously. Our prior knowledge is affected by, and subsequently affects, our visual perception.

PRIOR KNOWLEDGE AND ARTWORK

A person's prior knowledge can give them information to analyze an artwork differently than someone without that knowledge. Prior knowledge about an artist and their process or an art movement can help someone understand and appreciate an artwork more than someone who has no knowledge of these concepts. For example, someone not familiar with the artist Jackson Pollock and his method of action painting might dismiss his artworks as an unskilled mess. With prior knowledge of his intention and process, someone can appreciate his method of "action painting" and using his movements to express himself on canvas, moving away from figurative representation, as well as the tradition of putting his canvas on an easel. The background knowledge of Pollock's significance in art history, and the significance of his new process at the time, can affect how a viewer will perceive his artwork.

BELIEFS AND PERCEPTION

Our beliefs can affect our visual perception in many ways. One way that beliefs can affect visual perception is confirmation bias, which is when someone sees only evidence and information that will confirm their beliefs. Even if the visual information contradicts what someone already believes, confirmation bias can cause them to interpret visual information based on their biases and come to erroneous conclusions based on these biases. A person with strong religious beliefs might see religious symbols and religious significance in images and in their surroundings. Someone with racist or sexist attitudes could automatically view images of different cultures, or races, or images of women, in a negative way, without delving deeper into what they are seeing. To avoid judging visual input based on bias and beliefs, it can help to have background information and facts about the visual input and to have objective criteria to analyze and judge the visual input on.

BELIEFS AND ARTWORK

Beliefs can affect our perception of an artwork by bringing preconceived notions to our observations of the artwork and affecting our judgement of the work. A person with strong religious beliefs could enjoy and appreciate religious-themed artworks from medieval artists and understand the symbolism used throughout. On the other hand, someone without religious beliefs may immediately dismiss the artwork, finding it uninteresting. They would not appreciate the craftsmanship and the significance of these periods of art, based on their beliefs.

The understanding of the concept of art itself can also influence perception. If people believe that artwork is strictly painting, drawing, and sculpture, they would dismiss performance art or many of the new modern art genres as not actually being forms of artwork. Their beliefs about what constitutes authentic artwork would cause them to fail to examine these forms further, and they could not appreciate these artworks as they were intended.

OBSERVATION METHODS AND PERCEPTION

The way in which we observe visual stimuli can affect how we perceive them. When viewing an object from only one angle, the viewer can miss information that could be gained by looking at it from all sides. Looking at an object from high, or a bird's-eye view, can look very different from looking at it with a worm's-eye view, or from below. The distance from which an object is viewed can affect perception as well. Looking at something closely can give clues about the details of an object, whereas looking at it from a distance can give a better idea of the overall object. The length of time that an object is viewed can also affect perception. Looking at an object at a glance will give less visual information than taking the time to observe and study it.

OBSERVATION METHODS AND ARTWORK

Different observation methods can affect how a person perceives a sculpture. Sculptures are generally meant to be viewable and observed from all sides, and viewing a piece from one side, or from a certain angle can make the viewer miss information. If a large installation sculpture is viewed only from one angle, or only from close up, the viewer could miss the effect of the entire sculpture. It should be viewed from as many angles as possible, and as a whole in addition to close up.

A large painting can be viewed closely, to see the details of brushstrokes and layered color. Viewing a painting from a close distance can also show the perspective of the artist as they were creating it. It can also be viewed from a distance, to capture the entire artwork as a whole and get the effect that the artist was trying to communicate.

MULTISENSORY EXPERIENCES AND PERCEPTION

Our senses can affect each other, and they can even affect how we perceive things visually. Throughout the day, we are barraged by sights and sounds, and we must prioritize what we pay attention to and what we ignore. A sound that is recognized as alarming, such as a car horn or an ambulance siren, will take precedence over other sounds and at the same time draw our gaze. A pleasing or interesting sound can also attract our attention, encouraging us to look in its direction to see the source. If an artwork were to incorporate sound, the types of sounds and directions they are coming from can aid in directing the viewer's eye throughout the artwork and even create a focal point.

In other instances, sound can also be distracting. It will be easier to concentrate on the details of a painting in a quiet room, rather than in a noisy, crowded room. An outdoor sculptural installation near a noisy road can be more difficult to examine than one in a museum gallery.

VIEWPOINTS AND ARTWORK

Artwork can appear differently to different people depending on their viewpoints. Artwork can be viewed from a historical or personal perspective, or from a subjective or objective viewpoint. This painting, *Dance at Le Moulin de la Galette* from 1876 by Pierre-Auguste Renoir, can be analyzed in multiple ways. From a historical viewpoint, it is important to consider the significance of the artwork in the impressionist style, capturing a fleeting moment on a Sunday afternoon in Paris and the dappled light through the trees. From a personal perspective, someone might react favorably to the warm and inviting scene or unfavorably if they do not like crowds.

Objectively, this artwork can be analyzed using the elements and principles of art, as well as the skill used to execute the rendering. Subjectively, a person might prefer that paintings are rendered more realistically or that a subject is more posed instead of the artist capturing a casual scene.

CREATING MEANING

Meaning can be created in artwork in many different ways. Sometimes the meaning of an artwork is immediately obvious and uncontested, and other times it is more complex and subject to various interpretations. Understanding the culture and context in which the artwork is created, as well as the art movement it fits into, can provide clues to its meaning.

Symbols are used to add meaning in ways that are not immediately clear, and they are usually not the focal point of an artwork. Rather, the artist relies on the viewer to see and decipher the symbols. These can have obvious meanings or rely on background or historical knowledge to understand their significance. Subject matter can be used to convey meaning in a more obvious manner. The artist's choice of subject and how it is portrayed can show meaning and intent.

An artist can also use elements and principles to create meaning in their artwork. Colors can signify feelings and moods. Size, placement, emphasis, and repetition can all convey strong ideas or the dominance of one idea over another.

SYMBOLS

Symbols incorporated into artwork are interpreted by the viewer based on their knowledge of these clues and the context they are placed within. This artwork, *The Ambassadors* by Hans Holbein the Younger, was painted in 1533. At first glance, this seems to be a portrait of two men, likely ambassadors based on the title, dressed in fine clothing and posing in front of a small set of shelves. The shelves contain many seemingly random objects, but they were chosen and placed for their symbolic significance within the context of the painting. The globe and maps signify the age of exploration. The gloves and dagger held by the men symbolize authority and luxury at the time. The elongated shape on the floor is a stretched-out skull, which would look more correct when viewed from the bottom left of the painting. The skull generally symbolizes death. There are also symbols throughout the painting referring to the division between the Catholics and Protestants at the time: a mostly hidden crucifix in the top left and the hymnal juxtaposed with a lute with a broken string. Symbols placed throughout the artwork add meaning and intent to this seemingly innocuous portrait.

CREATIVITY AND CRITICAL THINKING

Artistic problems can be solved through creativity and innovation by brainstorming to come up with multiple solutions. Artists solve problems involved with what media and venue to use to express themselves and how to best get their message to their viewers. They decide how to use the elements and principles to convey their message, what subject to portray, what style to use, and even how to explain their artistic process to others. Problem solving using creativity and critical thinking can occur in many ways, including creating thumbnail sketches, keeping a notebook of ideas to draw from for artwork, and experimenting with materials. Artists can brainstorm ideas and come up with the best solution for their current problem. The artist should first assess the problem and decide what they are trying to solve. They can then come up with multiple ideas through writing, sketching, experimenting, and even viewing others' artwork, and then they can choose the best solution and build upon it.

AESTHETICS AND EXPRESSIVE FEATURES

Aesthetics is a philosophy in art that seeks to create non-subjective criteria for the judgement of beauty. Aesthetics asks questions such as "What is art?" "What is beauty?" and "What makes art beautiful?" Aesthetics in art also questions what makes a painting good and whether a realistic painting is "better" than an abstract one. The aesthetics movement of the late 19th century favored the beauty of art over practical or moral narratives.

Expressive features in artwork include how the artists uses the elements and principles to communicate mood and feeling. An artist can communicate through the composition of the artwork, imagery, text, color, or a juxtaposition of opposing elements, among other things. These are the characteristics of an artwork that stir emotion within the viewer. The viewer could feel conflict and opposition through strong, jagged lines or contrasts of colors. They could also feel peace and harmony through the use of analogous colors and soft, flowing elements throughout the artwork.

CONTEXT

Context describes the related conditions or circumstances around which something occurs. To understand an artwork, it helps to understand its context or the circumstances in which the artist was working in at the time. This can include their environment, the historical events and traditions that were happening, their cultural values, the social movements at the time, and even the artist's personal values and commitments. Recognizing art in context includes looking at it in perspective — not only of how you see it at the moment, but also how it fits into the history of art, what it was a reaction to, what movement it followed, and what it preceded. You could judge a piece of Dada art simply by its own merit and appearance, but understanding the context of it, the feelings of cynicism and sarcasm as well as their intention of creating antiart, will carry more meaning to your understanding of the artwork and give you a broader perspective of what the artist intended.

MEDIA AND TECHNIQUES

Media is the plural of medium, and it refers to the physical materials used by an artist to create artwork. Examples of media include paint, oil, clay, ink, metal, or any other material used to create artwork. Artistic media have changed and evolved throughout the years, with the invention and improvement of materials such as the advent of acrylic paint or the invention of tubes for paint portability.

Techniques for artwork include the ways in which an artist uses their technical skills to create artwork. This includes specialized methods for different media. Drawing techniques will differ from painting techniques, and they will also differ from the specialized methods used for printmaking or sculpting. An artist can explore new techniques, learn techniques from books, classes, or studying artwork, and use these techniques in their artwork to improve their methods or change the focus of their art.

MUSEUMS AND PRESERVATION

The profession of art conservation is devoted to the preservation of artwork for the future. Art conservators protect artwork from future deterioration and damage and restore damaged artwork to as closely to the original form as possible while preserving its integrity. They also examine and document the state of the artwork as it is discovered, or as it is acquired, and they seek to keep it from changing over time. Conservation includes controlling the environment in which art is exhibited, transported, or stored, including the light, temperature, and humidity. They prepare for disaster, control pests, and protect artwork from damage. A conservator must decide on the most appropriate actions that should be taken to restore or preserve an artwork. The process of preventative conservation, to minimize or prevent any further damage to artwork, relies on multidisciplinary fields including science, chemistry, biology, and engineering, as well as art.

GOLDEN MEAN AND HIERARCHICAL PROPORTION

The golden mean, also known as the golden ratio, golden number, or Fibonacci number, is a geometric proportion regarded as a way to add beauty, harmony, and balance to a composition. The proportion is 1 to 1.618, and this is used throughout art and architecture as a basis for design. Sometimes this is used as a single rectangle and a single square in these proportions, but this can be divided again and again to further subdivide the composition. These proportions were used by the ancient Greeks when designing the Parthenon and by Michelangelo in many of his works, among others.

Hierarchical proportion is a technique used by artists to emphasize parts of a sculpture or other artwork. The artist would use unnatural or unusual proportions to depict his or her subjects, bringing the viewer's attention to the more important figures depicted in the art. The artist might show a person of higher status as being larger than someone who is of lower status or who is subservient. Beginning in Renaissance times, artists began to depict their subjects in more realistic proportions in relation to each other.

JUXTAPOSITION, APPROPRIATION, AND TRANSFORMATION

Juxtaposition is the placement of contrasting elements next to each other to create an effect. Artists will contrast elements in their artwork to draw the viewer's eye, emphasizing the similarities and differences of the juxtaposed elements. An artist can also juxtapose imagery or concepts to relay their ideas. René Magritte's painting, *Memory of a Journey* from 1955, juxtaposes a giant feather against the Leaning Tower of Pisa, using scale to grab the viewer's attention.

Appropriation refers to the borrowing of preexisting objects or images in artwork with little to no transformation. Marcel Duchamp's "readymades" are an example of appropriation; he used preexisting objects in his works without changing them or changing them very little.

Transformation refers to the changing of an image or object to present it in a new way. Artists might start with a preexisting idea or object but transform it and use their own style and technique to make it their own artwork.

Visual Literacy and Analysis Skills

ELEMENTS OF ART

This painting, Mary Cassatt's *Young Girls* from 1867, shows effective use of the elements of art. Cassatt was an impressionist painter, and she used visible brushstrokes with soft edges to capture moments in time. Cassatt used yellows and orange-reds in the girls' dresses and greens in the background. The warm **colors** advance, whereas the cooler colored background recedes and helps the subjects stand out. The warmth of the colors in the skin tones gives life and vibrancy to the young girls. The rougher brushstrokes of the dresses, hair, and background show an implied **texture**. The implied **lines** surrounding the subjects in the foreground are softened and blurred, giving a softer feel to the subject. Cassatt used a wide range of light and dark **values** to give depth to this artwork. The darker background serves as negative **space**, whereas the subjects are the positive space. Mary Cassatt used the elements of art to successfully portray the soft, tender nature of youth and innocence in this painting.

PRINCIPLES OF DESIGN

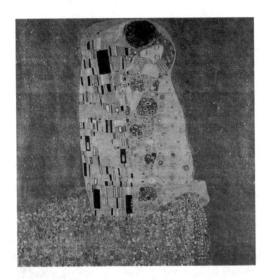

Gustav Klimt's *The Kiss* from 1907–1908 is a painting with gold leaf added. It depicts a couple embraced and entwined in a kiss. Klimt used asymmetrical **balance** in this painting, although the figures are centrally located. The patch of meadow underneath them is mainly on the left of the painting, and the darker squares in the clothing are also on the left. This is balanced by the **emphasis**, or focal point, of the woman's face, which draws the viewer's eye. There is **contrast** throughout, with circles, rectangles, and solid areas of color. There is also the contrast of the bright gold with the darker background, causing the figures to stand out. The clothing of both figures, as well as the flowers in the meadow, show different **patterns**. The repeated yellows and golds throughout the painting give a **unity** to the piece. Klimt successfully used the elements of art to create this eye-catching painting.

ROMANTIC LANDSCAPE

In Wassily Kandinsky's *Romantic Landscape* from 1911, he used the principles of design to successfully organize the elements of art. Although the artwork contains mainly darker and muted tones of **color**, such as darker blues and reds, as well as browns, grays and greens, he used one area of brighter orange in the top left. This small area of brighter color **contrasts** with the darker, more muted **values**, and it serves to **balance** the painting, while providing **emphasis** as a focal point to draw the eye. The **lines** and implied lines show **movement** in a triangle shape, leading the eye around the painting, from the upward sloping brown shape in the bottom left, leading up to a blue and whitish line at the top, then back down with a dark-gray line. He uses some dots of dark gray in different places to create **rhythm**, and the repeated colors throughout the painting provide **unity** to the artwork.

USING EXPERIENCE TO ANALYZE AN ARTWORK

Using experience to analyze an artwork can help the viewer relate to and understand the artwork by relating to the context surrounding it. Experience can help the viewer feel what the artist is trying to convey. In this example, *Snap the Whip* by Winslow Homer from 1862, children are playing a game outside in a grassy field. The game is called snap the whip; the children hold hands and the main player tries to run and spin to throw the children off at the end of the chain. If a viewer has experienced this game, or even a similar game such as "red rover," they will have a greater understanding of the fun and excitement conveyed by the artist. Someone who grew up in the city without playing in grassy fields will not be able to relate as closely to this image. Relating to an artwork with experience can help the viewer decide and analyze whether the artist as successfully conveyed their ideas.

USING OBSERVATION TO ANALYZE AN ARTWORK

Analyzing art can be done in many different ways. By observing artwork in various ways, the viewer can get a greater overview of the artwork and its message. Viewers can begin by standing back and taking in a wide view of the entire artwork. They can observe what catches their eye and how the artwork leads their eye around. After noting their initial impressions, viewers can take a closer look, observing details such as brushstrokes, use of color, lines, and blending or glazing. Viewers should also consider the subject and messages that the artist is trying to convey, deciding whether the portrayal is successful. In a sculptural form, viewers would look closely at the materials and walk around the sculpture to observe how their view changes from all sides. Keeping in mind the elements and principles of art and how the artist is using them, careful observation of the artwork can help the viewer analyze the success of the art.

EXPERIENCE, OBSERVATION, MEMORY, AND IMAGINATION

Artists will often use their own experiences and observations of their surroundings as sources for their artwork. An artist growing up by the ocean might use the beach as inspiration for their artwork, painting beach scenes and ocean life. A person who grew up in a crowded city might choose to portray the bustle of city life, tall buildings, or even homeless people because this is what they experienced. An artist can observe their surroundings and find the beauty in it, like the Hudson River School painters did when painting beautiful American landscapes. An artist could also draw on memories for inspiration, painting things that they remember from their past or their childhood. Imagination is a rich source of ideas too, and an artist can use their imagination to create new scenes, like surrealist painters often did. Surrealists used their imaginations to combine images in new ways, or even bend or distort ordinary objects. Experience, observation, memory, and imagination are all sources that artists use for their artwork.

EXPERIENCE AND PERCEPTION

A person's experiences can affect their perception of an artwork by influencing their ideas of what is, or isn't, art. This is an example of street art by Banksy, a well-known street artist whose work has become desirable to find and see. His identity is still unknown, and this mystique adds to the appeal of his art. Street art does have a negative connotation for many. Street art, or graffiti, is generally painted illegally on buildings and is often covered over. The illegal and unwanted aspect could make many people think that it is not an art form. If someone has experienced vandalism on their home or business, they would be less accepting of street art as an art form. If someone's neighborhood has been filled with unwanted graffiti, they might not want to see it on their own building or in other public places. On the other hand, people who are involved in creating street art view it as a positive experience, and they are accepting of it as an art form.

IMPROVING COMPOSITION

Although there are many ways to compose an artwork and lead the viewer's eye around the work, there are certain considerations that can improve the composition of a work. It is jarring to the eye to see two edges in a painting touch, but not overlap. In this case, the edge of the jug is touching the fruit, but they do not overlap. This causes a spatial ambiguity and does not make it clear that one object is in front of the other. Lines that are known, in the mind, to be straight should be made straight in the artwork. The edge of the table, in the back, does not make a straight line. From the perspective this artwork is composed, the table is tilted farther than the edges of the objects show, and this conflict makes it seem that the objects may slide off the table. The artwork is somewhere in between symmetrical and asymmetrical balance, with the objects placed in the center with similar sizes on each side, carrying similar visual weight, but slightly different. This composition could be improved by creating a purposeful asymmetrical balance, using three different-sized objects instead.

USE OF MEDIA

In this work by J. M. W. Turner from 1801, it is evident that the medium used is watercolor paint. Watercolor is by nature transparent, and painting with watercolor involves letting the white of the paper show through for lighter values. Darker colors are made by using less water for a denser color or by building up layers of colors upon each other. In this landscape painting, Turner used washes for the large areas of color in the top two-thirds of the painting. The colors are delicately built upon each other. A wet-on-wet technique, adding watercolor to already-wet paper, will yield soft edges for the colors. To achieve the edges of the mountains and cliffs, the layer beneath can dry before adding another color on top. These colors were thinned with a lot of water to let the white of the paper show through and create lighter hues. The details at the bottom of the painting would be done with a smaller brush and less water to achieve more detail and sharper lines.

TILTED ARC BY RICHARD SERRA

Richard Serra's site-specific sculpture from 1981, titled *Tilted Arc*, was installed in Manhattan in Foley Federal Plaza. This sculpture consisted of a 120-foot-long, 12-foot-high leaning plate of steel. This work, although seemingly nondescript, was actually described as ugly and an eyesore by critics. At the same time, it was deemed significant for its placement because it transformed the location it was placed in. By placing the sculpture in this plaza, Serra disrupted many people's daily routines as they walked through the area, causing them to change paths and walk around the sculpture. The sculpture was purposely located where it would redefine the space. Many people petitioned for its removal, but Serra countered that to move the sculpture would be to destroy it because it was created specifically for the site. Serra was able to successfully transform the space with his strategic sculpture placement. The sculpture was dismantled and removed in 1989

BRUSHSTROKES AND IMPASTO

Vincent van Gogh often used impasto, or thick layers of paint with prominent brushstrokes, in his paintings. Using this painting technique can add texture to a painting, and it can add to the other visual elements present in the artwork. In *Starry Night* (1889), van Gogh used the impasto technique and visible brushstrokes to create movement throughout the artwork. The swirls in the sky lead the eye throughout the painting, and the circles of brushstrokes around the stars and moon accentuate their presence in the sky. The prominent brushstrokes consist of colors placed next to each other, with dashes of color repeated throughout. This creates a repetition of pattern, as well as a visual texture, in addition to the actual texture of the thick paint. The brushstrokes add a visual interest and sense of movement that would be much different if he had simply painted the background in solid colors or blended the colors gradually. The brushstrokes and impasto technique are a significant part of the artwork, transforming a night scene into a vibrant, expressive work of art.

THE DECONSTRUCTION CRITICISM THEORY

The criticism theory of deconstruction focuses on examining the many potential meanings within an artwork, including ones that are possibly even conflicting with each other. This theory was first used in the 1970s by French philosopher Jacques Derrida. Deconstruction involves finding and recognizing the underlying meaning and implied messages within artwork. When delving into artwork in this way, it is difficult to find and agree upon just one meaning, and it can even challenge preconceived notions and previously agreed upon ideas. This aesthetic theory seeks what is hidden, omitted, or repressed to show how the initial impression is not the only interpretation nor is it necessarily the generally accepted meaning. There could be many unanswered questions within the artwork, such as the intentions of the artist, the significance of the objects or location, or the identities of the subjects, and this leads to ambiguity of meaning. Stereotypes must be set aside to look for a true meaning.

ANDY WARHOL'S MARILYN MONROE

Andy Warhol's screen printed images of Marilyn Monroe perpetuate the image of her well-known Hollywood persona. Marilyn Monroe was famous for being a beautiful and talented cultural icon, and the repeated image used by Warhol reinforces this image of her celebrity. To use the critical perspective of deconstruction to analyze this artwork, one must go past the initial impression and stereotypes, seeking what is hidden or omitted, looking for other meanings and interpretations. In addition to Monroe's exuberant celebrity personality, there was a darker, troubled side that eventually led to her suicide. The initial impression of this artwork is the superficial, smiling celebrity paparazzi image, with bright colors, repeated as it would have been seen everywhere in media. Delving further past this initial impression yields another possible interpretation, and it reinforces the idea that there is more than one possible way to view and understand this artwork.

THE FORMALISM AESTHETIC THEORY

The formalist criticism theory deals with analyzing the visual aspects of an artwork, including the elements and principles used. This theory attaches meaning in the artist's use of materials, focusing on how the artwork is made and how it looks, not the narrative it is attempting to convey or any social or historical context. Formalism is useful for analyzing nonrepresentational and abstract art, looking at the artist's use of elements, principles, composition, and media rather than trying to find meaning in the subject matter. With this approach, the critic is looking at the same things in a realistic, representational, or abstract painting, analyzing it in the same way to see if the artist successfully used media and visual elements in their artwork. An extreme form of formalism believes that everything necessary to analyze a work of art is already present in that work and no context or history is applicable to the analysis of artwork.

JAMES ABBOTT MCNEILL WHISTLER'S NOCTURNE IN BLACK AND GOLD

James Abbott McNeill Whistler's *Nocturne in Black and Gold: The Falling Rocket* (1875) captures the excitement of fireworks in the night sky. This is a loosely painted, abstracted work, getting away from realistic representation. From a formalism perspective, Whistler successfully used composition, as well as the elements and principles of art, in this work. For the composition, he used the rule of thirds and placed the horizon line at roughly one-third from the bottom of the painting. The emphasis, or focal point, is the brightest yellow in the lower left. Whistler used strong contrast to help the bright lights and fireworks stand out from the dark background. He used repetition of colors to create a unity throughout the work and lead the eye from each colored area. The brighter and lighter colors in the lower third are balanced by the darker hues and splatters of color higher in the painting.

THE CULTURAL PERSPECTIVE AESTHETIC THEORY

The cultural perspective aesthetic theory looks at an artwork with consideration to the cultural and social norms that are associated with it or the artist. Instead of focusing on the elements, principles, and form, or the hidden meaning in an artwork, this theory analyzes how an artwork expresses or fits into the cultural or social viewpoint. The concept of culture includes the customs, beliefs, and traditions of a group of people during a certain time. The cultural perspective aesthetic theory could be used on an American artwork, for example, and explain the perspective that is conveyed with consideration of the origin of the artwork. An artwork from another culture will convey different messages depending on its social norms and cultural ideas and looking at the artwork in this way can reveal these messages. Artists will often express themselves and their culture through their artwork.

AFRICAN MASK

Using the example of an African mask, analyzing this from a cultural perspective of aesthetic theory is much different than using a formalist or deconstruction theory. Instead of finding hidden meanings or analyzing only the visual components, the cultural perspective looks at the connection between the artwork and the culture in which it was made, analyzing how it expresses the culture. African masks were used in ceremonies for religious and social events. The combination of human and animal elements, in this case a human face with animal horns, symbolizes the closeness of humans with the natural environment. In some cases, the person wearing the mask is thought to either communicate with or become the figure that the mask represents. They can represent totem animals, or even the deceased. Masks are an important part of African culture, and they express the significance of cultural ideas through this art form.

THE EXPRESSION AESTHETIC THEORY

The expression aesthetic theory focuses on art as the artist's expression of emotions. It sees art as a process of expressing emotion, and the artist does not necessarily know what emotions they will be expressing before creation. Expression is not a calculated process; rather, it is something that occurs from how the artist created their work. To analyze artwork in this manner, the viewer should imagine the artist's process and attempt to experience the emotion that is being conveyed. As artists create the work, they are thought to move from a feeling of oppression to a sense of clarity and freeness by expressing their emotions. They figure out their own emotions while in the process of expressing them, turning it from a feeling into a visual expression. In evaluating artwork with this in mind, the viewer is looking for and understanding what the artist is expressing emotionally.

WASSILY KANDINSKY'S YELLOW-RED-BLUE

Wassily Kandinsky's *Yellow-Red-Blue* (1925) is an abstract painting filled with shapes and colors. To analyze it using the expression aesthetic theory, one would imagine the artist's process and think about what emotions are being expressed through this artwork. According to the theory, the artist is working out their own emotion while creating the artwork, and this emotion is not fully expressed until the artwork is completed. In this painting, Kandinsky used a combination of bright primary colors, abstract and geometric shapes, and a variety of lines. The eye is led throughout the piece with these lines, and the bright colors catch the eye as well. Primary colors give a sense of simplicity and straightforwardness, and the lines go back and forth from order to a more chaotic feel. The brighter yellow is balanced by the large, darker hues of red and blue, and emotionally the more geometric and brighter left side contrasts with the organic shapes and squiggles on the right, suggesting a contrasting inner turmoil.

THE FEMINIST ART MOVEMENT

The feminist art movement sought to establish a fair and equal place for women artists in the art world and to bring to light the accomplishments of prior women artists. These artists sought to transform stereotypes and change cultural attitudes about women, and they tried to do so through their artwork. The feminist art movement expanded the definition and scope of art, the artists we recognize, and who is included in the conversation of art making. Feminist artists gave credit to artists before them, and they introduced new media in their artwork. Because of the accomplishments of this movement, women artists no longer necessarily feel the need to identify themselves as such, or to specifically create artwork that addresses the perspective of women. Women artists began to express their individual concerns and feelings, rather than trying to address and contribute to the feminist viewpoint.

THE IMPRESSIONIST MOVEMENT

The impressionist movement marked a departure from the traditional notions of art. At the time, the narrow ideals of art were controlled by institutions such as the Salon and the French academy. These institutions also held control over the careers of artists. The impressionists cast the old rules aside and painted how they wanted to, capturing the changing qualities of light in new ways and scenes as they looked at a particular moment. They captured scenes as they saw them, on the spot, rather than taking sketches back to the studio to complete a painting. Impressionism also began when photography was catching on, and it served as an imitation of and reaction against it. Impressionism imitated the capturing of fleeting moments, while reacting against a faithful photographic reproduction of a scene. This art movement transformed landscape painting, and impressionism influenced artists to later express their artistic freedom and experiment with methods and media.

THE POSTIMPRESSIONIST MOVEMENT

Postimpressionist artists rejected the ideas of depicting the world around them, as the impressionists did, and instead sought to explore their emotions and memories to depict highly personal meanings through their artwork. Instead of showing scenes from life, as the impressionists did, postimpressionist artists wanted to go further and show their feelings through abstracted forms and new uses of color. They used symbolism and attempted to evoke emotion in their viewers. Postimpressionist artists did not seek to create a cohesive style; rather, the movement was more about the departure from a faithful depiction of the world or events, and it was about beginning to relay information from the artist's subconscious mind. Postimpressionists used saturated colors and unnatural hues to express emotion in their artwork, taking a new, imaginative approach to representing their subjects. The painterly quality and distinct brushstrokes added to the notion that this was not a faithful representation, but rather an interpretation.

MINIMALIST ART

The minimalist art movement, like many other movements, sought to challenge the boundaries and conventions of art. By removing themselves and their feelings from their artwork, minimalist artists distanced themselves from the work of the abstract expressionists who came before them. They were interested in creating a new kind of artwork that was unlike any other previous fine art, minimized to its simplest form. Minimalist artwork used prefabricated and construction-related materials, and it showed a preference for simple geometric forms. These artists wanted their art to show no evidence of the artist who created it and stand on its own instead of having personal elements. Paintings lacked brushstrokes and had flat fields of color, and sculptures had clean, straight lines and geometric shapes. The minimalism label referred to artists using a minimal number of colors, shapes, or forms in their artwork and the artwork was stripped of decoration and refined to its simplest form.

KARA WALKER'S SILHOUETTE ARTWORK

Kara Walker is an African-American artist known for her black-and-white silhouette artwork on gallery walls, exploring themes of gender, race, violence, sexuality, and identity. Walker is motivated by exposing racial stereotypes and historical narratives that have been glossed over by time. Through her artwork, she questions how skin color defines a person and how black people are represented in culture. From early on, as an artist she felt pressure to represent the "black experience" in a positive light; instead, she to represent it truthfully and expose historical issues. Her artwork has a tendency to make people uncomfortable, and she seeks to create this uncomfortable feeling, to take people out of their comfort zone of what they believe of race, gender, or identity. Her work has been called negative and revolting, and she has even had work covered due to its controversy. Despite the negative attention from some, it has not deterred Walker from portraying difficult subjects.

THE DADA ART MOVEMENT

The Dada art movement sought to reject the traditional methods and ideas of art creation and essentially to redefine art on its own terms. This wasn't so much of a cohesive style as it was a group of artists looking to collaborate and create art with spontaneity. This group actually mocked the established art scene, and they started debates about the definition of art. The "readymade" concept contributed to this debate because it was a departure from what was previously considered art. Some Dada artists also sought to debate politics with their artwork, especially rallying against the horrors of war. They issued publications and created photomontages to stand up against political ideas. Dada art critiqued society, politics, and previously established rules for

art, and their penchant for the strange, satirical, and irrational was later picked up and used by surrealist artists.

ANDY WARHOL AND POP ART

Andy Warhol explored the connections between popular culture and art, and he gained international attention for his artwork and for himself. He used many different media types, including painting, screen printing, and even computers, to create iconic pop art. The allure and mystery of his personal life, combined with his public persona, helped to keep him in the spotlight and create interest in him and his work. He reproduced images from mass media that nobody had thought to use before for artwork, and he successfully became synonymous with pop art. His work appealed to a large audience, and he created some the most widely recognized artworks ever made. Warhol also changed the concept of being an artist by using his factory concept to produce artwork. He predicted the quick rise and fall of celebrities with his "15 minutes of fame" concept, which became the new norm in popular culture.

THE SOCIAL REALISM MOVEMENT

Social realism began in the early 1900s with the aim of portraying everyday life, especially that of the working class. It became an important art movement in the 1930s in the United States during the Great Depression. At this time, urban areas were growing, and slums also grew. Social realism artists were motivated by reacting against the idealism of the romantic period. These artists revealed the realities of contemporary life, and they sympathized with the poor and working class. They recorded the realities of what they saw, without glorifying scenes or heightening emotions. While documenting the realities of the poor and working class, social realists were also critical of the government and structures that created these conditions. They wanted to use this new style as a weapon to fight against the government and capitalism, as well as the exploitation of workers, while transforming society.

SELF-CRITIQUE OF ARTWORK

Self-critique of artwork is useful for analyzing artistic processes and outcomes in order to improve the process and the final product. Self-critique involves thinking about what is successful in an artwork, as well as what could be improved. When doing a self-critique, artists can look at the composition, use of elements and principles, how they portrayed their subject, whether they expressed their ideas effectively, and their use of media. It is helpful to stop often in the artistic process and stand back to critique the work, to see how it is progressing and decide if it is going in the right direction. Sometimes it is also helpful to stop for a while and put the work away, and then look at it again with fresh eyes later. With self-critique, artists become more aware of their progress and improvements and will also learn how to critique other artists' work objectively. They will focus on improving their artwork and on finding ways to grow, rather than repeating mistakes and becoming frustrated.

Praxis Practice Test

Want to take this practice test in an online interactive format?
Check out the bonus page, which includes interactive practice questions and much more: **mometrix.com/bonus948/priiartck0134**

1. Which of the following architectural styles is known for the use of pointed arches, gargoyles, and a sense of upward visual movement?

    a. Classical
    b. Art Nouveau
    c. Gothic
    d. Baroque

2. Vincent van Gogh, Paul Cézanne, and Paul Gauguin are artists associated with which style of art?

    a. Post-Impressionism
    b. Surrealism
    c. Fauvism
    d. Cubism

3. Which of these terms refers to a performance or event created in the context of fine art?

    a. Happening
    b. Installation
    c. Sculpture
    d. Plein air

4. When a piece of clay is partially dry but not completely dry, it is _____.

    a. bisque
    b. greenware
    c. leather hard
    d. bone dry

5. Which of these painting techniques involves the application of thick layers of paint with visible brushstrokes?

    a. Sfumato
    b. Sgraffito
    c. Wash
    d. Impasto

6. In Leonardo da Vinci's *Mona Lisa,* he used a painting technique to give a smoky, cloudy appearance and soften the appearance of any hard lines. Which of the following techniques does this describe?

   a. Sgraffito
   b. Sfumato
   c. Velatura
   d. Imprimatura

7. Which of the following is an example of an accommodation in the classroom for a student with behavioral disabilities?

   a. Using large paper and taping it to the table
   b. Outlining a design with glue
   c. Using larger tools and offering choices of media
   d. Working with clay in a secluded area of the room

8. Claes Oldenburg was an American sculptor in the 1960s known for creating large scale Pop art sculptures, often of food items. How did his work challenge the traditional means of sculpture?

    a. He challenged the traditional media of metal and marble by sculpting with wire.
    b. He painted his sculptures, which was not traditionally done.
    c. He challenged the traditions of sculpture by using assistants to create his works.
    d. He changed the traditional hard medium of sculpture to a soft, changeable format.

9. Which type of assessment in the art classroom best reflects a student's ability to apply art-making skills?

    a. Performance
    b. Traditional
    c. Formative
    d. Summative

10. Which statement best describes the purpose of sculptures in the Classical period in ancient Greece?

    a. Sculptures sought to capture the true likeness of a person.
    b. Sculptures were made to honor gods and goddesses.
    c. Sculptures were used in fertility rituals.
    d. Sculptures were created to provide a resting place for a soul after death.

11. Of these architectural designs, which best embodies the theory of "form follows function"?

    a. An office building is designed inside a repurposed department store.
    b. A bank is designed with a facade to resemble a Greek temple.
    c. A stadium is designed to have room for spectators surrounding a central field for the players.
    d. A college campus is designed with walking paths that form intricate geometric designs.

12. Which of the following was NOT a goal of the artists of the Impressionist movement?

    a. To capture fleeting moments of time
    b. To portray the momentary effect of light on a scene or object
    c. To depart from depicting a scene in a realistic manner
    d. To portray exaggerated scenes and heightened emotions

13. Hierarchical proportion was used in many cultures to denote relative importance of figures, including Mayan, Renaissance, and Ancient Egyptian artwork. Which of the following describes the hierarchical proportion with which figures would be portrayed in Ancient Egyptian artwork?

    a. People of higher status are portrayed on a larger scale than those of lower status.
    b. People of higher status are portrayed on a diagonal higher than those of lower status.
    c. People of higher status are portrayed more realistically than those of lower status.
    d. People of higher status are portrayed with larger features than those of lower status.

14. Which method of layering these multimedia materials is correct for working with wax or oil-based media and water-based media?

    a. Layering acrylic paint over oil paint
    b. Layering watercolor paint over encaustic paint
    c. Layering tempera paint over oil pastels
    d. Layering crayon over watercolor paint

15. A tertiary color can be created by mixing which of the following?

    a. Red and yellow
    b. Yellow and orange
    c. Blue and yellow
    d. Orange and green

16. Which of the following was NOT an architectural need or advancement that led to the construction of skyscrapers?

    a. The invention of the first safe passenger elevator
    b. The development of load bearing walls for construction
    c. The refinement of the steel process which led to steel skeletons in buildings
    d. The need for more vertical buildings to create more space in cities

17. Which of the following art related careers will be least likely to depend on the use of computer graphics and image editing programs?

    a. Illustrator
    b. Photographer
    c. Curator
    d. Graphic designer

18. Which of the following would reinforce the goals of the Feminist art movement?

    a. Portraying women in a more abstract manner
    b. Creating artwork that supports stereotypes about traditional female roles
    c. Excluding modern art from the canon of female artwork
    d. Embracing materials in female artwork traditionally tied to their gender

19. **Which photographic technique will result in a clear and focused subject with a background out of focus, as in the following image?**

a. Using a larger aperture
b. Using a higher ISO
c. Using a slower shutter speed
d. Using a greater distance from the camera to the subject

20. This painting shows religious subject matter with elongated figures, unnatural poses, and dramatic lighting. During which art period or movement would this have most likely been painted?

    a. Medieval
    b. Renaissance
    c. Mannerism
    d. Romanticism

21. How was the Postmodernist art movement similar to the Dada art movement?

    a. They both sought to portray dream-like scenes with accuracy.
    b. They both sought to depart from the traditions and authority of previous art movements.
    c. They both sought to bring attention to the contributions of previously unrecognized artists.
    d. They both sought to explore the emotional response of the artist.

22. An elementary student in the art classroom has difficulty focusing on their project, and is often found wandering away from their desk, distracting other students. Which of the following would be the LEAST helpful accommodation for this student?

    a. The student's project should be broken down into smaller chunks.
    b. The student should should be given larger materials and larger paper to work with.
    c. The student should be given a secluded area in the room to work and concentrate.
    d. The student should be given frequent praise during the project.

23. A teacher writes their curriculum focusing first on setting the goals of instruction, then the assessment methods and the lesson plans. Which curriculum design method is this teacher using?
   a. Teaching for Artistic Behavior
   b. Discipline Based Art Education
   c. The TABA method
   d. Backward design

24. Which of the following describes a student's use of metacognitive skills in the art classroom?
   a. A student uses a rubric to assess their progress toward reaching their goals.
   b. A student answers an essay question about an artist's life.
   c. A student creates a sketch in their sketchbook drawn from real life.
   d. A student uses different media than they are used to for creating artwork.

25. An artist paints thin, transparent layers of oil paint on top of another layer of oil paint that has already dried. What is this technique called?
   a. Alla prima
   b. Impasto
   c. Glazing
   d. Plein air

26. Which of the following paint supports would be most ideal for an egg tempera painting?
   a. Canvas
   b. Paper
   c. Masonite
   d. Linen

27. Which of the following art skills would be most appropriate to students in Kindergarten through 3rd grade?
   a. Drawing with two-point perspective
   b. Mixing secondary colors
   c. Calligraphy
   d. Working with oil paints

28. Which of the following safety practices would NOT be done in the art classroom as a result of the MSDS sheets?
   a. A fire extinguisher is kept in the classroom due to flammable materials.
   b. An apron, gloves, and goggles are used with certain corrosive printmaking materials.
   c. Solvents are kept in a fireproof cabinet.
   d. The blade of a utility knife is retracted when not in use.

29. Which of the following art movements did NOT aim to portray life and people in an exaggerated or idealized way?
   a. The Ashcan School
   b. The Hudson River School
   c. Romanticism
   d. Neoclassical

30. What surface would have been used for this painting from the Byzantine era?

a. Wood panel
b. Linen
c. Canvas
d. Paper

31. A student evaluates a well-known artwork, finding the potential hidden meanings and implied messages within it. Which of the following criticism theories is the student using?

a. Formalism aesthetic theory
b. Cultural perspective aesthetic theory
c. Deconstruction criticism theory
d. Expression aesthetic theory

32. How did the Impressionism art movement react against the advent of photography in the art world?

a. Impressionist artists sought to capture fleeting moments and the play of light across objects.
b. Impressionist artists wanted to use minimal colors to capture a scene.
c. Impressionist artists wanted to work indoors rather than out in the field.
d. Impressionist artists sought to capture an impression of a scene rather than a faithful reproduction.

33. An art museum wishes to incorporate technology into their new exhibition showcasing Pop art. Which of the following would NOT be an effective way to incorporate this?

   a. Touchscreen technology could give the viewer more information about the artists.
   b. Multiple video screens showing the artists explaining their process could be set up together in the gallery.
   c. A docent-led tour could include a pre-arranged video call with an artist to discuss their work.
   d. Visitors could be provided headphones and a guide book for a self-led tour experience.

34. Which of the following statements accurately describes an ethical standard relating to artwork?

   a. Permission should be obtained if using source materials that are not public domain or out of copyright.
   b. Copyright for an artwork begins once the artist files for copyright.
   c. Copyright laws are the same in each of the 50 states, but vary by country.
   d. It is permissible to draw or paint a copy a famous artwork and sell copies of it.

35. Which of the following architectural elements is featured in this photograph?

   a. Triangulated pediment
   b. Flying buttress
   c. Ornamental parapet
   d. Transept

36. Which of the following painting techniques would NOT be used to create texture in an artwork?

    a. Sgraffito
    b. Dry brush
    c. Wash
    d. Impasto

37. Which of the following principles of design helps to create the focal point in this painting?

    a. Contrast
    b. Movement
    c. Balance
    d. Rhythm

38. Which of the following is NOT a tool commonly used for printmaking?

    a. Burnisher
    b. Brayer
    c. Gouge
    d. Mandrel

39. Which of the following was a significant contribution of artists during the Renaissance art period?

    a. Lost wax casting
    b. Linear perspective
    c. Paint in tubes
    d. Acrylic paint

40. A wooden sculpture of a youthful human figure shows symmetry and is visually abstracted. It is used for religious purposes. In which culture was this sculpture most likely created?

   a. Ancient Roman
   b. Mycenaean
   c. African
   d. Egyptian

41. Fresco was a technique often used in the Renaissance art period. Which of the following best describes this process?

   a. Oil paint was applied to wet plaster.
   b. Pigments mixed with plaster were applied to a surface.
   c. Tempera paint was applied to dry plaster.
   d. Pigments mixed with water were applied to wet plaster.

42. Which of the following is a technique used to create a more interesting composition in an artwork or a painting?

   a. Intaglio
   b. Rule of thirds
   c. Tromp l'oiel
   d. Middle ground

43. Which of the following best describes some of the characteristics of Baroque architecture?

   a. Pear-shaped domes, marble or faux finishing, and bronze gilding
   b. Hemispherical domes, columns, and decorative pilasters
   c. Semicircular arches, barrel or groin vaults, and thick walls
   d. Circular domes, pendentives, and mosaics

44. Which of the following is NOT an example of relating context to an artwork?

   a. Finding more information about the cultural values of African artists
   b. Reading about the social movements at the time of Harlem Renaissance artwork
   c. Practicing similar techniques of a Pointillist artist
   d. Researching a Dada artist's values and personal views

45. Which of the following is the best description of appropriation in artwork?

   a. Placing contrasting elements next to each other
   b. Using unusual proportions to emphasize a part of an artwork
   c. Borrowing and using pre-existing images with few or no changes
   d. Changing an image and presenting it in a new way

46. Which of the following recommendations is NOT a way to improve the composition of a still life?

   a. Arranging the items in a symmetrical grouping
   b. Overlapping items rather than having the edges touch
   c. Using accurate perspective
   d. Including a focal point in the arrangement

47. Which of the following describes a similarity between Minimalist art and Color Field painting?

a. The use of mainly primary colors
b. Paint extending onto the edges of the canvas
c. A focus on consumer items as the subject
d. Large, flat areas of color with minimal brush strokes

48. Which of the following best describes the mezzotint process?

a. The artist uses gouges to cut away the pieces of material that will not hold ink.
b. The artist works from dark to light, roughening and smoothing areas of a plate to change their ability to hold ink.
c. The artist melts fine particles of acid-resistant powdered rosin onto a metal plate, which is then dipped in acid.
d. The artist uses a burin to carve lines into a plate, and these lines hold the ink for printing.

49. Which of the following will most likely benefit a person seeking a career in graphic design?

a. Certification in programming languages such as Visual Basic, C++, or Java
b. An apprenticeship under an artist skilled in their chosen medium
c. A working knowledge of programs such as Photoshop, Illustrator, and Flash
d. Experience with pedagogy, assessment, and classroom management

50. Which of the following is NOT a common file format for images?

a. JPEG
b. GIF
c. AVI
d. PNG

51. Which of the following is an example of a triadic color scheme?

a. Orange, green, and purple
b. Blue, green, and purple
c. Red, yellow, and orange
d. Orange, blue, and green

52. This photograph, one of the first works of Modernism during a time of many immigrants coming to America, was captured by which photographer?

    a. Alfred Stieglitz
    b. Edward Weston
    c. Dorothea Lange
    d. Louis Daguerre

53. An artist is creating a drawing from life. They are keeping their eyes on the subject, and only glancing occasionally at their paper, creating an outline of the subject. Which type of drawing is this artist creating?

    a. Gesture drawing
    b. Blind contour drawing
    c. Perspective drawing
    d. Crosshatch drawing

54. Which of the following is NOT an accurate difference between acrylic paint and oil paint?

    a. Acrylic paint dries much more quickly than oil paint.
    b. Oil paint is more flexible than acrylic paint when dry.
    c. Acrylic paint can be cleaned with water, while oil paint requires solvents.
    d. Oil paint has no visible color shift when it dries, while acrylic paint becomes darker when it dries.

55. The concept of infinity is often used in patterns in Middle Eastern art. Why is this concept significant?

    a. To contrast the infinity with man's finite existence on earth
    b. To cover large areas of walls with the same pattern
    c. To allow different artists to easily copy the same pattern
    d. To represent the magnitude of the soul

56. Which of the following is NOT a characteristic of traditional Japanese woodblock printing?

    a. They often depicted landscapes, history, geishas, and scenes from everyday life.
    b. They used large, flat areas of color in the composition.
    c. They used primarily black for the prints.
    d. They began by drawing in ink then gluing it to the wood block for carving.

57. Which of the following is an accurate statement regarding digital photography versus film photography?

    a. Digital photography is slower and more expensive than film photography.
    b. Digital photography has more limited storage space than film photography.
    c. Digital photography requires specialized equipment for developing the photographs.
    d. Digital photography can be more easily edited than film photography.

58. An artist wants to create a pen and ink drawing with a lot of detailed work. Which surface would work best for this endeavor?

    a. Watercolor paper
    b. Canvas
    c. Illustration board
    d. Charcoal paper

59. Which of the following is NOT a common oil painting medium?

    a. Poppy oil
    b. Linseed oil
    c. Grapeseed oil
    d. Stand oil

60. Which of the following best describes the daguerreotype process?

    a. An image is created on paper coated with silver iodide.
    b. An image is created on a silvered copper plate.
    c. An image is created on a glass plate.
    d. An image is created on a tin plate.

61. **This metalworking technique involves forming metal threads into a lace pattern. Which of the following is the name of this technique?**

    a. Filigree
    b. Enameling
    c. Fusion
    d. Soldering

62. **Which of the following forms of printmaking was applied in this image?**

    a. Relief
    b. Serigraphy
    c. Lithography
    d. Intaglio

63. Which of the following watercolor techniques would this artist have used to create the hazy sky and clouds in this painting?

a. Dry brush
b. Wash
c. Crayon resist
d. Wet on wet

64. An art critic analyzes an artwork based on the use of elements and principles, not delving into the context associated with the artwork. Which of the following criticism theories is this critic using?

a. Formalism
b. Expressionism
c. Deconstructivism
d. Representationalism

65. An artist's oil painting has dried and the paint has begun to crack. Which of the following is a possible cause of this issue?

a. The artist varnished the oil painting after it dried.
b. The artist mixed linseed oil with their paint.
c. The artist did not prime the canvas before painting.
d. The artist worked in layers and used a glazing technique.

66. Which of the following pigments is NOT hazardous due to the use of toxic metals?

a. Cadmium red
b. Cadmium yellow hue
c. Cobalt blue
d. Flake white

67. If a graphic artist wanted to create a logo that could be resized for large banners without becoming pixelated, which of the following would be the best method?

    a. Creating a logo in Adobe Photoshop and saving it as a JPEG
    b. Drawing a logo by hand and scanning it, saving it as a GIF
    c. Creating a vector-based logo and saving it as an EPS
    d. Tracing a hand-drawn logo in Adobe Photoshop and saving it as a TIF

68. Which of the following was a reason that Baroque architecture spread throughout South America in the 1600s and 1700s?

    a. South American architects read about this style and began to use it.
    b. Spain colonized Central and South America.
    c. Architects from France emigrated to South America.
    d. Baroque architecture was a reaction against the previous Neoclassical architecture.

69. Which of the following video file formats would be the most ideal for saving and sharing a high-definition video?

    a. MP4
    b. WMV
    c. MPEG
    d. MOV

70. Which of the following is the correct name for this architectural element of a statue created for use as a column?

    a. Balustrade
    b. Pilaster
    c. Caryatid
    d. Obelisk

71. Which of the following is NOT an aim of video sculpture?

a. To integrate video aspects into an object, location or performance.
b. To diverge from the standard narrative video configuration.
c. To present videos in new and innovative ways.
d. To show a video in a linear format with a beginning and end.

72. If an artist wanted to create multiple prints using a printmaking technique, which of the following techniques would NOT be appropriate to use?

a. Linocut
b. Screen-printing
c. Intaglio
d. Monotype

73. How does the traditional creation of porcelain challenge the perception of the "Made in China" slogan, which calls to mind mass-produced products made inexpensively in China?

a. Porcelain is no longer made in China.
b. The creation of porcelain is labor intensive.
c. The materials used for porcelain are very expensive.
d. Porcelain can only be made by artisans.

74. This painting is an example of which of the following painting techniques?

a. Alla prima
b. Plein air
c. Tromp l'oeil
d. Sgraffito

75. During which of the following artistic movements would this painting have been created?

a. Neoclassical
b. Mannerism
c. Medieval
d. Post-Impressionism

76. Which of the following best describes a way that visual art has influenced popular culture?

a. Artists appropriated images from comic books to use in their artwork.
b. The bright colors and repetition of Pop art were subsequently used in fashion and advertising.
c. Mass-produced objects were a subject in the artworks.
d. Artists used commercial methods such as screen-printing.

77. Which of the following best describes why watercolor paper should be stretched before it is painted on?

a. So the paint will adhere to the surface
b. So the colors will mix properly
c. To make the paper into a larger surface
d. So that it will not warp

78. Which of the following principles of design is most evident in this painting?

a. Balance
b. Contrast
c. Emphasis
d. Rhythm

79. If an artist wanted to create a drawing with a great amount of detail, which of the following drawing instruments would be best suited for this?

a. Vine charcoal
b. Red conte crayon
c. 2H pencil
d. Black chalk

80. Which of the following is an instrument used to support and steady the artist's hand while painting or drawing?

a. Mahlstick
b. Tortillion
c. Frisket
d. T-square

81. If an artist wanted to use pen and ink to emulate the visual color blending of the Pointillism art movement, which of the following would be the most appropriate technique?

a. Stippling
b. Cross hatching
c. Hatching
d. Wash

82. Which of the following painting surfaces does NOT need to be primed with a primer before it is painted on?

    a. Wood panel, when using oil paints
    b. Canvas, when using acrylic paints
    c. Wood panel, when using egg tempera paints
    d. Watercolor paper, when using watercolor paints

83. An art critic analyzes this vase with deliberation over the meanings of the dragon, pine, and bamboo painted on the surface. Which of the following methods is this critic using?

    a. Formalism aesthetic theory
    b. Cultural perspective aesthetic theory
    c. Expressionism aesthetic theory
    d. Deconstructivism aesthetic theory

84. Which of the following describes the main issues that were expressed through the Muralism art movement of Latin America?

    a. The rights of women and children
    b. Freedom of speech and artistic expression
    c. The desire for better schools and education
    d. Political and social justice

85. An artist creates a sculpture from a block of marble, carefully removing pieces by use of a chisel. Which of the following sculptural techniques is this artist using?

    a. Casting
    b. Modeling
    c. Subtractive
    d. Assemblage

86. Which of the following terms describes the method with which this fiber art was created?

    a. Embroidery
    b. Weaving
    c. Knitting
    d. Crochet

87. Which of the following terms refers to hanging artworks in groupings on the wall at eye level as well as above and below eye level?

    a. Exhibition-style
    b. Gallery-style
    c. Salon-style
    d. Museum-style

88. Which of the following best describes why Ansel Adams created black and white environmental photographs instead of color?

    a. Color photography had not yet been invented.
    b. If the photographs were in color, they would be mainly green.
    c. He did not have experience with producing color photographs.
    d. He could control the outcome of the prints better with black and white.

89. Which of the following cultures would have produced this dot style painting?

a. Aboriginal
b. African
c. Chinese
d. Brazilian

90. Which of the following media was accepted as a fine art in the early to mid-1900s?

a. Oil painting
b. Photography
c. Performance art
d. Gouache

91. Which of the following theories of art would recognize the subject of this artwork as a girl playing the piano, and its importance as an extension of our perception?

    a. Expressionism
    b. Representationalism
    c. Formalism
    d. Deconstructivism

92. Which of the following image resolutions are considered ideal for printing an image versus publishing an image online?

    a. 300 dpi for printing, 72 dpi for online
    b. 720 dpi for printing, 100 dpi for online
    c. 100 dpi for printing, 75 dpi for online
    d. 500 dpi for printing, 250 dpi for online

93. Which of the following is a criticism of some environmental art, including Robert Smithson's "Spiral Jetty"?

    a. Environmental art should not be categorized as art.
    b. Environmental art should include other artistic media.
    c. Environmental art can neglect to focus on environmental issues.
    d. Environmental art can permanently damage the land it was created on.

94. Which of the following is NOT one of the names for this method of composition for art and architecture?

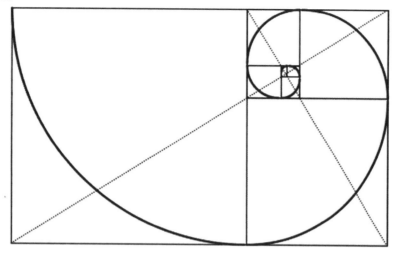

    a. Golden Mean
    b. Pi
    c. Golden Ratio
    d. Fibonacci number

95. In this painting, the larger area of red on the left is repeated in small amounts in different areas on the right. This is an example of which principle of design?

    a. Movement
    b. Contrast
    c. Symmetry
    d. Unity

Mometrix

96. Which of the following metals used for jewelry making is an alloy of antimony, tin and copper?

    a. Pewter
    b. Silver
    c. Aluminum
    d. Titanium

97. Which of the following terms is NOT associated with knitting?

    a. Chain stitch
    b. Purl
    c. Casting on
    d. Stockinette

98. Which of the following accurately describes characteristics of gouache paint?

    a. It can be thinned with turpentine or other solvents.
    b. It is only available in black, white, and primary colors.
    c. It cannot be re-wet or reworked.
    d. It is opaque and dries to a smooth, matte finish.

99. Which of the following types of clays is an earthenware that is generally a reddish-brown color, and is more porous and less durable than other types of clay?

    a. Stoneware
    b. Terra cotta
    c. Porcelain
    d. Raku

100. Which of the following artworks was instrumental in the acceptance of fiber arts as an artistic medium?

    a. Kara Walker's "Gone"
    b. Yayoi Kusama's "Dots Obsession"
    c. Judy Chicago's "The Dinner Party"
    d. Miriam Schapiro's "Big Ox No. 1"

Answer Key and Explanations

1. C: Gothic architecture, which was a style used in Europe from the mid-12th to the 16th century, is known for its tall designs with a sense of upward movement. This was a departure from the previously dark, damp buildings of the Romanesque style. Gargoyles were used as drainage spouts, and pointed arches were a commonly used visual element in this style.

2. A: Van Gogh, Cézanne, Seurat and Gauguin are all associated with the Post-Impressionism movement. This movement sought to explore the emotional response of the artist and was a departure from the naturalism of Impressionism. These artists used bold colors and while they portrayed real-life subjects, they also began to use distorted, geometric forms in their artwork. They sometimes used exaggerated colors and bold outlines as well.

3. A: A happening is a performance or event created in the context of fine art. These began in the 1950s, and they include audience participation as a main component. Happenings can be planned or improvised, and are meant to be a changing, unique work of art that cannot be preserved in a museum. Happenings might include music, dance, poetry, or performance, and can have a large or small audience depending on the artist's intentions.

4. C: When clay is partially but not completely dry, it is leather hard. At this stage the piece can still be carved or trimmed. When the piece is completely dry, it is considered bone dry. A bone-dry piece is fragile and cannot be carved or trimmed at this stage. An unfired ceramic piece is called greenware, and after the piece is fired once in a kiln it is considered bisque. A bisque ware piece can be glazed and fired again.

5. D: The impasto technique is the application of thick layers of paint, usually with oil or acrylics. The visible brushstrokes can become a visual element that leads the viewer's eye around the painting, and the paint can be applied by a brush or a palette knife. With this technique, the artist can create texture, and can control how the light reflects off of the layers of paint. Vincent van Gogh was known for working with this technique.

6. B: Sfumato is a technique in which the painter creates a hazy, smoky atmosphere, reducing the appearance of harsh lines in the artwork. *Mona Lisa* is an example of this, with soft transitions throughout the painting. Da Vinci masterfully built up layer upon layer of paint to create this soft appearance. This can also be used to represent objects in the distance, to create the appearance of atmospheric perspective and haziness.

7. D: Students with behavioral disabilities can benefit from the tactile feel of working with clay, and can also benefit from working in a secluded, quiet area of the room. These students can benefit from being free of distractions and noise and working with their hands. Using larger paper and tools can help students with physical disabilities or visual impairment and outlining a design with glue can be beneficial for students with visual impairments so that they can feel the design.

8. D: Claes Oldenburg was an American sculptor known for creating large scale Pop art sculptures. He created soft sculptures, often of food items, beginning in 1962. In doing this, he changed the traditional hard medium of sculpture to a soft, changeable format that challenged the idea of sculpture. Oldenburg was later known for his large-scale outdoor sculptures of ordinary objects, including a clothespin and a rubber stamp.

9. A: A performance assessment is an authentic task that focuses on the student's ability to demonstrate their art skills or their use of methods and materials. Traditional assessment consists of standard tests, such as multiple choice and essay tests. A formative assessment tests a student's understanding and progress throughout a course, while a summative assessment checks a student's knowledge at the end of a unit or lesson.

10. B: Sculptures in the Classical period in ancient Greece were made to honor their gods and goddesses. The technical skill of Greek sculptors allowed them to depict human anatomy with great accuracy, and at the same time they idealized the human figure. They often depicted figures and scenes from mythology and used sculptures to adorn temples. The statue of Zeus at Olympia was created during this period in ancient Greece.

11. C: The architectural term "form follows function" suggests that a building's design, or form, should be led by its function. If architecture is designed with its facade or looks primarily in mind, or if a new space is fit into a preexisting building, it does not follow this principle. When a stadium is designed with its form following its purpose, with room for spectators surrounding the central field, the form is following the function of the design.

12. D: Artists of the Impressionist movement sought to capture fleeting moments in time and the momentary effects of light. They were departing from the realistic depiction of previous art movements such as realism and using the newly invented paint in tubes to paint outside to portray these moments in a new way. Artists of the romanticism movement portrayed exaggerated scenes and heightened emotions.

13. A: In the hierarchical proportion used in artwork in ancient Egypt, scale was used to show the importance of people in relation to each other. People of higher status would often be sculpted or drawn as larger than those of lower status. This proportional organization would not necessarily be used in battle scenes or more chaotic portrayals of groups of people.

14. D: To prevent a water-based media from being resisted by an oil or wax-based media, it recommended to layer the water-based media underneath the oil or wax-based media. Acrylic, watercolor, and tempera are all water-based, while oil paint, encaustic, and crayons are oil and wax based, which will all resist the water-based media. Layering a water-based media on an oil or wax-based media can cause the top layer to not stick to the bottom layer.

15. B: A tertiary color is created by combining a primary color with a secondary color. The tertiary color will be named by combining the names of the two colors used. In this instance, the name of the tertiary color would be yellow-orange. The primary colors are red, yellow, and blue, while the secondary colors are orange, green, and purple or violet.

16. B: The refinement of the steel process, which led to steel skeletons for buildings, allowed buildings to be constructed at greater heights. The steel skeletons allowed builders to depart from load bearing walls, which did not allow for tall buildings such as these. The invention of the first safe passenger elevator, as well as the need for more vertical spaces to save room, also led to the construction of skyscrapers.

17. C: An illustrator will most likely need to be proficient at using computer graphics programs such as Adobe Photoshop and Illustrator for their work, although some work can be completed by hand as well. A photographer will use digital photo editing software to refine their photographs before printing or publishing them online. A graphic designer will use a range of computer graphics programs to create their designs. A curator would be the least likely to need proficiency in these programs.

18. D: In the Feminist art movement, female artists began to embrace and use materials that were traditionally tied to their gender, including embroidery and textiles. They sought to challenge stereotypes and cultural attitudes and bring attention to the contributions of female artists throughout history, including all art movements. They used new media that was not yet male-dominated to communicated with their viewers, and used self-portraits, appropriated images, collage, and other methods to get their messages across.

19. A: A larger aperture will result in a clear and focused subject with the background out of focus, otherwise known as a shallow depth of field, creating a clearer focal point in the photograph. To create a shallow depth of field, you would use a larger aperture, and decrease the distance from the camera to the subject. A higher ISO changes the sensitivity to light but does not affect depth of field and shutter speed can be slowed to blur motion, but will not affect the depth of field.

20. C: The Mannerism style, beginning at the end of the Renaissance in the 1520s, focused on mainly religious subject matter and included techniques such as elongated limbs, dramatic lighting, and unnatural, artificial poses. These artists departed from the compositional techniques of the Renaissance period and created compositions on a more flattened plane. They also experimented with portraying emotions in their artwork and using bright colors.

21. B: Both Postmodernism and Dada art sought to depart from the authority and traditions of previous art movements. Dada was considered "anti-art," challenging the previous ideas of art. Postmodernism was anti-authoritarian and refused to recognize the authority of any previous art movement, questioning authorship, originality, and subjectivity. They both wanted to move forward in their own way without relying on previous ideas and traditions.

22. B: In this situation, larger paper and larger materials would be the least likely accommodation to help this student. This accommodation is more often given to students with physical disabilities or vision impairment. A student with behavioral disabilities should be given a secluded area to work in, have their assignment broken down into smaller chunks with frequent check ins, and should be given frequent praise to help them stay on task during the class.

23. D: Backward design entails starting with the end point, or the goals of instruction, and then basing the assessments and the lessons around meeting those goals. The backward design method entails identifying what skills or knowledge the students should master by the end of the lesson or unit, then designing the instruction and assessments for the students to master the skills and information.

24. A: A student uses their metacognitive skills to assess their own learning, and this can include self-assessment and correcting their own work based on their self-assessment. When a student uses a rubric to check their progress toward reaching their goals, they are using their metacognitive skills. These skills help a student understand and regulate their own learning, and, when the student uses them, they can get themselves closer to their learning goals.

25. C: When an artist paints layers of transparent oil paint on top of one another, after each layer underneath has dried, this is called glazing. Glazing is a technique used to build up colors that will blend visually, without blending them on the palette. Glazing is often used to create complex colors such as skin tones. The artist needs to understand the transparency of different pigments to use this technique.

26. C: Egg tempera requires a rigid support so that the paint will not crack or flake off the support. Masonite or a wood panel would be the most ideal support for this paint. On paper or a fabric such as canvas or linen, the paint will crack and flake. To use these flexible supports, the paint also needs to be able to flex to some degree.

27. B: Mixing secondary colors is an appropriate skill to be introduced in these early grades. Students should be learning to name and recognize the primary and secondary colors and begin to mix the secondary colors as well. Using two-point perspective, hand-lettering, and using oil paints are all skills appropriate to introduce in later grades, such as middle or high school.

28. D: The safety while using a utility knife is not dictated by the MSDS sheets. The Materials Safety Data Sheets explain the hazards associated with certain materials, and what precautions should be taken because of these hazards. This includes flammable or corrosive materials that are used in the art classroom. Students should understand how to properly use, clean up, and store each material that they are using.

29. A: The Ashcan School sought to portray life and people in a realistic, unidealized manner, and thought the working class was a worthy subject. Artists of the Romanticism movement portrayed scenes with exaggerated and heightened emotions, while artists of the Neoclassical movement portrayed people with themes of heroism and classical mythology. The Hudson River School depicted idealized landscapes of the views surrounding the Hudson River Valley.

30. A: A painting from the Byzantine era would have been made on a wood panel, for several reasons. Canvas and paper were not used yet for paintings. Canvas became popular during the Renaissance times since canvases were able to support larger works and make them lighter. This painting would have been done with tempera, which will crack if flexed, so using a non-flexible surface like a wood panel would be ideal for the medium.

31. C: The deconstruction criticism theory involves finding hidden meanings and implied messages within an artwork. This theory seeks to analyze what is hidden, omitted, or repressed within the artwork, and shows that the initial impression of the artwork is just one of many potential interpretations. The artist's intentions, and the significance of subjects, objects or locations, could all lead to different interpretations of the artwork.

32. D: While the artists of the Impressionism movement tried to capture fleeting moments in time, like photography, they also reacted against photography by capturing an impression instead of a faithful reproduction. Impressionist artists often worked outdoors to capture the play of light on the scene and used a wide range of colors to imitate the light they saw. Their loose brushstrokes and vivid colors captured the impression of a scene rather than a realistic reproduction of it.

33. B: While video screens showing the artists discussing their artwork or showing video artwork are effective ways of incorporating technology in an exhibit, having multiple screens playing in one gallery can be distracting. One video screen per gallery, or video screens in separate viewing rooms, would be preferable so that they do not distract the visitors from each other or from another artwork.

34. A: If not using your own source material, and the source material is not out of copyright or in the public domain, you should obtain permission from the source. Copyright for an artwork begins once the artwork is completed. Copyright laws vary by state and country, so it is important to always check. It is not permitted to sell a copy of a famous artwork as your own.

35. B: This photograph features a pair of flying buttresses, which are masonry supports that transmit the thrust of a roof or vault into the outer support. The flying buttress is an inclined bar that flies out from the wall to carry the weight of the vault or roof. This type of support was developed in Gothic architecture, departing from the previously hidden supports. The flying buttress was instrumental in supporting the high ceilings characteristic of Gothic churches.

36. C: A wash is a large, flat area of color. Sgraffito involves scratching through paint to reveal the layer or surface underneath, and this can add texture to a painting. With dry brush, the artist loads paint onto the brush with minimal water or oil medium, and this can create a scratchy texture in the painting where the brushstrokes are visible. Impasto painting involves layers of thick paint, which can create a texture.

37. A: This artist used contrast to create the focal point of the painting. The light value of the bar, coupled with the bright red of the clothing, draw the viewer's eye. These both contrast heavily with the dark background and the muted colors throughout the rest of the artwork. Together the light line and red clothing catch the viewer's attention and emphasize the tightrope walker in the painting.

38. D: A mandrel is a tool used to size and shape a ring for jewelry making. It is a tapered piece of metal on which rings fit. A burnisher is a smooth metal tool used to smooth the surface of the plate for intaglio printmaking. A brayer is a rubber roller used to roll ink onto a surface for printmaking. A gouge is a tool used for relief printmaking, used to cut away parts of the surface before applying ink.

39. B: Renaissance artists were the first to use linear perspective in their artwork, giving it greater realism and more accurate depth. Prior to this, artists were aware of the relation of sizes for objects close up or far away, but Flippo Brunelleschi is credited with discovering geometric perspective in 1413, and artists began using vanishing points and horizon lines following this discovery.

40. C: African sculptors often used wood to create masks and sculptures of human figures. They emphasized symmetry and pattern, and would stylize, or visually abstract, the figure rather than depicting the figure in a naturalistic way. These sculptures were often used for religious purposes including display on altars or use in rituals. They would emphasize youthful characteristics as well as health and physical strength.

41. D: The fresco technique involved mixing pigments with water and applying the mixture to wet plaster. Once the plaster dried, the pigments would be visible. This made the pigments and the painting into a permanent part of the wall. The painting technique is time sensitive since the paint must be applied while the plaster is still wet. This technique was used by Michelangelo on the Sistine Chapel ceiling.

42. B: The rule of thirds is a compositional technique used in painting, photography and other two-dimensional artwork to add visual interest to the composition by not putting the subject in the center. The scene is divided into three parts both horizontally and vertically, the subject is centered on a point where those dividing lines intersect. In a landscape, the horizon line will often fall on the lower line.

43. A: Baroque architecture is characterized by pear shaped domes, marble or faux finishing, and bronze gilding, among other things. It originated in Italy in the late 16th century. Hemispherical domes, columns and decorative pilasters are characteristics of Renaissance architecture. Semicircular arches, barrel or groin vaults, and thick walls are characteristics of Romanesque architecture. Circular domes, pendentives, and mosaics are characteristics of Byzantine architecture.

44. C: Context describes the related conditions or circumstances around which something occurs. Understanding the context can help a person understand the artwork better, by looking at the circumstances in which the artist was working in at the time. This can include their environment, the historical events and traditions happening, their cultural values, the social movements at the time, and even the artist's personal values and commitments.

45. C: Appropriation involves using pre-existing images or objects in an artwork with few or no changes. Marcel Duchamp's "ready-mades" are one example of this. Transformation is changing an object or image and presenting it in a new way. Juxtaposition involves placing contrasting elements next to each other. Hierarchical proportion uses unusual proportion to draw a viewer's eye to the more important figures in an artwork.

46. A: A still life arrangement will have a better and more interesting composition when it is asymmetrical. It can be centered but should still have elements of asymmetry. Using incorrect perspective can be distracting to the viewer. Having edges of objects touch rather than overlap causes spatial ambiguity rather than showing which object is closer. A focal point should be included in the arrangement to draw the viewer's eye.

47. D: Color Field painters and Minimalist artists both used large, flat areas of paint in their artwork with minimal brush strokes. Color Field painting is also characterized by the extension of the paint to the edges of the canvas, suggesting the colors go on for infinity. Neither groups focused on using primary colors, although the De Stijl art movement did. Pop art used popular and consumer items as their subjects.

48. B: For a mezzotint, the artist will roughen and smooth areas of a plate to change their ability to hold ink. The artist works from dark to light, roughening parts for shading, and smoothing parts for lighter areas. Using gouges to cut away material describes linocut and woodcut. Melting fine particles of acid resistant material onto a plate describes aquatint. The use of a burin to carve lines describes the intaglio process.

49. C: A graphic designer will be responsible for the design of print and digital items. They would not need certification in programming languages, or an apprenticeship under an artist or designer. They also would not need experience with pedagogy, assessment and classroom management. A graphic designer will benefit from a working knowledge of the programs they will likely use for their job, including Adobe Photoshop, Adobe Illustrator and Adobe Flash, among others.

50. C: AVI is one of the oldest video formats and is not an image format. JPEG, GIF, and PNG are all common image file formats. JPEG stands for Joint Photographic Experts Group. GIF and PNG files both use lossless compression, while JPEG is highly compressed and lossy. They can each be used for specific purposes while saving image files, depending on the desired final product.

51. A: A triadic color scheme is composed of three colors that are evenly spaced around the color wheel. This could be comprised of the three primary colors, or the three secondary colors, as in this example. This would not include analogous, which are next to each other, or complementary colors, which are directly across from each other on the color wheel.

52. A: This photograph, titled *The Steerage*, is Alfred Stieglitz's most famous work. Taken in 1907, this photograph depicts families on the lower deck of a boat leaving America and traveling to Germany. This has been often been interpreted as an "immigration to America" photograph, although it is not. Stieglitz was on the upper deck of the ship, and he had a view of the lower deck, known as the steerage. From here, he was able to get this view and take this photograph.

53. B: A blind contour drawing involves the artist keeping their eyes on the subject, only occasionally checking to see where their pencil is on the paper. The artist is strengthening their hand-eye coordination and creating a contour drawing of the subject while keeping their gaze on the subject. This is typically used as a drawing exercise rather than a way to faithfully capture a subject or scene.

54. B: When acrylic paint dries, it becomes a sort of plastic that is flexible and will not crack when bent. This makes acrylic ideal for painting on multiple surfaces. Oil paint is less flexible and is prone to crack when flexed. Acrylic does dry much more quickly than oil, and it can be cleaned up with water. It does dry slightly darker when the white binder in the paint turns clear.

55. A: Artists in the Middle East often repeat a pattern in a way that could go to infinity. This is used to contrast against man's finite existence on earth, and to disregard this temporary presence. These patterns were also used on surfaces to represent the dissolution of matter, which is another important concept for these artists. These patterns could be highly intricate and ornate.

56. C: While strong black outlines were often used, Japanese woodblock prints used a rich palette of colors. The water-based inks used by these artists provide a large range of colors that could be vivid and transparent. When multiple layers were used, they had to be placed with precision as subsequent areas were carved out of the wood and more ink was applied to the prints.

57. D: Film photography is slower and more expensive to work with than digital photography. It requires specialized equipment to produce the prints from film. The storage space is limited to how many exposures are available on the film. Digital photography is easier to edit and manipulate than film photography, due to the availability of photo editing software. There are both free and paid programs that can be used to edit the photographs.

58. C: Watercolor paper and charcoal paper will both have a rough surface that is not suitable for detailed pen and ink work. Canvas is not suitable to draw on unless primed, and even then, it will have a rough surface. Illustration board is a firm, smooth surface that is made for detailed illustration work. It would be the most suitable choice out of these.

59. C: Poppy oil, linseed oil, and stand oil are all used in oil painting. Linseed oil is the most commonly used, and it gives the colors a glossy effect while slowing drying time. Poppy oil is good for lighter colors, as it is less likely to yellow than linseed oil. Stand oil will dry more quickly than linseed oil and can be used to thin oil paint.

60. B: For the daguerreotype process, an image is created on a silvered copper plate. The subject had to stay still for 15-30 minutes. A calotype creates an image on paper coated in silver iodide. An ambrotype involves creating a print on a glass plate, while a tintype involves creating a print on a tin plate. These were all used before the film camera was invented.

61. A: This technique of creating a lace pattern from thin strips of metal is called filigree. Creating a filigree piece involves careful bending of wire. A filigreed piece can be simple or ornate and complex. Many pieces of metal can be combined in this technique. The metal first needs to be annealed, or heated then cooled slowly, to make it easier to bend and work with.

62. D: This example is of etching, which is a form of intaglio printing. Intaglio is from the Italian word *intagliare* meaning "to carve or cut," and it involves carving or cutting lines into a metal plate. Intaglio methods also include drypoint, mezzotint, aquatint, and engraving. The artist uses a sharp tool to carve into the surface, and then he or she rubs ink into the surface and prints the ink onto the paper to produce the print.

63. D: This painting shows the wet-on-wet technique, where the artist adds wet paint to the already wet paper. This produces hazy edges instead of crisp edges, and allows colors to bleed into one another. A wash would be one solid or gradient. Dry brush would produce sharp edges, and a crayon resist would reveal a drawing underneath the paint.

64. A: This critic would be using the formalism aesthetic theory to analyze this artwork. This is concerned primarily with how the artwork looks, including the use of elements and principles, and does not take into account the context or narrative related to the artwork. With this theory, all artwork would be approached and analyzed in the same way, so it is especially useful when analyzing non-representational and abstract artwork.

65. C: Painting on an unprimed canvas can cause cracking as the fabric pulls the oils out of the paint. A canvas or board should always be primed with a quality primer to produce the best results. Varnishing the painting after it has dried, mixing linseed oil with oil paint, and working in layers using a glazing technique will produce good results as long as they are done properly.

66. B: When a paint is labeled as 'hue,' it is created to look as visually similar to its hazardous counterpart as possible but created without the toxic metals. Cadmium orange hue will be similar to cadmium orange in color but will not contain a hazardous metal. Flake white contains lead which is a hazardous metal. Cadmium and cobalt are also toxic metals and should be handled with care.

67. C: To create a scalable logo that will not become pixelated at any size, it is important to create a vector-based logo. This can be done in Adobe Illustrator or other programs. An image in vector format can be rescaled to very large or very small without any loss of quality, unlike a raster image that is made up of pixels. A raster image can generally only be scaled down without loss of quality.

68. B: When Spain colonized parts of Central and South America in the 1600s, they began to influence the architecture of those regions. The highly ornate Baroque style was used in many shrines and cathedrals. Mexico was the wealthiest of these colonies, and they created some intricate and extravagant cathedrals using the Baroque style. This style was also used in Peru, Portugal, and Brazil.

69. A: An MP4 file will have the best combination of smaller file size and high-quality video output. A .WMV file, or Windows Media Video, is a very small file which is good for sharing, but as a result is compressed and will be of low quality. An MPEG will be a small file and low in quality. An MOV file is an Apple Quicktime Movie file. They are fairly large files and will have a higher quality than many other formats.

70. C: A caryatid is a sculpture of a draped female that is created as a column. This architectural element was first used in Greek architecture. A balustrade is a series of pillars that support a rail, sometimes on a balcony. A pilaster is a flat, upright element that appears as a column attached to a wall. An obelisk is a tall, freestanding four-sided structure that ends in a pyramidal point.

71. D: Video sculpture artists seek to use video in new and innovative ways. They incorporate video into objects, places or performances, and diverge from the traditional narrative video format that has a beginning and an end. Video sculpture originated with artist Nam June Paik in 1963. It now allows performance artists to have a greater degree of permanence to their performances.

72. D: The monotype method of printing is not used to make multiple prints. To create a monotype print, the artist draws or paints on a smooth, nonabsorbent surface, then the media is transferred to a sheet of paper. This is done by hand or with a printing press. Linocut, intaglio, and screen-printing are all printmaking methods used to make multiple prints.

73. B: The traditional creation of porcelain in China is very labor intensive and can involve a 30-step process from the beginning to the end. Highly skilled artisans create traditional porcelain, and this takes time as well as specialized knowledge. This process challenges the perception of the "Made in China" slogan, which calls to mind mass-produced items that are made quickly and cheaply. Porcelain parts, however, can be mass-produced in factories.

74. C: This painting is an example of tromp l'oeil, which means "to deceive the eye" in French. The painting is made to look realistic, as if they are actual objects on a wooden surface. The artist would have great skill and mastery of their media to create this optical illusion. Alla prima is a wet-on-wet technique, and plein air is when the artist paints outdoors. Sgraffito involves scratching through the surface of paint to reveal the surface underneath.

75. A: This painting by French artist Jean Auguste Dominique Ingres is called *Virgil Reading the Aeneid before Augustus, Octavia and Livia*. This was painted in the Neoclassical style, which was a departure from the highly ornate Baroque style. Neoclassical artists were attempting to revive the subjects and styles of the Classical period, including Greek and Roman art.

76. B: Pop art was an art movement that used comic images, and items from popular culture. This movement subsequently influenced popular culture with its bright colors and designs, as well as its use of mass-produced items in the artwork.

77. D: Prior to using watercolor paper for a watercolor painting, it is best to stretch the paper. This is done by taping it to a surface, wetting it, and allowing it to dry. Then the paper is painted on. This helps to keep the paper from warping when the painting is completed. This can also be accomplished with a pad of watercolor paper that is glued on all sides.

78. D: The principle of design most evident in this painting is rhythm. Rhythm is the repetition of an element, but with some variance, unlike pattern which is an exact repetition. In this artwork, the trees are repeated in different sizes and distances, and slightly different shapes. It creates a rhythm throughout the artwork. Balance, contrast and emphasis are not as pronounced in this artwork as the rhythm is.

79. C: Pencils come in many degrees of hardness, but a 2H pencil will be hard enough to keep a sharp point and allow the artist to create a detailed drawing. Vine charcoal, conte crayon, and chalk will all be much softer and will not keep a sharp point. They are more suited to sketches and looser drawings than a pencil with a hard lead.

80. A: A mahlstick, or maulstick, is a stick with a padded top that an artist can use to rest and steady their hand when drawing or painting. This also keeps the artist from touching or resting their hand on the artwork. A tortillion is rolled paper used for blending pencil or charcoal, and frisket is a liquid or plastic that is used for masking. A t-square is used for drawing horizontal lines.

81. A: Stippling would be the best technique to use to emulate pointillism. Stippling involves creating dots with the pen and ink, and if an artist used different colors for these dots, the eye would visually blend the colors, much like the dots of paint in pointillism. Cross hatching and hatching involve lines, while a wash is a flat area of color.

82. D: Oil paint, acrylic paint, and egg tempera will all work best with using a primer to prepare the surface before painting. This also keeps the paints from soaking into the surface, and in some cases, eating away at the surface. Many canvases and supports are now available pre-primed. Watercolor paint does not require a primed surface, it is best used directly on watercolor paper. Watercolor paper is made for this purpose.

83. B: The critic is using the cultural perspective aesthetic theory to analyze the symbols painted on this vase. The dragon, bamboo, pine and other symbols hold cultural significance to the Chinese people. The dragon can represent fortune and luck, while pine is a symbol of longevity. Bamboo represents virtue. This theory is concerned with the cultural norms associated with the artist and how they express them in their work.

84. D: The Muralism art movement allowed artists in Latin America to express their ideas about political and social justice. The movement included artist Diego Rivera, among others, and was popular in Mexico as well as other countries in Latin America. This mural movement resulted in colorful and expressive public works of art that artists also used to depict their cultural background.

85. C: The subtractive method of sculpting involves removing pieces of material to create the sculpture. Chiseling marble or other stone, and carving wood or other materials would all be considered subtractive. Casting involves melted material such as metal that is poured into a mold. Modeling involves adding materials to build the sculpture, and assemblage is joining different materials together.

86. A: This fiber artwork was created with the embroidery method. Embroidery involves decorating fabric by using a needle to add yarn or thread in blocks of color or decorative patterns. Embroidery can be used for simple lines and patterns, or more complex representational images, as shown here. It can be used to decorate clothing or household items, or to create decorative artwork.

87. C: Salon-style exhibition involves hanging the artwork at, above and below eye level in groupings. This is different than the standard museum style of a single row of artworks with the center of each work at average eye level. This originated in 1667 at the Royal Academy salon in Paris, where there were too many works to hang in a single row. Thus, the works crowded the wall from floor to ceiling instead.

88. D: Although Adams initially experimented with color photography, he was able to control the results of his black and white prints better than color prints. He had high standards for his work and the black and white process suited these standards better at the time. He did look forward to a time when he would be able to apply these same high standards to color photography.

89. A: Aboriginal dot painting began in the early 1970s in Papunya, Australia. The artists would abstract their designs by filling in the designs with dots, to try to conceal any secret or sacred meanings within them from outsiders. Acrylic paints have allowed them to use brilliant colors in these designs. These paintings might also have stripes, lines, and other geometric patterns.

90. B: Photography began to be accepted as a fine art rather than a craft in the early to mid-1900s. Alfred Stieglitz and Ansel Adams were both instrumental in leading the charge for this acceptance. Since its invention, photography was used to capture family photographs and historical events, and was used for photojournalism, all of which were considered craft instead of art.

91. B: The representationalism theory of art claims that artwork needs represent something that exists to be art. This makes artwork an extension of our perception. The representation does not need to be literal, but the audience should understand the representation. In this painting, Renoir simply and clearly used the subject of a girl playing a piano, which is something the audience will recognize as a representation of something that exists.

92. A: The ideal and standard resolution for printing a digital image is 300 dpi. At this resolution the image should come out clear and not pixelated. The resolution can be much lower for publishing online—72 dpi—and it will appear clear on the screen. A lower resolution than this can appear pixelated on the screen, and an image saved at screen resolution is not suitable for printing.

93. D: A criticism of some environmental art, including Smithson's "Spiral Jetty," is that it can permanently damage the land on which it was created. Environmental art is considered art, although it is difficult to exhibit in a gallery as-is, and usually this is done by displaying photos of the artwork. It will often focus on environmental issues, and it does contain parts of the surrounding environment to create the artwork.

94. B: In addition to this proportional composition aid being called the Golden Mean, Golden Ratio, and Fibonacci Number, it can also be referred to as the Golden Number or Phi. This was used in ancient Greek architecture including the Parthenon. It can also be seen in da Vinci's "The Last Supper," and is thought of as a way to effectively compose an artwork or the proportions of a work of architecture.

95. D: Unity is a principle that takes an element of art and uses it to draw the artwork together in a cohesive manner. In this example, Van Gogh's artwork uses a large area of bright red on the left, and it is repeated in smaller areas on the right. This helps to unify the piece while creating a focal point on the left to draw the viewer's eye toward the figure. The bright red throughout the work helped to lead the viewer's eyes around.

96. A: Pewter is an alloy of tin, antimony and copper. An alloy is a combination of a metal and an element, or of different metals. Tin is too soft for many uses, so when it is combined with other metals it can be stronger and used for other purposes. Silver is an element as well as a precious metal, and aluminum and titanium are both elements too.

97. A: A chain stitch is associated with crochet, not knitting. A chain stitch is created, for example, as the first row of an afghan, and the subsequent row is worked off of this chain. Purl, stockinette, and cast on are all terms associated with knitting. Casting on is creating the first stitch on the knitting needle. The main stitches are knit and purl, and the basic pattern is stockinette.

98. D: Gouache is a paint medium that is often used for illustration due to its opaque colors and smooth, matte finish. It also dries quickly which is an advantage in illustration. Gouache can be rewet and reworked and comes in a wide range of colors. It is water soluble, meaning it only needs water for thinning and cleaning. Turpentine and other solvents would not be used with gouache.

99. B: Terra cotta is easily identified by its reddish-brown color. It is a type of earthenware, fired below 1200°C. Stoneware is a mid- to high fire clay, with colors ranging from light gray to brown, and it is more durable than terra cotta. Porcelain is a high fire clay made with kaolin, and it is generally white when fired. Raku is a firing technique that uses a wide variety of clays, including stoneware clays.

100. C: Judy Chicago's "The Dinner Party" was instrumental in fiber art's acceptance as an artistic medium rather than a craft. This artwork celebrated the accomplishments of women from history and included needlepoint and embroidery among the materials. This helped to elevate the status of fiber arts to something liberating and fun for artistic purposes, rather than a traditional craft used by women.

Praxis Practice Test #1

1. Which of the following architectural styles is known for the use of pointed arches, gargoyles, and a sense of upward visual movement?

    a. Classical
    b. Art Nouveau
    c. Gothic
    d. Baroque

2. Vincent van Gogh, Paul Cézanne, and Paul Gauguin are artists associated with which style of art?

    a. Post-Impressionism
    b. Surrealism
    c. Fauvism
    d. Cubism

3. Which of these terms refers to a performance or event created in the context of fine art?

    a. Happening
    b. Installation
    c. Sculpture
    d. Plein air

4. When a piece of clay is partially dry but not completely dry, it is _____.

    a. bisque
    b. greenware
    c. leather hard
    d. bone dry

5. Which of these painting techniques involves the application of thick layers of paint with visible brushstrokes?

    a. Sfumato
    b. Sgraffito
    c. Wash
    d. Impasto

6. In Leonardo da Vinci's *Mona Lisa,* he used a painting technique to give a smoky, cloudy appearance and soften the appearance of any hard lines. Which of the following techniques does this describe?

    a. Sgraffito
    b. Sfumato
    c. Velatura
    d. Imprimatura

7. Which of the following is an example of an accommodation in the classroom for a student with behavioral disabilities?

    a. Using large paper and taping it to the table
    b. Outlining a design with glue
    c. Using larger tools and offering choices of media
    d. Working with clay in a secluded area of the room

8. Claes Oldenburg was an American sculptor in the 1960s known for creating large scale Pop art sculptures, often of food items. How did his work challenge the traditional means of sculpture?

    a. He challenged the traditional media of metal and marble by sculpting with wire.
    b. He painted his sculptures, which was not traditionally done.
    c. He challenged the traditions of sculpture by using assistants to create his works.
    d. He changed the traditional hard medium of sculpture to a soft, changeable format.

9. Which type of assessment in the art classroom best reflects a student's ability to apply art-making skills?

    a. Performance
    b. Traditional
    c. Formative
    d. Summative

10. Which statement best describes the purpose of sculptures in the Classical period in ancient Greece?

    a. Sculptures sought to capture the true likeness of a person.
    b. Sculptures were made to honor gods and goddesses.
    c. Sculptures were used in fertility rituals.
    d. Sculptures were created to provide a resting place for a soul after death.

11. Of these architectural designs, which best embodies the theory of "form follows function"?

    a. An office building is designed inside a repurposed department store.
    b. A bank is designed with a facade to resemble a Greek temple.
    c. A stadium is designed to have room for spectators surrounding a central field for the players.
    d. A college campus is designed with walking paths that form intricate geometric designs.

12. Which of the following was NOT a goal of the artists of the Impressionist movement?

    a. To capture fleeting moments of time
    b. To portray the momentary effect of light on a scene or object
    c. To depart from depicting a scene in a realistic manner
    d. To portray exaggerated scenes and heightened emotions

13. Hierarchical proportion was used in many cultures to denote relative importance of figures, including Mayan, Renaissance, and Ancient Egyptian artwork. Which of the following describes the hierarchical proportion with which figures would be portrayed in Ancient Egyptian artwork?

    a. People of higher status are portrayed on a larger scale than those of lower status.
    b. People of higher status are portrayed on a diagonal higher than those of lower status.
    c. People of higher status are portrayed more realistically than those of lower status.
    d. People of higher status are portrayed with larger features than those of lower status.

14. Which method of layering these multimedia materials is correct for working with wax or oil-based media and water-based media?

    a. Layering acrylic paint over oil paint

    b. Layering watercolor paint over encaustic paint

    c. Layering tempera paint over oil pastels

    d. Layering crayon over watercolor paint

15. A tertiary color can be created by mixing which of the following?

    a. Red and yellow

    b. Yellow and orange

    c. Blue and yellow

    d. Orange and green

16. Which of the following was NOT an architectural need or advancement that led to the construction of skyscrapers?

    a. The invention of the first safe passenger elevator

    b. The development of load bearing walls for construction

    c. The refinement of the steel process which led to steel skeletons in buildings

    d. The need for more vertical buildings to create more space in cities

17. Which of the following art related careers will be least likely to depend on the use of computer graphics and image editing programs?

    a. Illustrator

    b. Photographer

    c. Curator

    d. Graphic designer

18. Which of the following would reinforce the goals of the Feminist art movement?

    a. Portraying women in a more abstract manner

    b. Creating artwork that supports stereotypes about traditional female roles

    c. Excluding modern art from the canon of female artwork

    d. Embracing materials in female artwork traditionally tied to their gender

19. Which photographic technique will result in a clear and focused subject with a background out of focus, as in the following image?

a. Using a larger aperture
b. Using a higher ISO
c. Using a slower shutter speed
d. Using a greater distance from the camera to the subject

20. This painting shows religious subject matter with elongated figures, unnatural poses, and dramatic lighting. During which art period or movement would this have most likely been painted?

  a. Medieval
  b. Renaissance
  c. Mannerism
  d. Romanticism

21. How was the Postmodernist art movement similar to the Dada art movement?

  a. They both sought to portray dream-like scenes with accuracy.
  b. They both sought to depart from the traditions and authority of previous art movements.
  c. They both sought to bring attention to the contributions of previously unrecognized artists.
  d. They both sought to explore the emotional response of the artist.

22. An elementary student in the art classroom has difficulty focusing on their project, and is often found wandering away from their desk, distracting other students. Which of the following would be the LEAST helpful accommodation for this student?

  a. The student's project should be broken down into smaller chunks.
  b. The student should should be given larger materials and larger paper to work with.
  c. The student should be given a secluded area in the room to work and concentrate.
  d. The student should be given frequent praise during the project.

23. A teacher writes their curriculum focusing first on setting the goals of instruction, then the assessment methods and the lesson plans. Which curriculum design method is this teacher using?

    a. Teaching for Artistic Behavior

    b. Discipline Based Art Education

    c. The TABA method

    d. Backward design

24. Which of the following describes a student's use of metacognitive skills in the art classroom?

    a. A student uses a rubric to assess their progress toward reaching their goals.

    b. A student answers an essay question about an artist's life.

    c. A student creates a sketch in their sketchbook drawn from real life.

    d. A student uses different media than they are used to for creating artwork.

25. An artist paints thin, transparent layers of oil paint on top of another layer of oil paint that has already dried. What is this technique called?

    a. Alla prima

    b. Impasto

    c. Glazing

    d. Plein air

26. Which of the following paint supports would be most ideal for an egg tempera painting?

    a. Canvas

    b. Paper

    c. Masonite

    d. Linen

27. Which of the following art skills would be most appropriate to students in Kindergarten through 3rd grade?

    a. Drawing with two-point perspective

    b. Mixing secondary colors

    c. Calligraphy

    d. Working with oil paints

28. Which of the following safety practices would NOT be done in the art classroom as a result of the MSDS sheets?

    a. A fire extinguisher is kept in the classroom due to flammable materials.

    b. An apron, gloves, and goggles are used with certain corrosive printmaking materials.

    c. Solvents are kept in a fireproof cabinet.

    d. The blade of a utility knife is retracted when not in use.

29. Which of the following art movements did NOT aim to portray life and people in an exaggerated or idealized way?

    a. The Ashcan School

    b. The Hudson River School

    c. Romanticism

    d. Neoclassical

30. What surface would have been used for this painting from the Byzantine era?

a. Wood panel
b. Linen
c. Canvas
d. Paper

31. A student evaluates a well-known artwork, finding the potential hidden meanings and implied messages within it. Which of the following criticism theories is the student using?

a. Formalism aesthetic theory
b. Cultural perspective aesthetic theory
c. Deconstruction criticism theory
d. Expression aesthetic theory

32. How did the Impressionism art movement react against the advent of photography in the art world?

a. Impressionist artists sought to capture fleeting moments and the play of light across objects.
b. Impressionist artists wanted to use minimal colors to capture a scene.
c. Impressionist artists wanted to work indoors rather than out in the field.
d. Impressionist artists sought to capture an impression of a scene rather than a faithful reproduction.

33. An art museum wishes to incorporate technology into their new exhibition showcasing Pop art. Which of the following would NOT be an effective way to incorporate this?

    a. Touchscreen technology could give the viewer more information about the artists.

    b. Multiple video screens showing the artists explaining their process could be set up together in the gallery.

    c. A docent-led tour could include a pre-arranged video call with an artist to discuss their work.

    d. Visitors could be provided headphones and a guide book for a self-led tour experience.

34. Which of the following statements accurately describes an ethical standard relating to artwork?

    a. Permission should be obtained if using source materials that are not public domain or out of copyright.

    b. Copyright for an artwork begins once the artist files for copyright.

    c. Copyright laws are the same in each of the 50 states, but vary by country.

    d. It is permissible to draw or paint a copy a famous artwork and sell copies of it.

35. Which of the following architectural elements is featured in this photograph?

    a. Triangulated pediment

    b. Flying buttress

    c. Ornamental parapet

    d. Transept

36. Which of the following painting techniques would NOT be used to create texture in an artwork?

   a. Sgraffito
   b. Dry brush
   c. Wash
   d. Impasto

37. Which of the following principles of design helps to create the focal point in this painting?

   a. Contrast
   b. Movement
   c. Balance
   d. Rhythm

38. Which of the following is NOT a tool commonly used for printmaking?

   a. Burnisher
   b. Brayer
   c. Gouge
   d. Mandrel

39. Which of the following was a significant contribution of artists during the Renaissance art period?

   a. Lost wax casting
   b. Linear perspective
   c. Paint in tubes
   d. Acrylic paint

40. A wooden sculpture of a youthful human figure shows symmetry and is visually abstracted. It is used for religious purposes. In which culture was this sculpture most likely created?

    a. Ancient Roman
    b. Mycenaean
    c. African
    d. Egyptian

41. Fresco was a technique often used in the Renaissance art period. Which of the following best describes this process?

    a. Oil paint was applied to wet plaster.
    b. Pigments mixed with plaster were applied to a surface.
    c. Tempera paint was applied to dry plaster.
    d. Pigments mixed with water were applied to wet plaster.

42. Which of the following is a technique used to create a more interesting composition in an artwork or a painting?

    a. Intaglio
    b. Rule of thirds
    c. Tromp l'oiel
    d. Middle ground

43. Which of the following best describes some of the characteristics of Baroque architecture?

    a. Pear-shaped domes, marble or faux finishing, and bronze gilding
    b. Hemispherical domes, columns, and decorative pilasters
    c. Semicircular arches, barrel or groin vaults, and thick walls
    d. Circular domes, pendentives, and mosaics

44. Which of the following is NOT an example of relating context to an artwork?

    a. Finding more information about the cultural values of African artists
    b. Reading about the social movements at the time of Harlem Renaissance artwork
    c. Practicing similar techniques of a Pointillist artist
    d. Researching a Dada artist's values and personal views

45. Which of the following is the best description of appropriation in artwork?

    a. Placing contrasting elements next to each other
    b. Using unusual proportions to emphasize a part of an artwork
    c. Borrowing and using pre-existing images with few or no changes
    d. Changing an image and presenting it in a new way

46. Which of the following recommendations is NOT a way to improve the composition of a still life?

    a. Arranging the items in a symmetrical grouping
    b. Overlapping items rather than having the edges touch
    c. Using accurate perspective
    d. Including a focal point in the arrangement

47. Which of the following describes a similarity between Minimalist art and Color Field painting?

a. The use of mainly primary colors
b. Paint extending onto the edges of the canvas
c. A focus on consumer items as the subject
d. Large, flat areas of color with minimal brush strokes

48. Which of the following best describes the mezzotint process?

a. The artist uses gouges to cut away the pieces of material that will not hold ink.
b. The artist works from dark to light, roughening and smoothing areas of a plate to change their ability to hold ink.
c. The artist melts fine particles of acid-resistant powdered rosin onto a metal plate, which is then dipped in acid.
d. The artist uses a burin to carve lines into a plate, and these lines hold the ink for printing.

49. Which of the following will most likely benefit a person seeking a career in graphic design?

a. Certification in programming languages such as Visual Basic, C++, or Java
b. An apprenticeship under an artist skilled in their chosen medium
c. A working knowledge of programs such as Photoshop, Illustrator, and Flash
d. Experience with pedagogy, assessment, and classroom management

50. Which of the following is NOT a common file format for images?

a. JPEG
b. GIF
c. AVI
d. PNG

51. Which of the following is an example of a triadic color scheme?

a. Orange, green, and purple
b. Blue, green, and purple
c. Red, yellow, and orange
d. Orange, blue, and green

52. This photograph, one of the first works of Modernism during a time of many immigrants coming to America, was captured by which photographer?

a. Alfred Stieglitz
b. Edward Weston
c. Dorothea Lange
d. Louis Daguerre

53. An artist is creating a drawing from life. They are keeping their eyes on the subject, and only glancing occasionally at their paper, creating an outline of the subject. Which type of drawing is this artist creating?

a. Gesture drawing
b. Blind contour drawing
c. Perspective drawing
d. Crosshatch drawing

54. Which of the following is NOT an accurate difference between acrylic paint and oil paint?

a. Acrylic paint dries much more quickly than oil paint.
b. Oil paint is more flexible than acrylic paint when dry.
c. Acrylic paint can be cleaned with water, while oil paint requires solvents.
d. Oil paint has no visible color shift when it dries, while acrylic paint becomes darker when it dries.

55. The concept of infinity is often used in patterns in Middle Eastern art. Why is this concept significant?
   a. To contrast the infinity with man's finite existence on earth
   b. To cover large areas of walls with the same pattern
   c. To allow different artists to easily copy the same pattern
   d. To represent the magnitude of the soul

56. Which of the following is NOT a characteristic of traditional Japanese woodblock printing?
   a. They often depicted landscapes, history, geishas, and scenes from everyday life.
   b. They used large, flat areas of color in the composition.
   c. They used primarily black for the prints.
   d. They began by drawing in ink then gluing it to the wood block for carving.

57. Which of the following is an accurate statement regarding digital photography versus film photography?
   a. Digital photography is slower and more expensive than film photography.
   b. Digital photography has more limited storage space than film photography.
   c. Digital photography requires specialized equipment for developing the photographs.
   d. Digital photography can be more easily edited than film photography.

58. An artist wants to create a pen and ink drawing with a lot of detailed work. Which surface would work best for this endeavor?
   a. Watercolor paper
   b. Canvas
   c. Illustration board
   d. Charcoal paper

59. Which of the following is NOT a common oil painting medium?
   a. Poppy oil
   b. Linseed oil
   c. Grapeseed oil
   d. Stand oil

60. Which of the following best describes the daguerreotype process?
   a. An image is created on paper coated with silver iodide.
   b. An image is created on a silvered copper plate.
   c. An image is created on a glass plate.
   d. An image is created on a tin plate.

61. This metalworking technique involves forming metal threads into a lace pattern. Which of the following is the name of this technique?

    a. Filigree
    b. Enameling
    c. Fusion
    d. Soldering

62. Which of the following forms of printmaking was applied in this image?

    a. Relief
    b. Serigraphy
    c. Lithography
    d. Intaglio

63. Which of the following watercolor techniques would this artist have used to create the hazy sky and clouds in this painting?

a. Dry brush
b. Wash
c. Crayon resist
d. Wet on wet

64. An art critic analyzes an artwork based on the use of elements and principles, not delving into the context associated with the artwork. Which of the following criticism theories is this critic using?

a. Formalism
b. Expressionism
c. Deconstructivism
d. Representationalism

65. An artist's oil painting has dried and the paint has begun to crack. Which of the following is a possible cause of this issue?

a. The artist varnished the oil painting after it dried.
b. The artist mixed linseed oil with their paint.
c. The artist did not prime the canvas before painting.
d. The artist worked in layers and used a glazing technique.

66. Which of the following pigments is NOT hazardous due to the use of toxic metals?

a. Cadmium red
b. Cadmium yellow hue
c. Cobalt blue
d. Flake white

181

67. If a graphic artist wanted to create a logo that could be resized for large banners without becoming pixelated, which of the following would be the best method?

    a. Creating a logo in Adobe Photoshop and saving it as a JPEG

    b. Drawing a logo by hand and scanning it, saving it as a GIF

    c. Creating a vector-based logo and saving it as an EPS

    d. Tracing a hand-drawn logo in Adobe Photoshop and saving it as a TIF

68. Which of the following was a reason that Baroque architecture spread throughout South America in the 1600s and 1700s?

    a. South American architects read about this style and began to use it.

    b. Spain colonized Central and South America.

    c. Architects from France emigrated to South America.

    d. Baroque architecture was a reaction against the previous Neoclassical architecture.

69. Which of the following video file formats would be the most ideal for saving and sharing a high-definition video?

    a. MP4

    b. WMV

    c. MPEG

    d. MOV

70. Which of the following is the correct name for this architectural element of a statue created for use as a column?

    a. Balustrade

    b. Pilaster

    c. Caryatid

    d. Obelisk

71. Which of the following is NOT an aim of video sculpture?

    a. To integrate video aspects into an object, location or performance.
    b. To diverge from the standard narrative video configuration.
    c. To present videos in new and innovative ways.
    d. To show a video in a linear format with a beginning and end.

72. If an artist wanted to create multiple prints using a printmaking technique, which of the following techniques would NOT be appropriate to use?

    a. Linocut
    b. Screen-printing
    c. Intaglio
    d. Monotype

73. How does the traditional creation of porcelain challenge the perception of the "Made in China" slogan, which calls to mind mass-produced products made inexpensively in China?

    a. Porcelain is no longer made in China.
    b. The creation of porcelain is labor intensive.
    c. The materials used for porcelain are very expensive.
    d. Porcelain can only be made by artisans.

74. This painting is an example of which of the following painting techniques?

    a. Alla prima
    b. Plein air
    c. Tromp l'oeil
    d. Sgraffito

75. During which of the following artistic movements would this painting have been created?

a. Neoclassical
b. Mannerism
c. Medieval
d. Post-Impressionism

76. Which of the following best describes a way that visual art has influenced popular culture?

a. Artists appropriated images from comic books to use in their artwork.
b. The bright colors and repetition of Pop art were subsequently used in fashion and advertising.
c. Mass-produced objects were a subject in the artworks.
d. Artists used commercial methods such as screen-printing.

77. Which of the following best describes why watercolor paper should be stretched before it is painted on?

a. So the paint will adhere to the surface
b. So the colors will mix properly
c. To make the paper into a larger surface
d. So that it will not warp

78. Which of the following principles of design is most evident in this painting?

a. Balance
b. Contrast
c. Emphasis
d. Rhythm

79. If an artist wanted to create a drawing with a great amount of detail, which of the following drawing instruments would be best suited for this?

a. Vine charcoal
b. Red conte crayon
c. 2H pencil
d. Black chalk

80. Which of the following is an instrument used to support and steady the artist's hand while painting or drawing?

a. Mahlstick
b. Tortillion
c. Frisket
d. T-square

81. If an artist wanted to use pen and ink to emulate the visual color blending of the Pointillism art movement, which of the following would be the most appropriate technique?

a. Stippling
b. Cross hatching
c. Hatching
d. Wash

185

82. Which of the following painting surfaces does NOT need to be primed with a primer before it is painted on?

a. Wood panel, when using oil paints
b. Canvas, when using acrylic paints
c. Wood panel, when using egg tempera paints
d. Watercolor paper, when using watercolor paints

83. An art critic analyzes this vase with deliberation over the meanings of the dragon, pine, and bamboo painted on the surface. Which of the following methods is this critic using?

a. Formalism aesthetic theory
b. Cultural perspective aesthetic theory
c. Expressionism aesthetic theory
d. Deconstructivism aesthetic theory

84. Which of the following describes the main issues that were expressed through the Muralism art movement of Latin America?

a. The rights of women and children
b. Freedom of speech and artistic expression
c. The desire for better schools and education
d. Political and social justice

85. An artist creates a sculpture from a block of marble, carefully removing pieces by use of a chisel. Which of the following sculptural techniques is this artist using?

a. Casting
b. Modeling
c. Subtractive
d. Assemblage

86. Which of the following terms describes the method with which this fiber art was created?

- a. Embroidery
- b. Weaving
- c. Knitting
- d. Crochet

87. Which of the following terms refers to hanging artworks in groupings on the wall at eye level as well as above and below eye level?

- a. Exhibition-style
- b. Gallery-style
- c. Salon-style
- d. Museum-style

88. Which of the following best describes why Ansel Adams created black and white environmental photographs instead of color?

- a. Color photography had not yet been invented.
- b. If the photographs were in color, they would be mainly green.
- c. He did not have experience with producing color photographs.
- d. He could control the outcome of the prints better with black and white.

89. Which of the following cultures would have produced this dot style painting?

a. Aboriginal
b. African
c. Chinese
d. Brazilian

90. Which of the following media was accepted as a fine art in the early to mid-1900s?

a. Oil painting
b. Photography
c. Performance art
d. Gouache

91. Which of the following theories of art would recognize the subject of this artwork as a girl playing the piano, and its importance as an extension of our perception?

   a. Expressionism
   b. Representationalism
   c. Formalism
   d. Deconstructivism

92. Which of the following image resolutions are considered ideal for printing an image versus publishing an image online?

   a. 300 dpi for printing, 72 dpi for online
   b. 720 dpi for printing, 100 dpi for online
   c. 100 dpi for printing, 75 dpi for online
   d. 500 dpi for printing, 250 dpi for online

93. Which of the following is a criticism of some environmental art, including Robert Smithson's "Spiral Jetty"?

   a. Environmental art should not be categorized as art.
   b. Environmental art should include other artistic media.
   c. Environmental art can neglect to focus on environmental issues.
   d. Environmental art can permanently damage the land it was created on.

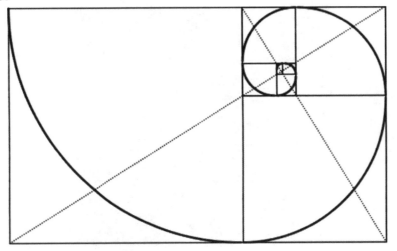

94. Which of the following is NOT one of the names for this method of composition for art and architecture?

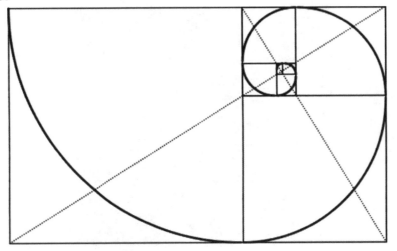

    a. Golden Mean
    b. Pi
    c. Golden Ratio
    d. Fibonacci number

95. In this painting, the larger area of red on the left is repeated in small amounts in different areas on the right. This is an example of which principle of design?

    a. Movement
    b. Contrast
    c. Symmetry
    d. Unity

96. Which of the following metals used for jewelry making is an alloy of antimony, tin and copper?

    a. Pewter
    b. Silver
    c. Aluminum
    d. Titanium

97. Which of the following terms is NOT associated with knitting?

    a. Chain stitch
    b. Purl
    c. Casting on
    d. Stockinette

98. Which of the following accurately describes characteristics of gouache paint?

    a. It can be thinned with turpentine or other solvents.
    b. It is only available in black, white, and primary colors.
    c. It cannot be re-wet or reworked.
    d. It is opaque and dries to a smooth, matte finish.

99. Which of the following types of clays is an earthenware that is generally a reddish-brown color, and is more porous and less durable than other types of clay?

    a. Stoneware
    b. Terra cotta
    c. Porcelain
    d. Raku

100. Which of the following artworks was instrumental in the acceptance of fiber arts as an artistic medium?

    a. Kara Walker's "Gone"
    b. Yayoi Kusama's "Dots Obsession"
    c. Judy Chicago's "The Dinner Party"
    d. Miriam Schapiro's "Big Ox No. 1"

Answer Key and Explanations

1. C: Gothic architecture, which was a style used in Europe from the mid-12th to the 16th century, is known for its tall designs with a sense of upward movement. This was a departure from the previously dark, damp buildings of the Romanesque style. Gargoyles were used as drainage spouts, and pointed arches were a commonly used visual element in this style.

2. A: Van Gogh, Cézanne, Seurat and Gauguin are all associated with the Post-Impressionism movement. This movement sought to explore the emotional response of the artist and was a departure from the naturalism of Impressionism. These artists used bold colors and while they portrayed real-life subjects, they also began to use distorted, geometric forms in their artwork. They sometimes used exaggerated colors and bold outlines as well.

3. A: A happening is a performance or event created in the context of fine art. These began in the 1950s, and they include audience participation as a main component. Happenings can be planned or improvised, and are meant to be a changing, unique work of art that cannot be preserved in a museum. Happenings might include music, dance, poetry, or performance, and can have a large or small audience depending on the artist's intentions.

4. C: When clay is partially but not completely dry, it is leather hard. At this stage the piece can still be carved or trimmed. When the piece is completely dry, it is considered bone dry. A bone-dry piece is fragile and cannot be carved or trimmed at this stage. An unfired ceramic piece is called greenware, and after the piece is fired once in a kiln it is considered bisque. A bisque ware piece can be glazed and fired again.

5. D: The impasto technique is the application of thick layers of paint, usually with oil or acrylics. The visible brushstrokes can become a visual element that leads the viewer's eye around the painting, and the paint can be applied by a brush or a palette knife. With this technique, the artist can create texture, and can control how the light reflects off of the layers of paint. Vincent van Gogh was known for working with this technique.

6. B: Sfumato is a technique in which the painter creates a hazy, smoky atmosphere, reducing the appearance of harsh lines in the artwork. *Mona Lisa* is an example of this, with soft transitions throughout the painting. Da Vinci masterfully built up layer upon layer of paint to create this soft appearance. This can also be used to represent objects in the distance, to create the appearance of atmospheric perspective and haziness.

7. D: Students with behavioral disabilities can benefit from the tactile feel of working with clay, and can also benefit from working in a secluded, quiet area of the room. These students can benefit from being free of distractions and noise and working with their hands. Using larger paper and tools can help students with physical disabilities or visual impairment and outlining a design with glue can be beneficial for students with visual impairments so that they can feel the design.

8. D: Claes Oldenburg was an American sculptor known for creating large scale Pop art sculptures. He created soft sculptures, often of food items, beginning in 1962. In doing this, he changed the traditional hard medium of sculpture to a soft, changeable format that challenged the idea of sculpture. Oldenburg was later known for his large-scale outdoor sculptures of ordinary objects, including a clothespin and a rubber stamp.

192

9. A: A performance assessment is an authentic task that focuses on the student's ability to demonstrate their art skills or their use of methods and materials. Traditional assessment consists of standard tests, such as multiple choice and essay tests. A formative assessment tests a student's understanding and progress throughout a course, while a summative assessment checks a student's knowledge at the end of a unit or lesson.

10. B: Sculptures in the Classical period in ancient Greece were made to honor their gods and goddesses. The technical skill of Greek sculptors allowed them to depict human anatomy with great accuracy, and at the same time they idealized the human figure. They often depicted figures and scenes from mythology and used sculptures to adorn temples. The statue of Zeus at Olympia was created during this period in ancient Greece.

11. C: The architectural term "form follows function" suggests that a building's design, or form, should be led by its function. If architecture is designed with its facade or looks primarily in mind, or if a new space is fit into a preexisting building, it does not follow this principle. When a stadium is designed with its form following its purpose, with room for spectators surrounding the central field, the form is following the function of the design.

12. D: Artists of the Impressionist movement sought to capture fleeting moments in time and the momentary effects of light. They were departing from the realistic depiction of previous art movements such as realism and using the newly invented paint in tubes to paint outside to portray these moments in a new way. Artists of the romanticism movement portrayed exaggerated scenes and heightened emotions.

13. A: In the hierarchical proportion used in artwork in ancient Egypt, scale was used to show the importance of people in relation to each other. People of higher status would often be sculpted or drawn as larger than those of lower status. This proportional organization would not necessarily be used in battle scenes or more chaotic portrayals of groups of people.

14. D: To prevent a water-based media from being resisted by an oil or wax-based media, it recommended to layer the water-based media underneath the oil or wax-based media. Acrylic, watercolor, and tempera are all water-based, while oil paint, encaustic, and crayons are oil and wax based, which will all resist the water-based media. Layering a water-based media on an oil or wax-based media can cause the top layer to not stick to the bottom layer.

15. B: A tertiary color is created by combining a primary color with a secondary color. The tertiary color will be named by combining the names of the two colors used. In this instance, the name of the tertiary color would be yellow-orange. The primary colors are red, yellow, and blue, while the secondary colors are orange, green, and purple or violet.

16. B: The refinement of the steel process, which led to steel skeletons for buildings, allowed buildings to be constructed at greater heights. The steel skeletons allowed builders to depart from load bearing walls, which did not allow for tall buildings such as these. The invention of the first safe passenger elevator, as well as the need for more vertical spaces to save room, also led to the construction of skyscrapers.

17. C: An illustrator will most likely need to be proficient at using computer graphics programs such as Adobe Photoshop and Illustrator for their work, although some work can be completed by hand as well. A photographer will use digital photo editing software to refine their photographs before printing or publishing them online. A graphic designer will use a range of computer graphics programs to create their designs. A curator would be the least likely to need proficiency in these programs.

18. D: In the Feminist art movement, female artists began to embrace and use materials that were traditionally tied to their gender, including embroidery and textiles. They sought to challenge stereotypes and cultural attitudes and bring attention to the contributions of female artists throughout history, including all art movements. They used new media that was not yet male-dominated to communicated with their viewers, and used self-portraits, appropriated images, collage, and other methods to get their messages across.

19. A: A larger aperture will result in a clear and focused subject with the background out of focus, otherwise known as a shallow depth of field, creating a clearer focal point in the photograph. To create a shallow depth of field, you would use a larger aperture, and decrease the distance from the camera to the subject. A higher ISO changes the sensitivity to light but does not affect depth of field and shutter speed can be slowed to blur motion, but will not affect the depth of field.

20. C: The Mannerism style, beginning at the end of the Renaissance in the 1520s, focused on mainly religious subject matter and included techniques such as elongated limbs, dramatic lighting, and unnatural, artificial poses. These artists departed from the compositional techniques of the Renaissance period and created compositions on a more flattened plane. They also experimented with portraying emotions in their artwork and using bright colors.

21. B: Both Postmodernism and Dada art sought to depart from the authority and traditions of previous art movements. Dada was considered "anti-art," challenging the previous ideas of art. Postmodernism was anti-authoritarian and refused to recognize the authority of any previous art movement, questioning authorship, originality, and subjectivity. They both wanted to move forward in their own way without relying on previous ideas and traditions.

22. B: In this situation, larger paper and larger materials would be the least likely accommodation to help this student. This accommodation is more often given to students with physical disabilities or vision impairment. A student with behavioral disabilities should be given a secluded area to work in, have their assignment broken down into smaller chunks with frequent check ins, and should be given frequent praise to help them stay on task during the class.

23. D: Backward design entails starting with the end point, or the goals of instruction, and then basing the assessments and the lessons around meeting those goals. The backward design method entails identifying what skills or knowledge the students should master by the end of the lesson or unit, then designing the instruction and assessments for the students to master the skills and information.

24. A: A student uses their metacognitive skills to assess their own learning, and this can include self-assessment and correcting their own work based on their self-assessment. When a student uses a rubric to check their progress toward reaching their goals, they are using their metacognitive skills. These skills help a student understand and regulate their own learning, and, when the student uses them, they can get themselves closer to their learning goals.

25. C: When an artist paints layers of transparent oil paint on top of one another, after each layer underneath has dried, this is called glazing. Glazing is a technique used to build up colors that will blend visually, without blending them on the palette. Glazing is often used to create complex colors such as skin tones. The artist needs to understand the transparency of different pigments to use this technique.

26. C: Egg tempera requires a rigid support so that the paint will not crack or flake off the support. Masonite or a wood panel would be the most ideal support for this paint. On paper or a fabric such as canvas or linen, the paint will crack and flake. To use these flexible supports, the paint also needs to be able to flex to some degree.

27. B: Mixing secondary colors is an appropriate skill to be introduced in these early grades. Students should be learning to name and recognize the primary and secondary colors and begin to mix the secondary colors as well. Using two-point perspective, hand-lettering, and using oil paints are all skills appropriate to introduce in later grades, such as middle or high school.

28. D: The safety while using a utility knife is not dictated by the MSDS sheets. The Materials Safety Data Sheets explain the hazards associated with certain materials, and what precautions should be taken because of these hazards. This includes flammable or corrosive materials that are used in the art classroom. Students should understand how to properly use, clean up, and store each material that they are using.

29. A: The Ashcan School sought to portray life and people in a realistic, unidealized manner, and thought the working class was a worthy subject. Artists of the Romanticism movement portrayed scenes with exaggerated and heightened emotions, while artists of the Neoclassical movement portrayed people with themes of heroism and classical mythology. The Hudson River School depicted idealized landscapes of the views surrounding the Hudson River Valley.

30. A: A painting from the Byzantine era would have been made on a wood panel, for several reasons. Canvas and paper were not used yet for paintings. Canvas became popular during the Renaissance times since canvases were able to support larger works and make them lighter. This painting would have been done with tempera, which will crack if flexed, so using a non-flexible surface like a wood panel would be ideal for the medium.

31. C: The deconstruction criticism theory involves finding hidden meanings and implied messages within an artwork. This theory seeks to analyze what is hidden, omitted, or repressed within the artwork, and shows that the initial impression of the artwork is just one of many potential interpretations. The artist's intentions, and the significance of subjects, objects or locations, could all lead to different interpretations of the artwork.

32. D: While the artists of the Impressionism movement tried to capture fleeting moments in time, like photography, they also reacted against photography by capturing an impression instead of a faithful reproduction. Impressionist artists often worked outdoors to capture the play of light on the scene and used a wide range of colors to imitate the light they saw. Their loose brushstrokes and vivid colors captured the impression of a scene rather than a realistic reproduction of it.

33. B: While video screens showing the artists discussing their artwork or showing video artwork are effective ways of incorporating technology in an exhibit, having multiple screens playing in one gallery can be distracting. One video screen per gallery, or video screens in separate viewing rooms, would be preferable so that they do not distract the visitors from each other or from another artwork.

34. A: If not using your own source material, and the source material is not out of copyright or in the public domain, you should obtain permission from the source. Copyright for an artwork begins once the artwork is completed. Copyright laws vary by state and country, so it is important to always check. It is not permitted to sell a copy of a famous artwork as your own.

35. B: This photograph features a pair of flying buttresses, which are masonry supports that transmit the thrust of a roof or vault into the outer support. The flying buttress is an inclined bar that flies out from the wall to carry the weight of the vault or roof. This type of support was developed in Gothic architecture, departing from the previously hidden supports. The flying buttress was instrumental in supporting the high ceilings characteristic of Gothic churches.

36. C: A wash is a large, flat area of color. Sgraffito involves scratching through paint to reveal the layer or surface underneath, and this can add texture to a painting. With dry brush, the artist loads paint onto the brush with minimal water or oil medium, and this can create a scratchy texture in the painting where the brushstrokes are visible. Impasto painting involves layers of thick paint, which can create a texture.

37. A: This artist used contrast to create the focal point of the painting. The light value of the bar, coupled with the bright red of the clothing, draw the viewer's eye. These both contrast heavily with the dark background and the muted colors throughout the rest of the artwork. Together the light line and red clothing catch the viewer's attention and emphasize the tightrope walker in the painting.

38. D: A mandrel is a tool used to size and shape a ring for jewelry making. It is a tapered piece of metal on which rings fit. A burnisher is a smooth metal tool used to smooth the surface of the plate for intaglio printmaking. A brayer is a rubber roller used to roll ink onto a surface for printmaking. A gouge is a tool used for relief printmaking, used to cut away parts of the surface before applying ink.

39. B: Renaissance artists were the first to use linear perspective in their artwork, giving it greater realism and more accurate depth. Prior to this, artists were aware of the relation of sizes for objects close up or far away, but Flippo Brunelleschi is credited with discovering geometric perspective in 1413, and artists began using vanishing points and horizon lines following this discovery.

40. C: African sculptors often used wood to create masks and sculptures of human figures. They emphasized symmetry and pattern, and would stylize, or visually abstract, the figure rather than depicting the figure in a naturalistic way. These sculptures were often used for religious purposes including display on altars or use in rituals. They would emphasize youthful characteristics as well as health and physical strength.

41. D: The fresco technique involved mixing pigments with water and applying the mixture to wet plaster. Once the plaster dried, the pigments would be visible. This made the pigments and the painting into a permanent part of the wall. The painting technique is time sensitive since the paint must be applied while the plaster is still wet. This technique was used by Michelangelo on the Sistine Chapel ceiling.

42. B: The rule of thirds is a compositional technique used in painting, photography and other two-dimensional artwork to add visual interest to the composition by not putting the subject in the center. The scene is divided into three parts both horizontally and vertically, the subject is centered on a point where those dividing lines intersect. In a landscape, the horizon line will often fall on the lower line.

43. A: Baroque architecture is characterized by pear shaped domes, marble or faux finishing, and bronze gilding, among other things. It originated in Italy in the late 16th century. Hemispherical domes, columns and decorative pilasters are characteristics of Renaissance architecture. Semicircular arches, barrel or groin vaults, and thick walls are characteristics of Romanesque architecture. Circular domes, pendentives, and mosaics are characteristics of Byzantine architecture.

44. C: Context describes the related conditions or circumstances around which something occurs. Understanding the context can help a person understand the artwork better, by looking at the circumstances in which the artist was working in at the time. This can include their environment, the historical events and traditions happening, their cultural values, the social movements at the time, and even the artist's personal values and commitments.

45. C: Appropriation involves using pre-existing images or objects in an artwork with few or no changes. Marcel Duchamp's "ready-mades" are one example of this. Transformation is changing an object or image and presenting it in a new way. Juxtaposition involves placing contrasting elements next to each other. Hierarchical proportion uses unusual proportion to draw a viewer's eye to the more important figures in an artwork.

46. A: A still life arrangement will have a better and more interesting composition when it is asymmetrical. It can be centered but should still have elements of asymmetry. Using incorrect perspective can be distracting to the viewer. Having edges of objects touch rather than overlap causes spatial ambiguity rather than showing which object is closer. A focal point should be included in the arrangement to draw the viewer's eye.

47. D: Color Field painters and Minimalist artists both used large, flat areas of paint in their artwork with minimal brush strokes. Color Field painting is also characterized by the extension of the paint to the edges of the canvas, suggesting the colors go on for infinity. Neither groups focused on using primary colors, although the De Stijl art movement did. Pop art used popular and consumer items as their subjects.

48. B: For a mezzotint, the artist will roughen and smooth areas of a plate to change their ability to hold ink. The artist works from dark to light, roughening parts for shading, and smoothing parts for lighter areas. Using gouges to cut away material describes linocut and woodcut. Melting fine particles of acid resistant material onto a plate describes aquatint. The use of a burin to carve lines describes the intaglio process.

49. C: A graphic designer will be responsible for the design of print and digital items. They would not need certification in programming languages, or an apprenticeship under an artist or designer. They also would not need experience with pedagogy, assessment and classroom management. A graphic designer will benefit from a working knowledge of the programs they will likely use for their job, including Adobe Photoshop, Adobe Illustrator and Adobe Flash, among others.

50. C: AVI is one of the oldest video formats and is not an image format. JPEG, GIF, and PNG are all common image file formats. JPEG stands for Joint Photographic Experts Group. GIF and PNG files both use lossless compression, while JPEG is highly compressed and lossy. They can each be used for specific purposes while saving image files, depending on the desired final product.

51. A: A triadic color scheme is composed of three colors that are evenly spaced around the color wheel. This could be comprised of the three primary colors, or the three secondary colors, as in this example. This would not include analogous, which are next to each other, or complementary colors, which are directly across from each other on the color wheel.

52. A: This photograph, titled *The Steerage*, is Alfred Stieglitz's most famous work. Taken in 1907, this photograph depicts families on the lower deck of a boat leaving America and traveling to Germany. This has been often been interpreted as an "immigration to America" photograph, although it is not. Stieglitz was on the upper deck of the ship, and he had a view of the lower deck, known as the steerage. From here, he was able to get this view and take this photograph.

53. B: A blind contour drawing involves the artist keeping their eyes on the subject, only occasionally checking to see where their pencil is on the paper. The artist is strengthening their hand-eye coordination and creating a contour drawing of the subject while keeping their gaze on the subject. This is typically used as a drawing exercise rather than a way to faithfully capture a subject or scene.

54. B: When acrylic paint dries, it becomes a sort of plastic that is flexible and will not crack when bent. This makes acrylic ideal for painting on multiple surfaces. Oil paint is less flexible and is prone to crack when flexed. Acrylic does dry much more quickly than oil, and it can be cleaned up with water. It does dry slightly darker when the white binder in the paint turns clear.

55. A: Artists in the Middle East often repeat a pattern in a way that could go to infinity. This is used to contrast against man's finite existence on earth, and to disregard this temporary presence. These patterns were also used on surfaces to represent the dissolution of matter, which is another important concept for these artists. These patterns could be highly intricate and ornate.

56. C: While strong black outlines were often used, Japanese woodblock prints used a rich palette of colors. The water-based inks used by these artists provide a large range of colors that could be vivid and transparent. When multiple layers were used, they had to be placed with precision as subsequent areas were carved out of the wood and more ink was applied to the prints.

57. D: Film photography is slower and more expensive to work with than digital photography. It requires specialized equipment to produce the prints from film. The storage space is limited to how many exposures are available on the film. Digital photography is easier to edit and manipulate than film photography, due to the availability of photo editing software. There are both free and paid programs that can be used to edit the photographs.

58. C: Watercolor paper and charcoal paper will both have a rough surface that is not suitable for detailed pen and ink work. Canvas is not suitable to draw on unless primed, and even then, it will have a rough surface. Illustration board is a firm, smooth surface that is made for detailed illustration work. It would be the most suitable choice out of these.

59. C: Poppy oil, linseed oil, and stand oil are all used in oil painting. Linseed oil is the most commonly used, and it gives the colors a glossy effect while slowing drying time. Poppy oil is good for lighter colors, as it is less likely to yellow than linseed oil. Stand oil will dry more quickly than linseed oil and can be used to thin oil paint.

60. B: For the daguerreotype process, an image is created on a silvered copper plate. The subject had to stay still for 15-30 minutes. A calotype creates an image on paper coated in silver iodide. An ambrotype involves creating a print on a glass plate, while a tintype involves creating a print on a tin plate. These were all used before the film camera was invented.

61. A: This technique of creating a lace pattern from thin strips of metal is called filigree. Creating a filigree piece involves careful bending of wire. A filigreed piece can be simple or ornate and complex. Many pieces of metal can be combined in this technique. The metal first needs to be annealed, or heated then cooled slowly, to make it easier to bend and work with.

62. D: This example is of etching, which is a form of intaglio printing. Intaglio is from the Italian word *intagliare* meaning "to carve or cut," and it involves carving or cutting lines into a metal plate. Intaglio methods also include drypoint, mezzotint, aquatint, and engraving. The artist uses a sharp tool to carve into the surface, and then he or she rubs ink into the surface and prints the ink onto the paper to produce the print.

63. D: This painting shows the wet-on-wet technique, where the artist adds wet paint to the already wet paper. This produces hazy edges instead of crisp edges, and allows colors to bleed into one another. A wash would be one solid or gradient. Dry brush would produce sharp edges, and a crayon resist would reveal a drawing underneath the paint.

64. A: This critic would be using the formalism aesthetic theory to analyze this artwork. This is concerned primarily with how the artwork looks, including the use of elements and principles, and does not take into account the context or narrative related to the artwork. With this theory, all artwork would be approached and analyzed in the same way, so it is especially useful when analyzing non-representational and abstract artwork.

65. C: Painting on an unprimed canvas can cause cracking as the fabric pulls the oils out of the paint. A canvas or board should always be primed with a quality primer to produce the best results. Varnishing the painting after it has dried, mixing linseed oil with oil paint, and working in layers using a glazing technique will produce good results as long as they are done properly.

66. B: When a paint is labeled as 'hue,' it is created to look as visually similar to its hazardous counterpart as possible but created without the toxic metals. Cadmium orange hue will be similar to cadmium orange in color but will not contain a hazardous metal. Flake white contains lead which is a hazardous metal. Cadmium and cobalt are also toxic metals and should be handled with care.

67. C: To create a scalable logo that will not become pixelated at any size, it is important to create a vector-based logo. This can be done in Adobe Illustrator or other programs. An image in vector format can be rescaled to very large or very small without any loss of quality, unlike a raster image that is made up of pixels. A raster image can generally only be scaled down without loss of quality.

68. B: When Spain colonized parts of Central and South America in the 1600s, they began to influence the architecture of those regions. The highly ornate Baroque style was used in many shrines and cathedrals. Mexico was the wealthiest of these colonies, and they created some intricate and extravagant cathedrals using the Baroque style. This style was also used in Peru, Portugal, and Brazil.

69. A: An MP4 file will have the best combination of smaller file size and high-quality video output. A .WMV file, or Windows Media Video, is a very small file which is good for sharing, but as a result is compressed and will be of low quality. An MPEG will be a small file and low in quality. An MOV file is an Apple Quicktime Movie file. They are fairly large files and will have a higher quality than many other formats.

70. C: A caryatid is a sculpture of a draped female that is created as a column. This architectural element was first used in Greek architecture. A balustrade is a series of pillars that support a rail, sometimes on a balcony. A pilaster is a flat, upright element that appears as a column attached to a wall. An obelisk is a tall, freestanding four-sided structure that ends in a pyramidal point.

71. D: Video sculpture artists seek to use video in new and innovative ways. They incorporate video into objects, places or performances, and diverge from the traditional narrative video format that has a beginning and an end. Video sculpture originated with artist Nam June Paik in 1963. It now allows performance artists to have a greater degree of permanence to their performances.

72. D: The monotype method of printing is not used to make multiple prints. To create a monotype print, the artist draws or paints on a smooth, nonabsorbent surface, then the media is transferred to a sheet of paper. This is done by hand or with a printing press. Linocut, intaglio, and screen-printing are all printmaking methods used to make multiple prints.

73. B: The traditional creation of porcelain in China is very labor intensive and can involve a 30-step process from the beginning to the end. Highly skilled artisans create traditional porcelain, and this takes time as well as specialized knowledge. This process challenges the perception of the "Made in China" slogan, which calls to mind mass-produced items that are made quickly and cheaply. Porcelain parts, however, can be mass-produced in factories.

74. C: This painting is an example of tromp l'oeil, which means "to deceive the eye" in French. The painting is made to look realistic, as if they are actual objects on a wooden surface. The artist would have great skill and mastery of their media to create this optical illusion. Alla prima is a wet-on-wet technique, and plein air is when the artist paints outdoors. Sgraffito involves scratching through the surface of paint to reveal the surface underneath.

75. A: This painting by French artist Jean Auguste Dominique Ingres is called *Virgil Reading the Aeneid before Augustus, Octavia and Livia*. This was painted in the Neoclassical style, which was a departure from the highly ornate Baroque style. Neoclassical artists were attempting to revive the subjects and styles of the Classical period, including Greek and Roman art.

76. B: Pop art was an art movement that used comic images, and items from popular culture. This movement subsequently influenced popular culture with its bright colors and designs, as well as its use of mass-produced items in the artwork.

77. D: Prior to using watercolor paper for a watercolor painting, it is best to stretch the paper. This is done by taping it to a surface, wetting it, and allowing it to dry. Then the paper is painted on. This helps to keep the paper from warping when the painting is completed. This can also be accomplished with a pad of watercolor paper that is glued on all sides.

78. D: The principle of design most evident in this painting is rhythm. Rhythm is the repetition of an element, but with some variance, unlike pattern which is an exact repetition. In this artwork, the trees are repeated in different sizes and distances, and slightly different shapes. It creates a rhythm throughout the artwork. Balance, contrast and emphasis are not as pronounced in this artwork as the rhythm is.

79. C: Pencils come in many degrees of hardness, but a 2H pencil will be hard enough to keep a sharp point and allow the artist to create a detailed drawing. Vine charcoal, conte crayon, and chalk will all be much softer and will not keep a sharp point. They are more suited to sketches and looser drawings than a pencil with a hard lead.

80. A: A mahlstick, or maulstick, is a stick with a padded top that an artist can use to rest and steady their hand when drawing or painting. This also keeps the artist from touching or resting their hand on the artwork. A tortillion is rolled paper used for blending pencil or charcoal, and frisket is a liquid or plastic that is used for masking. A t-square is used for drawing horizontal lines.

81. A: Stippling would be the best technique to use to emulate pointillism. Stippling involves creating dots with the pen and ink, and if an artist used different colors for these dots, the eye would visually blend the colors, much like the dots of paint in pointillism. Cross hatching and hatching involve lines, while a wash is a flat area of color.

82. D: Oil paint, acrylic paint, and egg tempera will all work best with using a primer to prepare the surface before painting. This also keeps the paints from soaking into the surface, and in some cases, eating away at the surface. Many canvases and supports are now available pre-primed. Watercolor paint does not require a primed surface, it is best used directly on watercolor paper. Watercolor paper is made for this purpose.

83. B: The critic is using the cultural perspective aesthetic theory to analyze the symbols painted on this vase. The dragon, bamboo, pine and other symbols hold cultural significance to the Chinese people. The dragon can represent fortune and luck, while pine is a symbol of longevity. Bamboo represents virtue. This theory is concerned with the cultural norms associated with the artist and how they express them in their work.

84. D: The Muralism art movement allowed artists in Latin America to express their ideas about political and social justice. The movement included artist Diego Rivera, among others, and was popular in Mexico as well as other countries in Latin America. This mural movement resulted in colorful and expressive public works of art that artists also used to depict their cultural background.

85. C: The subtractive method of sculpting involves removing pieces of material to create the sculpture. Chiseling marble or other stone, and carving wood or other materials would all be considered subtractive. Casting involves melted material such as metal that is poured into a mold. Modeling involves adding materials to build the sculpture, and assemblage is joining different materials together.

86. A: This fiber artwork was created with the embroidery method. Embroidery involves decorating fabric by using a needle to add yarn or thread in blocks of color or decorative patterns. Embroidery can be used for simple lines and patterns, or more complex representational images, as shown here. It can be used to decorate clothing or household items, or to create decorative artwork.

87. C: Salon-style exhibition involves hanging the artwork at, above and below eye level in groupings. This is different than the standard museum style of a single row of artworks with the center of each work at average eye level. This originated in 1667 at the Royal Academy salon in Paris, where there were too many works to hang in a single row. Thus, the works crowded the wall from floor to ceiling instead.

88. D: Although Adams initially experimented with color photography, he was able to control the results of his black and white prints better than color prints. He had high standards for his work and the black and white process suited these standards better at the time. He did look forward to a time when he would be able to apply these same high standards to color photography.

89. A: Aboriginal dot painting began in the early 1970s in Papunya, Australia. The artists would abstract their designs by filling in the designs with dots, to try to conceal any secret or sacred meanings within them from outsiders. Acrylic paints have allowed them to use brilliant colors in these designs. These paintings might also have stripes, lines, and other geometric patterns.

90. B: Photography began to be accepted as a fine art rather than a craft in the early to mid-1900s. Alfred Stieglitz and Ansel Adams were both instrumental in leading the charge for this acceptance. Since its invention, photography was used to capture family photographs and historical events, and was used for photojournalism, all of which were considered craft instead of art.

91. B: The representationalism theory of art claims that artwork needs represent something that exists to be art. This makes artwork an extension of our perception. The representation does not need to be literal, but the audience should understand the representation. In this painting, Renoir simply and clearly used the subject of a girl playing a piano, which is something the audience will recognize as a representation of something that exists.

92. A: The ideal and standard resolution for printing a digital image is 300 dpi. At this resolution the image should come out clear and not pixelated. The resolution can be much lower for publishing online—72 dpi—and it will appear clear on the screen. A lower resolution than this can appear pixelated on the screen, and an image saved at screen resolution is not suitable for printing.

93. D: A criticism of some environmental art, including Smithson's "Spiral Jetty," is that it can permanently damage the land on which it was created. Environmental art is considered art, although it is difficult to exhibit in a gallery as-is, and usually this is done by displaying photos of the artwork. It will often focus on environmental issues, and it does contain parts of the surrounding environment to create the artwork.

94. B: In addition to this proportional composition aid being called the Golden Mean, Golden Ratio, and Fibonacci Number, it can also be referred to as the Golden Number or Phi. This was used in ancient Greek architecture including the Parthenon. It can also be seen in da Vinci's "The Last Supper," and is thought of as a way to effectively compose an artwork or the proportions of a work of architecture.

95. D: Unity is a principle that takes an element of art and uses it to draw the artwork together in a cohesive manner. In this example, Van Gogh's artwork uses a large area of bright red on the left, and it is repeated in smaller areas on the right. This helps to unify the piece while creating a focal point on the left to draw the viewer's eye toward the figure. The bright red throughout the work helped to lead the viewer's eyes around.

96. A: Pewter is an alloy of tin, antimony and copper. An alloy is a combination of a metal and an element, or of different metals. Tin is too soft for many uses, so when it is combined with other metals it can be stronger and used for other purposes. Silver is an element as well as a precious metal, and aluminum and titanium are both elements too.

97. A: A chain stitch is associated with crochet, not knitting. A chain stitch is created, for example, as the first row of an afghan, and the subsequent row is worked off of this chain. Purl, stockinette, and cast on are all terms associated with knitting. Casting on is creating the first stitch on the knitting needle. The main stitches are knit and purl, and the basic pattern is stockinette.

98. D: Gouache is a paint medium that is often used for illustration due to its opaque colors and smooth, matte finish. It also dries quickly which is an advantage in illustration. Gouache can be rewet and reworked and comes in a wide range of colors. It is water soluble, meaning it only needs water for thinning and cleaning. Turpentine and other solvents would not be used with gouache.

99. B: Terra cotta is easily identified by its reddish-brown color. It is a type of earthenware, fired below 1200°C. Stoneware is a mid- to high fire clay, with colors ranging from light gray to brown, and it is more durable than terra cotta. Porcelain is a high fire clay made with kaolin, and it is generally white when fired. Raku is a firing technique that uses a wide variety of clays, including stoneware clays.

100. C: Judy Chicago's "The Dinner Party" was instrumental in fiber art's acceptance as an artistic medium rather than a craft. This artwork celebrated the accomplishments of women from history and included needlepoint and embroidery among the materials. This helped to elevate the status of fiber arts to something liberating and fun for artistic purposes, rather than a traditional craft used by women.

Praxis Practice Test #2

1. Which of the following best describes how Fauvism artists departed from previous styles?

    a. They used small dots of pure color to let the eye blend the colors together, rather than mixing colors on the palette.

    b. They used intense, unnatural colors and disregarded proportions rather than using realistic colors and portraying proportions accurately.

    c. They portrayed nonrepresentational subjects rather than portraying recognizable subjects in their artwork.

    d. They reduced subjects into geometric shapes and primary colors rather than faithfully representing recognizable subjects.

2. Which of the following best describes form, which is an element of art?

    a. The positive and negative areas of an artwork

    b. A flat element with height and width

    c. The way things feel or look like they may feel in an artwork

    d. A three-dimensional shape that has width, depth, and height

3. Which of the following types of architectural vaults is shown in this image?

    a. Groin vault
    b. Barrel vault
    c. Rib vault
    d. Tunnel vault

4. Which of the following artists did NOT paint in the color field style?

    a. Vladimir Tatlin
    b. Mark Rothko
    c. Clyfford Still
    d. Frank Stella

5. Which of the following is NOT a function of linseed oil when used for oil painting?

    a. Helps to maintain the flexibility of oil paint
    b. Makes the oil paint more fluid and transparent
    c. Cleans and conditions paintbrushes
    d. Increases the drying time of oil paint

6. Which of the following best describes what willow charcoal is composed of?

    a. Graphite shaped into thin sticks
    b. Pigment bound with gum arabic
    c. Organic materials bound with a wax binder
    d. Sticks burnt in a kiln without air

7. Which of the following best describes this sculpture as analyzed with the formalism aesthetic theory?

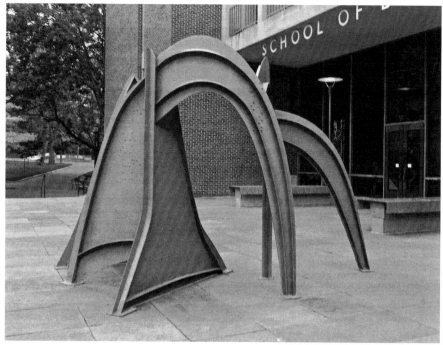

a. This sculpture evokes feelings of warmth and closeness due to its color and form.
b. This monochromatic sculpture is red, and it is asymmetrically balanced, leading the eye in arcs toward the ground.
c. This sculpture would be more successful if it represented a recognizable object.
d. This large sculpture is intimidating; the red color adds to the menacing appearance.

8. Which of the following most accurately describes the art technique of pouncing?

a. A decorative method of writing that involves a broad-tipped pen
b. A method similar to tracing that involves pricking holes in paper and forcing a powder through those holes
c. A method of sketching that involves large, broad gestures with the arm and hand to capture the subject
d. A method of drawing that involves creating lines perpendicular to each other to create values

9. Which of the following does NOT describe an advantage of creating an artwork on a toned paper or canvas, instead of the usual white ground?

a. A dark-toned ground can serve as the darker tones in the artwork.
b. A toned ground can be less intimidating to begin working on than a white ground.
c. A toned ground will often be less expensive than a white ground for artwork.
d. A medium-toned ground can allow the artist to build up both highlights and shadows in the artwork.

10. Which of the following architectural styles is characterized by decorative timbering and a steeply pitched roof, as shown in this image?

    a. Tudor
    b. Queen Anne
    c. Art Deco
    d. Italianate

11. Which of the following best describes the aquatint printmaking process?
    a. Melting fine particles of acid-resistant material onto a metal plate, then etching the plate with acid
    b. Alternately scraping smooth and roughening a metal plate to create light areas and shading
    c. Carving a block with a gouge, leaving the raised parts of the block as the positive image
    d. Arranging materials onto a surface to create a raised textured print

12. Which of the following terms best describes the contrast of the figure on the right with dark clothes and skin, placed next to the figure with pale skin and white clothing?
    a. Transformation
    b. Contextualization
    c. Appropriation
    d. Juxtaposition

13. Which of the following best describes the motivations of the Expressionist artists?
    a. To minimize their concepts into simple geometric forms
    b. To present their ideas subjectively and express emotions through their artwork
    c. To capture the effects of light on their subject through color
    d. To elevate popular culture in artwork and challenge the traditions of art

14. Which of the following themes did Keith Haring often address in his murals and artwork?

a. Global warming
b. Immigration and social justice
c. Acquired immunodeficiency syndrome (AIDS) and homosexuality
d. Industry and progress

15. Which of the following metals is usually added to silver to create sterling silver?

a. Copper
b. Bronze
c. Gold
d. Pewter

16. This painting shows a strong contrast between the dark background and the highlights on the subject. Which of the following is this technique an example of?

a. Chiaroscuro
b. Sfumato
c. Fresco
d. Intonaco

17. Which of the following color combinations could be used to create an analogous color scheme?

    a. Red, yellow, and blue
    b. Red, orange, green, and blue
    c. Yellow, red-violet, and blue-violet
    d. Green, blue-green, and blue

18. Which of the following describes how a student could use their metacognitive skills in the art classroom?

    a. Answering selected response questions about a period of art history
    b. Tracing a drawing made by a famous artist
    c. Creating an artwork with two different materials
    d. Making revisions on their sketches after revisiting their goals for an artwork

19. Which of the following was NOT an innovation contributed to the art world during the Renaissance period?

    a. Linear perspective
    b. Egg tempera
    c. Foreshortening
    d. Sfumato

20. An artist wishes to mask off an area of an artwork to prevent paint from changing that area. Which of the following materials would they use?

    a. Tissue paper
    b. Rice paper
    c. Frisket
    d. Linseed oil

21. Which of the following best describes what a camera's ISO setting adjusts?

    a. The size of the lens opening
    b. The image sensor's sensitivity to light
    c. The depth of field
    d. The shutter speed

22. An artist wants to use an oil- or wax-based media and a water-based media in one project. Which of the following describes the best way to layer these media?

    a. Oil paint layered on top of acrylic paint
    b. Gouache layered on top of oil pastels
    c. Watercolor layered on top of encaustic
    d. Tempera layered on top of crayon

23. Which of the following best describes the work of Romare Bearden?

    a. Detailed collages of African-American life
    b. Life-sized silhouettes of slave scenes
    c. Miniature sculptures encouraging social justice
    d. Street art highlighting the plight of poor neighborhoods

24. Which of the following pigments is NOT considered hazardous due to its use of toxic metals?

    a. Cadmium red
    b. Chrome yellow
    c. Yellow ochre
    d. Cobalt blue

25. Which of the following best describes the difference between watercolor paint and gouache paint?

    a. Gouache is used in a thick impasto technique, whereas watercolor is painted in thin layers
    b. Gouache is available only in neutral tones, whereas watercolor is available in a full range of colors
    c. Gouache is used for illustration work, whereas watercolor is used for fine art
    d. Gouache is opaque, whereas watercolor is transparent.

26. This woman is using a wax-resist dyeing method to decorate fabric. Which of the following is the correct term for this technique?

    a. Intaglio
    b. Batik
    c. Etching
    d. Inlay

27. Artists Eugène Delacroix, Théodore Géricault, and Thomas Cole are all associated with which of the following art movements?

    a. Romanticism
    b. Surrealism
    c. Art Nouveau
    d. Neoclassicism

28. This painting gives the illusion of viewing space from below on a ceiling, using foreshortened figures. Which of the following is the correct term for this technique?

    a. Chiaroscuro
    b. Di sotto in su
    c. Fresco
    d. Pentimento

29. Of these architectural designs, which best describes an Art Nouveau-style building?

    a. A symmetrical design with a pediment and Corinthian columns
    b. An open floor plan with a low-pitched roof, strings of windows, and long horizontal lines
    c. A rectangular, utilitarian plan with solid walls and without ornamentation
    d. An asymmetrical facade with decorations including butterflies, orchids, and water lilies

30. In this still life, which technique does the artist use to create visual interest?

   a. The arrangement in the artwork forms a pattern.
   b. The still life is comprised of an analogous color scheme.
   c. A variety of shapes are arranged throughout the work.
   d. The objects in the still life are arranged asymmetrically.

31. Which of the following is NOT an advantage of using acrylic paint instead of oil paint?

   a. Acrylic paint can be cleaned up with soap and water, instead of needing solvents for cleaning.
   b. Acrylic paint can be thinned with water, whereas oil paints require oils and solvents.
   c. Acrylic paints are all nontoxic, unlike oil paints.
   d. Acrylic paints dry much more quickly than oil paints, allowing artists to produce work more quickly.

32. A watercolor artist wishes to stretch their watercolor paper prior to starting a painting. Which of the following best describes a proper method to stretch the paper?

   a. The paper is soaked with water, then manually stretched by hand in all directions.
   b. The paper is soaked with water, placed on a board, then taped around the edges with gummed paper tape and allowed to dry overnight.
   c. The paper is soaked with water, then hung with clips from a rail, and weights are hung off the bottom of the paper.
   d. The paper is soaked with water, then rolled with a wooden pin to remove the excess water.

33. An artist needs to be able to erase various parts of a drawing without leaving pieces of eraser on the paper and without harming the surface. Which type of eraser would work best for this purpose?

   a. Kneaded eraser
   b. Art gum eraser
   c. Pink pearl eraser
   d. Vinyl eraser

34. Which of the following best describes the purpose of artwork in Ancient Egypt?

    a. It was mostly created for tombs and for the afterlife.
    b. Artwork was created to decorate the pyramids.
    c. It was mainly jewelry to be worn by the rulers of Egypt.
    d. Artwork was mostly in the form of paintings to decorate the walls of palaces.

35. Which of the following describes correctly following an ethical standard related to creating artwork?

    a. Using public domain images without checking the fine print for restrictions
    b. Avoiding copyright issues by working from life or using your own photographs
    c. Copying a famous artwork and publishing it as your own work
    d. Using another artist's ideas without asking for permission beforehand

36. Which of the following cultures would this sculpture have originated from?

    a. Europe
    b. Asia
    c. Africa
    d. North America

37. Which of the following best describes the stage of clay called slip?

    a. Clay that is partially dry, but not yet completely dry
    b. Clay that is completely dry but has not been fired yet
    c. Clay that has been fired once in a kiln
    d. A mix of clay and water, with a runny consistency

38. Which of the following best describes the significance of the Armory Show in 1913?

a. It was the first exhibition to showcase Realist artists in Europe.
b. It was the first art show that showcased mainly Minimalist artists.
c. It was the first art show to take place in a major military location.
d. It was the first major modern art exhibition in America.

39. Which of the following types of perspective is shown in this image?

a. One-point perspective
b. Two-point perspective
c. Three-point perspective
d. Four-point perspective

40. Which of the following best describes the nave of a church?

a. A center aisle
b. A vaulted, semicircular structure at the end of the aisle
c. A circular opening in the center of a dome
d. A flat, upright column inset in a wall

41. Which of the following best describes the process of enameling?

a. Two metals are joined together to create a stronger type of metal.
b. Sheets of glass are melted with metal leading in between.
c. Liquid glaze is fired onto a ceramic piece, which then forms into a shiny glaze.
d. Powdered glass is fused to a surface and melted to a smooth, shiny coating.

42. Which of the following metalworking techniques is shown in this image?

a. Etching
b. Lost wax casting
c. Stamping
d. Filigree

43. On a camera, what is the name of this part where the flash would attach to?

a. F-stop
b. Hot shoe
c. Shutter release
d. Emulsion plate

44. Which of the following best describes context as related to artwork?

a. The physical materials used by an artist to create an artwork
b. The elements or principles used within a work
c. The conditions or circumstances around which something is made
d. The ways in which an artist uses their skills to create a work

45. Which of the following genres of photography was NOT accepted as fine art prior to the 1970s?

    a. Nudes
    b. Fashion
    c. Portraits
    d. Landscapes

46. Which of the following best describes the mass tone of a paint pigment?

    a. The color of a paint straight from the tube
    b. The name of the color of the paint
    c. The opacity of the pigment
    d. How permanent the pigment is

47. Which of the following issues could occur if an oil painting is varnished too early?

    a. The varnish could peel off of the painting.
    b. The varnish could be too easily removable.
    c. The varnish could bring a more even sheen to the surface.
    d. The varnish could turn tacky and not dry.

48. Which of the following was NOT a role of an apprentice to a master artist during the Renaissance?

    a. Communicating with patrons
    b. Cleaning paintbrushes
    c. Grinding pigments
    d. Preparing surfaces for paintings

49. In intaglio printmaking, ink is squeegeed across the plate, forcing the ink into the lines. Which of the following steps would come next in this process?

    a. A dampened sheet of etching paper is laid on top of the plate.
    b. Felt blankets are placed on top of the paper.
    c. The plate is then wiped with a rag.
    d. The plate is rolled between two steel rollers on an etching press.

50. The artists Willem de Kooning, Jackson Pollock, and Franz Kline are all associated with which art movement?

    a. De Stijl
    b. Abstract Expressionism
    c. Dada
    d. Minimalism

51. Which of the following would be the correct method of creating a tint of the color red?

    a. Adding black to red
    b. Adding white to red
    c. Adding blue to red
    d. Adding yellow to red

52. The line in this artwork where the sky meets the ground is called which of the following?

    a. The proportional line
    b. The perspective line
    c. The axis line
    d. The horizon line

53. Which of the following describes a bas relief sculpture?

    a. A sculpture created in the round to be viewed from all angles
    b. A sculpture created around a framework or armature
    c. A sculpture attached to a back slab and projecting slightly
    d. A sculpture attached to a back slab and projecting significantly

54. Which of the following is the name given to the small Paleolithic sculptures shaped like women with enlarged stomachs and breasts that were likely used as fertility symbols?

    a. Junos
    b. Jupiters
    c. Venuses
    d. Mercuries

216

55. Which of the following is the correct name for this decorated semicircular alcove in a wall of a mosque, indicating the point nearest to Mecca?

a. Mihrab
b. Arabesque
c. Madrasa
d. Minbar

56. Which of the following best describes a motivation behind the iconoclasm in the Byzantine Empire in the 700s?

a. Christian images were seen as idols, which opposed the Old Testament prohibition of idolatry.
b. Artists began to purposely depict Christianity incorrectly, so the artwork was prohibited.
c. Artwork depicting Christianity had been a focus for so long that it was time to focus artwork on new subjects.
d. In light of debates of whether artwork was correctly depicting scenes from Christianity, these scenes were subsequently banned.

57. Which of the following best describes proportion in an artwork?

a. A way that forms are organized in space
b. A line along which forms are organized
c. The relationships of sizes of various elements within the artwork
d. The shape of the subject in an artwork

58. Which of the following accurately describes a difference between alkyd paints and traditional oil paints?

 a. Alkyds blend more easily than oils.
 b. Alkyds are thicker than oils.
 c. Alkyds dry glossier than oils.
 d. Alkyds dry more quickly than oils.

59. Which of the following best describes the difference between a gargoyle and a grotesque?

 a. A gargoyle depicts a creature with wings, whereas a grotesque depicts a person.
 b. A gargoyle is situated at the top of a building, whereas a grotesque can decorate any part of a building.
 c. A gargoyle is only on the corner of buildings, whereas a grotesque can line any wall of a building.
 d. A gargoyle has a waterspout, whereas a grotesque does not.

60. In this image, the figure has a dynamic pose, with the weight on one leg and the shoulders at an opposite angle from the hips. This pose is called which one of the following?

 a. Sprezzatura
 b. Pentimento
 c. Chiaroscuro
 d. Contrapposto

61. Which of the following was NOT a commonality among the artists of the New York School in the 1940s?

    a. They agreed on styles and theories of art.
    b. They were nearly all in their twenties and thirties.
    c. Many of them had worked on the WPA.
    d. They all believed in the individuality of the artist.

62. Which of the following describes how Frank Stella purposely removed expressive content from his artwork?

    a. He used straight edges rather than any curved forms.
    b. He eliminated visible brushstrokes, gesture, and definition of the surface.
    c. He only used one color at a time on each painting.
    d. He worked only in grayscale, without using any other colors in his artwork.

63. If an artist wishes to use an opaque paint to create an illustration with a matte sheen that could be reworked with water if needed, which of the following paints would be most appropriate to use?

    a. Acrylic
    b. Watercolor
    c. Oil
    d. Gouache

64. Which of the following cultures would include this figure as a sculptural form?

a. China
b. Egypt
c. India
d. Mongolia

65. Which of the following best describes the photography process of exposure bracketing?

a. Setting the exposure for your photograph prior to taking the photo
b. The process of deciding on the exposure for your photograph using a device to measure the light
c. Taking one photograph at the correct exposure, one overexposed, and one underexposed
d. Programming the digital camera to take the photograph using the proper exposure

66. Which of the following graphic file formats should be used if you need a web graphic with transparency?

a. .jpg
b. .gif
c. .tif
d. .raw

67. Which of the following would a hake brush be best suited for when painting?

a. Laying large, flat areas of color in a watercolor painting
b. Adding small areas of detail in an oil painting
c. Painting repeated layers of egg tempera
d. Creating an acrylic painting from start to finish

68. Which of the following English artists was NOT credited with establishing watercolor as an independent painting medium?

    a. Thomas Girtin
    b. Paul Sandby
    c. Joseph Mallord William Turner
    d. William H. Bartlett

69. Which of the following is a stipulation of the cultural heritage sites that UNESCO protects and preserves?

    a. They must be man-made.
    b. They must be more than 1 million years old.
    c. They must be made only of natural materials.
    d. They must be made within a certain distance of a major city.

70. Which of the following is the correct term for this four-sided architectural element with a pyramidal top?

    a. Caryatid
    b. Entablature
    c. Peristyle
    d. Obelisk

71. **Which of the following best describes the traditional Japanese aesthetic of wabi-sabi?**

    a. A concentration on simple forms
    b. A portrayal of transcendent landscapes
    c. An acceptance of imperfections
    d. A focus on curving lines rather than straight

72. **If an artwork is analyzed by the formalism aesthetic theory, which of the following would NOT be included in the analysis?**

    a. The artist used primarily warm and neutral colors in the painting.
    b. The trompe l'oeil technique creates an optical illusion in this painting.
    c. The lighter objects contrast against the dark background.
    d. The ribbons and feather have a smooth implied texture.

73. **Which of the following describes the symmetry that would be found in a rose window of a Gothic-style cathedral?**

    a. Asymmetrical
    b. Radial
    c. Reflexion
    d. Reciprocal

74. **Which of the following painters was NOT an artist in the Hudson River School?**

    a. Thomas Cole
    b. Albert Bierstadt
    c. Frederic Edwin Church
    d. Hans Fredrik Gude

75. Which of the following would NOT be recommended to improve this still life?

    a. Include only two of the objects shown, instead of three.
    b. Flatten the table a bit so the objects do not look like they will slide off.
    c. More consistently round the edges of the rounded objects.
    d. Make objects that are close together either overlap more or not touch at all, rather than barely touch.

76. Which of the following elements of art did Keith Haring's artwork most focus on?

    a. Color
    b. Line
    c. Value
    d. Texture

77. Which of the following best describes the difference between the principles of design pattern and rhythm?

    a. A pattern repeats elements in the same order, whereas rhythm repeats elements with variation.
    b. A pattern focuses on shapes, whereas rhythm focuses on line.
    c. A pattern will add elements as it progresses, whereas rhythm will repeat the same elements.
    d. A pattern will repeat elements in a grid, whereas rhythm repeats elements in a line.

78. Which of the following best describes Philip Pearlstein's artistic process?

    a. Applying drips and splatters of paint to a horizontal canvas
    b. Copying photographs using a grid system
    c. Creating photorealistic paintings from live models
    d. Creating large areas of color that reach the edges of the canvas

79. **Which of the following is a theme that Cindy Sherman has explored in a photographic series?**
    a. The homeless population in major cities
    b. Deviant and marginalized people
    c. The impact of businesses on the environment
    d. The roles of women in society

80. **If an artist is said to be a contemporary of another artist, which of the following is true?**
    a. The artists worked with the same materials.
    b. The artists worked in the same style.
    c. The artists lived at the same time.
    d. The artists lived in the same country.

81. **Which of the following is an example of appropriation?**
    a. Kara Walker's use of silhouettes in her artwork *Darkytown Rebellion*
    b. The Guerrilla Girls' use of the *Grande Odalisque* in *Do Women Have to Be Naked to Get into the Met. Museum?*
    c. David Smith's use of stainless steel in *Cubi XII*
    d. Alexander Calder's use of moving parts in his mobile sculptures

82. Which of the following types of domes are shown in this image?

a. Onion domes
b. Geodesic domes
c. Monolithic domes
d. Beehive domes

83. Which of the following best describes the goal of Surrealist art?

a. To bypass reason and unlock ideas from the unconscious mind
b. To capture the effect of lighting on a scene
c. To simultaneously show interlocking planes used to construct a scene
d. To react against the bourgeois and depart from traditional values of art

84. Which of the following best describes fine art versus applied art?

a. Fine art includes paintings and drawings, whereas applied art includes all forms of sculpture.
b. Fine art includes any art shown in museums, whereas applied art is done at home.
c. Fine art is created by artists with a formal education, whereas applied art is created by self-taught artists.
d. Fine art has no purpose other than being aesthetically pleasing, whereas applied art serves a purpose.

85. Which of the following would have been created with a subtractive sculpture technique?

a. Robert Rauschenberg's *Bed*
b. Claes Oldenburg and Coosje van Bruggen's *Spoonbridge and Cherry*
c. Jeff Koons' *Balloon Dog*
d. Michelangelo's *David*

86. Which of the following types of paints would have been used on this illuminated manuscript from the Middle Ages?

a. Gouache
b. Acrylic
c. Tempera
d. Oil

87. Which of the following best describes the drawing tool called a tortillon?

a. A thicker type of drawing paper that is available in hot pressed or cold pressed
b. A tightly rolled piece of paper, tapered at one end, used for blending
c. A pouch of powdered gum eraser in a mesh fabric bag
d. A flat metal sheet with various shapes cut into it for erasing

88. Which of the following types of paints replaced egg tempera in popularity in the 1500s?

a. Oil
b. Watercolor
c. Acrylic
d. Gouache

89. Which of the following is NOT an accurate safety recommendation when working with a ceramics kiln?

    a. Remove all combustible materials from the kiln area.
    b. Unload the kiln as soon as it is turned off.
    c. Always unplug the kiln before working on electrical components.
    d. Use protective glasses when looking into the kiln for long periods of time.

90. Which of the following is the correct description for repoussé metalwork?

    a. Reshaping metal by removing parts to alter its shape
    b. Molten metal poured into a die and then allowed to cool
    c. Metal wires that are bent to form intricate lacework designs
    d. Hammering a design into metal in a low relief on the reverse side

91. This type of depiction of the Virgin Mary holding the dead body of Christ is called which of the following terms?

    a. Pietà
    b. Predella
    c. Cassone
    d. Campanile

92. Which of the following is the correct term for the natural color of an object without it being affected by lighting or other factors?

    a. Absolute color
    b. Actual color
    c. Local color
    d. Real color

93. Which of the following would be considering a figurative artwork?

    a. *Broadway Boogie-Woogie* by Piet Mondrian
    b. *Green and Maroon* by Mark Rothko
    c. *Oath of the Horatii* by Jacques-Louis David
    d. *On White II* by Wassily Kandinsky

94. Which of the following best describes the concept of repoussoir in a two-dimensional artwork?

    a. Disturbing images created by juxtaposing the supernatural in a mundane setting
    b. Creating tonal effects by grouping closely placed parallel lines
    c. Using shading and perspective to create the illusion that the subject is three-dimensional and deceiving the eye
    d. An object in the side foreground that frames the edge and directs the viewer's eye into the composition

95. Which of the following is the correct term for this mark used in graphic arts?

    a. Alignment mark
    b. Registration mark
    c. Calibration mark
    d. Positioning mark

96. Which of the following art movements relied heavily on optical color mixing?

    a. Pointillism
    b. Fauvism
    c. Dada
    d. Postmodernism

97. Which of the following is another word for a substance added to oils or varnishes to make them dry more quickly?

    a. Sinopia
    b. Retardataire
    c. Siccative
    d. Trucage

98. Which of the following best describes the printmaking technique of cerography?

    a. A raised surface, sometimes linoleum or wood, is used to create the print.
    b. An image is engraved into a layer of wax on a metal surface.
    c. An image is carved into a metal surface, and the ink is held in these lines.
    d. Ink is pressed through a fine mesh screen to produce a print.

99. Which of the following best describes the ideals of the Aesthetic movement of the mid-19th century?

    a. Pursuing authenticity by depicting immigrants and working-class people
    b. A belief that artists would be fulfilled by producing things that would be useful
    c. A desire to unearth people's desires and fears while showing intense creativity
    d. Rebellion against industrialism and maintaining that art should be a part of everyday life

100. Which of the following accurately lists the four stages of art criticism?

    a. Description, analysis, interpretation, and judgment
    b. Analysis, investigation, understanding, and summary
    c. Dissection, inquiry, perception, and resolution
    d. Itemization, classification, itemization, and recommendation

Answer Key and Explanations

1. B: Fauvism was a departure from previous movements in that artists focused on bright, unnatural colors, bold lines, and distorting geometric figures. Previous movements wanted to portray subjects more faithfully and use more natural colors. Impressionism, for example, sought to show the fleeting effects of light on objects and scenes, but artists still used colors that more faithfully depicted the scene and used accurate proportions as well.

2. D: Form is the space that an object takes up in three dimensions and can include geometric or organic shapes. Shape is a two-dimensional area that is flat and can also include geometric or organic shapes. Space refers to the positive and negative areas in an artwork and can include the sense of depth within the piece. The way things feel in an artwork, or appear that they would feel, is texture.

3. A: This is an example of a groin vault, which is formed when two barrel vaults intersect perpendicularly. This can also be known as a cross vault or a double-barrel vault. The edges of the intersecting vaults form the groin, which can be rounded or pointed. A barrel vault, or tunnel vault, has the appearance of a tunnel with a rounded ceiling. A rib vault, or ribbed vault, is any vault supported by masonry ribs.

4. A: Clyfford Still, Mark Rothko, and Frank Stella are artists who worked in the color field movement. This movement was characterized by large abstract fields of flat color that reach the edges of the canvas, implying that they continue past the edge. Vladimir Tatlin is best known for his work in Constructivism, which emphasized the construction of art and reflecting modern industry through abstracted artwork.

5. C: Linseed oil has many uses when working with oil paint. When mixed with oil paint, it can help to maintain the flexibility of the film, it can make the paint more fluid and transparent for blending and glazing, and it can even increase the drying time of the paint. It is not, however, used to clean and condition paintbrushes. To clean oil paints out of paintbrushes, a solvent must be used, such as turpentine or mineral spirits.

6. D: Willow charcoal is a long, thin form of charcoal made by burning willow sticks in a kiln without air. Vine charcoal is similar, made by burning grape vines in a similar manner. Compressed charcoal is a combination of organic materials pressed with a gum arabic or wax binder into a hard stick. Willow and vine charcoal are used for quick sketches and are easy to blend. They are also easy to lift, meaning erasing parts with a kneaded eraser.

7. B: The formalism aesthetic theory is based on analyzing the artwork's success of using the elements and principles; it does not analyze the feelings or intentions behind it or even the abstraction or representational nature of the art. The emotionalism aesthetic theories investigate the expressive qualities of the artwork. Imitationalism looks at whether an artwork successfully represents what it sets out to represent.

8. B: Pouncing is a method similar to tracing, which has been used to transfer images since Renaissance times. A thin, paper-like tissue or tracing paper is laid over the original drawing, and small holes are pricked along the lines of the drawing either manually or with a pounce wheel. The drawing is then transferred by using a powder, such as chalk or charcoal, which is pushed through the holes making a dotted outline of the drawing onto a new surface.

Copyright © Mometrix Media. You have been licensed one copy of this document for personal use only. Any other reproduction or redistribution is strictly prohibited. All rights reserved.
This content is provided for test preparation purposes only and does not imply an endorsement by Mometrix of any particular political, scientific, or religious point of view.

9. C: There are many reasons to begin with a toned ground for artwork, but cost would not be a factor. Canvas is most commonly available in white, and the artist often will tone the ground to suit their needs. Using a toned ground can be less intimidating to start working on for many artists, and it can provide a middle ground for the artist to build both light and dark tones upon. The artist can also use a dark-toned ground as the darker tones in the artwork.

10. A: The Tudor style is characterized by, among other things, half-timber framing and steep roofs. The dark half-timber framing juxtaposed against a light exterior is shown here. Other characteristics of the Tudor style of architecture include diamond-shaped window panes with lead casing (also evident here), as well as dormer windows, flagstone floors, and tall, narrow windows and doors. This style was the final phase of Medieval architecture in England, during the dynasty of the House of Tudor.

11. A: An aquatint print is made by first melting fine particles of acid-resistant material onto a metal plate. The plate is then etched with acid, and the resulting print can resemble a watercolor painting. When a plate is scraped smooth for light areas and roughened for dark areas, and then printed, this is called a mezzotint. A wood or linoleum block can be carved with a gouge for a relief print. A relief print can also be created using various raised textures.

12. D: Juxtaposition is a term for placing two contrasting elements side by side to call attention to the contrast. In this example, the figure with dark clothing and dark skin is placed next to the figure with pale skin and white clothing. The poses of the figures also contrast, with one sitting in a compact manner and the other stretched out on the ground. The artist used these contrasts to create a juxtaposition to capture the viewer's eye.

13. B: Artists of the Expressionist movement sought to present their ideas subjectively and express emotions through artwork. They did this by distorting subjects and exaggerating colors, such as in Edvard Munch's *The Scream.* Minimalist artists minimized their subjects into simple forms and colors. Impressionist artists sought to capture the effects of light on their subject through color. Pop artists challenged the traditions of art and sought to elevate popular culture in artwork.

14. C: Keith Haring addressed many political and social themes in his artwork, but one of the main themes that he repeatedly addressed was acquired immunodeficiency syndrome (AIDS) and homosexuality. Haring was openly gay and was diagnosed with AIDS in 1988. After this, he used his artwork to increase awareness of AIDS. He also established a foundation to provide funding to AIDS organizations, among other causes. He died in 1990 of complications of AIDS.

15. A: Sterling silver is a combination of 92.5% silver combined with 7.5% of another metal, usually copper. A blend of two metals is called an alloy, and this is usually done to increase a metal's strength and hardness. Fine silver, which is 99.9% pure silver, is much softer than this alloy. Silver can also be mixed with other metals, such as zinc or platinum, to reduce its ability to tarnish.

16. A: Chiaroscuro emphasizes the contrast between light and dark. In this example, the artist used a dark background to contrast against the highlights on the subject. This technique was pioneered by artists such as Rembrandt, Caravaggio, and da Vinci, and it is also used to emphasize the modeling when portraying three-dimensional figures. In this example, the contrast accentuates the subject, as if a spotlight was used to dramatize the lighting.

17. D: An analogous color scheme consists of colors next to each other on the color wheel. In this example, green, blue-green, and blue could be used for an analogous color scheme. Red, yellow, and blue are the primary colors. Red, orange, green, and blue could be a tetradic color scheme, forming a rectangle on the color wheel. Yellow, red-violet, and blue-violet would be a split complementary color scheme.

18. D: Metacognition is a process of thinking about one's own thought process and analyzing one's own learning. When a student revisits their sketches and aligns them to their goals in an artwork, they are thinking about the process of their own learning and analyzing their progress toward a goal. Another metacognitive skill would be for the student to analyze their artwork after it is finished, and reflect on their progress toward their end product.

19. B: The Renaissance period brought many artistic innovations, including linear perspective, foreshortening, and the sfumato technique. Egg tempera was already in use well before the Renaissance era, and it was a popular medium throughout the Middle Ages. Egg tempera reached its peak during the Renaissance period, and it fell out of favor with the growing popularity of oil paint.

20. C: Frisket is a material that prevents an area of an artwork from being altered. On a watercolor painting, a liquid frisket might be used to preserve the white of the paper so the artist can paint over it. The frisket dries like a rubber and is then rubbed off after the painting dries, exposing the paper underneath. On an airbrush painting, an artist can use a thin adhesive film to cut and adhere to the surface, masking off an area of the artwork.

21. B: The ISO (ISO stands for the International Organization of Standardization, which is the governing body that standardizes camera sensitivity ratings) setting on a camera adjusts the image sensor's sensitivity to light. A higher ISO number will increase this sensitivity. This allows photographs to be taken with less light. A lower ISO number will decrease the image sensor's sensitivity for situations with more light. A higher ISO might be desirable in an indoor setting with a fast-moving subject. A lower ISO might be desirable in an outdoor setting with plenty of natural light.

22. A: When layering oil- or wax-based media with water-based media, it is always best to layer the oil- or waxed-based media on top of a water-based medium for maximum adhesion because oil or wax will repel water. In this situation, oil paints layered on top of acrylic paint will work best. Gouache, watercolors, and tempera are all water-based media, and oil pastels, encaustic, and crayon are oil- or wax-based media.

23. A: Romare Bearden was best known for his detailed collages depicting African-American life. He used clippings from magazines and created elaborate scenes of neighborhoods and other scenes including Harlem, jazz and blues musicians, and spirituality. Although he began as a painter, he later used his collage technique to express his ideas using found materials in a method similar to patchwork quilting.

24. C: Cadmium red, chrome yellow, and cobalt blue all contain toxic metals and should be handled with care. Paints should be kept separate from food or drink, and all materials should be washed after using. These paints should be kept off of skin if possible. If using a powdered pigment, a dust mask should be used. Yellow ochre is an earth pigment that contains iron oxide, which contributes to its hue.

25. D: Gouache is similar to watercolor, but it is opaque whereas watercolor is transparent. Both are water-based media. They are each used in thin layers, painted flat on the surface, and they would not be used in an impasto technique. Gouache and watercolors are both available in a full range of colors, and they are each used for fine art, although gouache is also used for commercial illustration work due to is tendency to lay in flat areas of color.

26. B: Batik is a wax-resist method used for decorating fabric. The resist is drawn onto the fabric with a tool called a canting, or it is printed on with a stamp. The artist can then dye the cloth, and the resist will keep those parts of the fabric from being dyed as well. The resist is then removed from the fabric by scraping or boiling it off. The word batik is of Javanese origin, although the process is used in many cultures for clothing and other fabrics.

27. A: Eugène Delacroix, Théodore Géricault, and Thomas Cole are all associated with the Romanticism movement, which was a movement not only in art but also in music and literature from the late 1700s to the mid-1800s. Romanticism was characterized by an emphasis on the individual and a glorification of nature and the past. In art, Romanticism focused on nature and dramatic scenes with strong lighting, evoking feelings and emotions.

28. B: Di sotto in su is an Italian term that means "seen from below." This technique involves creating a painting on a ceiling that employs foreshortened figures and/or a vanishing point to give the correct perspective as it would be seen from below. Chiaroscuro is a technique for the arrangement of light and dark in a work. Fresco is a painting technique involving wet plaster on a wall surface. Pentimento is an image concealed in a painting by a change made by the artist.

29. D: An Art Nouveau-style building would have an asymmetrical facade with ornamentation based on plant, animal, or flower designs such as peacocks, butterflies, orchids, or water lilies. The design would have curving forms and an eclectic style. The architect might also design the entire interior of the building, including the furniture, all with the same Art Nouveau ornamental forms and curving designs.

30. D: To create visual interest in this artwork, the artist Claude Monet arranged the still life asymmetrically. This is an effective method of creating a visually interesting composition. The arrangement does not form a pattern, nor does it use an analogous color scheme. The shapes used throughout the still life are primarily circles, seen in the various fruits spread out on the table.

31. C: Like oil paints, acrylic paints use toxic pigments and nontoxic pigments, depending on the colors being used by the artist. The artist must check each pigment to see how safe it is to use and what precautions they should take. Acrylic paints do dry much more quickly than oils, allowing the artist to work more quickly. Acrylics can be cleaned up with soap and water, and they can also be thinned with water, unlike oil paints.

32. B: An artist will often stretch their watercolor paper prior to starting a painting, which will keep the paper from warping when water and paint are applied. One method is to soak it with water, then tape it to a board with a gummed paper tape. The paper is then allowed to dry overnight. When it dries, the paper stretches and it will not warp when it is painted on. Alternately, an artist can buy a prestretched block of watercolor paper and peel each sheet off after using it.

33. A: Although an art gum eraser will also be gentle on the paper, the kneaded eraser is the only one that will not leave crumbs of eraser on the paper. A kneaded eraser can be molded to change its shape for various areas on a drawing, erasing small details and larger areas. It will not leave pieces behind, and it will not damage the paper. A pink pearl eraser, vinyl eraser, and art gum eraser will all leave crumbs of eraser behind on the paper when used.

34. A: Artwork in Ancient Egypt was mainly created for tombs and for a person's afterlife. Tombs were stockpiled with not only food and supplies, but also artwork and jewelry for a person's afterlife, especially for the wealthy. They used metals such as copper, gold, bronze, and silver, as well as stones including lapis lazuli, amethyst, quartz, and jasper for their jewelry. They also made carvings from a variety of native wood species.

35. B: It is important to correctly follow ethical standards involving copyright when creating artwork. If using other people's images, it is always important to read the fine print. It is best for the artist to use their own photographs or work from life. The artist should always get permission if using someone else's images or ideas and never copy someone else's artwork or ideas and present it as their own. If copying a famous work, it should be as an exercise only, and not be placed for sale.

36. C: Art and sculpture from Africa include an emphasis on the human figure, as well as visual stylization rather than representing them naturalistically. African art also focuses on symmetry and geometry, and figures often emphasize physical strength and youthfulness, as shown in this sculpture. Although some African art, such as this sculpture, is made from bronze, other African sculpture and masks are made from wood.

37. D: Slip is a mix of clay and water that has a runny consistency. It is used to join pieces of clay, by scoring the pieces and then applying the slip as a glue between them prior to joining. It can also be used to decorate ceramic pieces, by brushing, dipping, spraying, or building up the slip in intricate designs onto the surface. Slip can even be used for casting in a mold, as a solid cast, or as a hollow cast depending on the purpose.

38. D: The Armory Show in 1913 was significant because it was the first major modern art show in America. It was also known as the International Exhibition of Modern Art, and it took place at National Guard armories in several major cities. Prior to this, Americans were accustomed to realistic and representational art and found this exhibition to be full of new, shocking, and exciting ideas. The exhibition was a huge success and showcased many well-known artists.

39. B: This image shows two-point perspective, in which two vanishing points are on the horizon line. In this case, the vanishing points would be on either side of the building and the street and buildings would vanish into these vanishing points into the distance. The closest part of the building, from this perspective, is the front corner, and the horizon line is obscured by the buildings. The lines of the roof, ground, sidewalks, and windows could all be drawn back to the vanishing points.

40. A: The nave of a church is its center aisle, which usually extends from the main entrance to the apse or chancel. The apse or chancel is the vaulted, semicircular structure at the end of the aisle. A circular opening in the center of a dome is called an oculus, which is Latin for eye. A flat upright column inset in a wall is called a pilaster. It gives the appearance of a column without creating the same type of structural support that a column provides.

41. D: Enameling is a technique that involves melting powdered glass onto a surface at a heat of 750–850°C, which forms a shiny glass surface. This is often done on a metal surface, but enameling can also be done on glass or ceramic. The powdered glass is called frit, and it is colored by the addition of various minerals. Enameling can be transparent, opaque, or translucent once it is melted onto the surface.

42. D: Filigree is a metalworking technique that involves forming metal threads to create a lace pattern. The filigree technique requires skillful bending of wire to create simple or intricate patterns out of metal. The metal is first annealed prior to the filigree technique, which is a process of heating the metal then cooling it slowly, to make it easier to work with. The basket in this image was created from many pieces of metal bent to form a delicate pattern.

43. B: A hot shoe on a camera is a mounting point where a flash would attach. It is a squared U-shaped piece of metal with a metal contact point in the center. Modern cameras might have an accessory shoe without the function of creating an electrical circuit and will have the ability to be triggered wirelessly without using the contacts. A microphone, viewfinder, satellite positioning unit, or other accessories might be positioned at this point.

44. C: The context of an artwork is the conditions or circumstances around which it was created. This could include historical events; the environment in which the artist was working; the artist's background, traditions, and values; and other factors. The physical materials used by an artist to create artwork are called media. The ways in which an artist uses their skills to create a work are called techniques.

45. B: Up until the 1970s, the main genres accepted as fine art photography were nudes, landscapes, and portraits. In the early and mid-1900s, several photographers including Ansel Adams worked to advance the acceptance of photography as a fine art. Photographs had the potential to record detail, but they were also seen as a threat and shortcut to artwork, so their acceptance as fine art was a struggle for some time.

46. A: Mass tone is the color of a pigment straight from the tube of paint. This differs from the undertone of a paint, which is the color when applied thinly. A paint color can be very different when applied straight from the tube and applied thinly, or it can have the same characteristics. Some colors are naturally opaque, whereas others are naturally transparent. These characteristics all depend on the color's pigment.

47. D: If an oil painting is varnished too early, before the paint is completely dry, several things could happen. The varnish could crack, or it could turn tacky and not dry. If it is a matte varnish, it could sink and the matting agent could leave a white deposit on the paint surface. The varnish could sink into the paint and change the color of the paint. Any attempt to remove the varnish could also remove paint from the support.

48. A: During the Renaissance, artists would begin their career as an apprentice to a master artist. They would perform duties such as cleaning paintbrushes, grinding pigments, and preparing surfaces for paintings. They would slowly learn to sketch and transfer sketches to surfaces for frescoes and learn how to paint like their master artist. Communicating with patrons was left to the master artist, whereas apprentices performed lesser tasks.

49. C: After the ink is forced into the lines on the plate, the plate is wiped with a rag to remove the ink from the raised areas of the plate, leaving the ink only in the recessed lines and areas of the plate so that the plate is ready for printing. Then the plate is placed onto the etching press, and a dampened sheet of etching paper is placed on the plate. Felt blankets are placed on top of the paper, and they are all run through the etching press between the steel rollers to create the print.

50. B: Willem de Kooning, Jackson Pollock, and Franz Kline are all associated with the Abstract Expressionism movement. This movement developed in New York in the 1940s, after World War II, and it was the first American movement to have international influence. Abstract Expressionist artists emphasized spontaneous and subconscious creation, gestural forms, abstraction, and emotion.

51. B: A tint of a color is a light value made by mixing a hue, or a color, with white. A shade, on the other hand, is a darker value made by mixing a hue or color with black. To make a tint of red, red would be mixed with white. A variety of tints could be made from red to white by mixing different amounts of red and white, just as a variety of shades could be made by mixing different amounts of red and black.

52. D: The horizon line is the line where the ground meets the sky in a landscape. When using this to create a perspective drawing, vanishing points are placed along the horizon line. The horizon line is also sometimes referred to as eye level, depending on the perspective used in an artwork. When using vanishing points, objects become smaller as they are closer to a vanishing point, and they are larger as they are farther away from a vanishing point.

53. C: A bas relief, or low-relief sculpture, is a sculpture that is attached to a slab or wall and projects only slightly from the surface. A high-relief sculpture, on the other hand, will project significantly from its attached slab or wall, and parts may even be detached from the surface. Neither a high- nor a low-relief sculpture is meant to be viewed from all sides, unlike a sculpture created in the round.

54. C: The Venuses were small Paleolithic sculptures made of stone and animal bone that depicted women with oversized stomachs and breasts and were likely fertility symbols. The most famous of these is the *Venus of Willendorf* found in Austria, c. 28,000–23,000 BC. The anatomy of the figure is exaggerated, the head is obscured with curly hair, and the anatomy seems to represent all of women, not just one woman, or possibly the idea of fertility.

55. A: A mihrab is a semicircular niche in a wall of a mosque, indicating the point in the mosque nearest to Mecca. This is used to indicate the direction to be faced when praying. Arabesque is an ornamental design used in Arabic artwork, using flowing lines and vines. It often covers a surface in a repeating pattern. A madrasa is a college for Islamic instruction, and a minbar is a short flight of steps used in a mosque by the preacher.

56. A: One of the reasons for the iconoclasm during the 700s in the Byzantine Empire was the belief that the Old Testament prohibited idolatry, and the Christian images depicted idols and should be banned as such. Iconoclasm refers to the destruction of these icons because of the hostility toward these representations for a number of reasons. This might have also been a way to restrain the growing wealth and power of the monasteries who produced these icons.

57. C: Proportion is the relationship of the sizes of various elements within an artwork. The way in which forms are organized in space is perspective. The line along which forms are organized in an artwork is the axis. The shape of the subject in an artwork is its form. Proportion deals with the difference between parts of a whole or the space between different elements of something such as a face.

58. D: The main difference between alkyds and traditional oil paints is that alkyds dry much more quickly than oil paints. Alkyds are compatible to use with oils, and they will have the same sheen, blending qualities, and thickness, but the drying time is much shorter. They will still give a longer working time than acrylics. Alkyds should not be layered over oil paints because the film will be less flexible and more likely to crack.

59. D: Gargoyles and grotesques will look similar and also have similar placement. The main difference between them is that the gargoyle will be functional with a waterspout whereas a grotesque is not functional and does not have a water spout. These can be stone carvings of fantastic or mythical creatures. Gargoyles are specifically designed to have a waterspout to convey water away from the side of a building.

60. D: Contrapposto, or "counterpose," is a pose that departs from a stiff and formal sculptural pose. Contrapposto is when a figure is putting their weight on one leg, and has the other leg bent. Their hips and shoulders are at opposite angles. The figures appear more lifelike and natural than previously used poses, and it adds a dynamic feel to the sculptures. This was first used with Ancient Greek statues and was often used in Renaissance sculptures, including Michelangelo's *David*.

61. A: The artists of the New York School of the 1940s had many commonalities, including their age (except Hans Hofmann, who was in his fifties at the time). Many of them had worked on the WPA, or Works Progress Administration, prior to the New York School. They all believed in the individuality of the artist and had their own individual styles and theories of art. Due to this, they disagreed on styles and theories. For instance, Hofmann disliked surrealism, and de Kooning and Pollock used painting as a process of discovery.

62. B: Frank Stella removed expressive content from his artwork by eliminating visible brushstrokes, gesture, and definition of the surface. According to Stella, "… what you see is what you see." The viewer was not intended to read any other information into the artwork that wasn't there, and he reduced the artwork to the simplest form possible by detaching himself from his art and making the surface as flat as possible.

63. D: Gouache paint is often used for illustration due to its opacity and flat, matte sheen, its ability to be reworked with water, and its wide range of colors. Gouache is more opaque than watercolor, is thinner than acrylics, and comes in smaller tubes like watercolor paints. Gouache, watercolor, and acrylics are all water based, but only gouache and watercolor can be reworked with water once the paint has dried. Oil paint is oil based and cannot be mixed with water.

64. C: This statue of *Shiva as the Lord of Dance* is from the Chola Dynasty in India from c. 950–1000. Shiva is associated with dance and music and is often represented with a third eye, four arms, and a serpent around the neck. Shiva is a major deity of the Hindu religion, as part of the triumvirate including Brahma and Vishnu. Shiva's four arms represent the four cardinal directions, and Shiva has the weapon of a trident.

65. C: Exposure bracketing in photography means taking three photographs — one at the correct exposure, one underexposed, and one overexposed. With a digital camera with an automatic setting for exposure bracketing, this can be done automatically. This technique can be helpful in a difficult lighting situation, so the photographer will have the choice of several different exposures after the photographs have been taken.

66. B: A web graphic should have a small file size and load quickly. It does not need to have a high resolution for printing. A .jpg file does not have a transparency channel, so it must have a solid color background. A .gif image can have a transparent background, and it can be compressed to a small file, making it ideal for a web graphic. A .tif file can also be transparent, but it is a lossless raster format that is a larger size and not good for web publishing. A .raw file is also a large file by default.

67. A: A hake brush is a large, flat, oriental-style wash brush used to lay flat areas of color in a watercolor painting or ink wash. It has soft bristles, usually made from squirrel, goat, or ox hair. It could also be used for wetting the surface of the paper or for absorbing excess water from the paper. It would not be used for detail work or for any acrylic or oil painting. It would also not be used for egg tempera because egg tempera use requires small, short dabs of color that dry quickly.

68. D: Three English painters were credited with establishing watercolor painting as a credible artistic medium: Paul Sandby, Thomas Girtin, and Joseph Mallord William Turner. These men worked in watercolor in the late 18th century, and Sandby is credited as being the father of the English watercolor. William H. Bartlett was an artist in the Hudson River School of landscape artists in the United States during the 19th century.

69. A: The United Nations Educational, Scientific, and Cultural Organization (UNESCO) has a program that preserves cultural heritage sites including the Taj Mahal, Stonehenge, and the Eiffel Tower. One stipulation is that the site must be man-made. A cultural heritage site protected by UNESCO must be an excellent example of settlement, architecture, or technology that represents a stage in human history.

70. D: This architectural element, with four sides and a pyramidal top, is an obelisk. The Washington Monument is an example of an obelisk. A caryatid is a stone carving, usually of the figure of a woman, used in place of a column as a support. An entablature is the horizontal lintel on a classical building that is above the columns and below the triangulated pediment. A peristyle is a row of columns lining a space such as a courtyard.

71. C: The traditional Japanese aesthetic of wabi-sabi is an acceptance of imperfections. It is shown in artwork through asymmetry, incompleteness, simplicity, and modesty. The simple, rustic forms of Japanese teaware embody the idea of wabi-sabi. This is also shown in clayware with asymmetry or unrefined finishing. Wabi-sabi can also suggest melancholy and solitude or serenity and beauty.

72. B: The formalism aesthetic theory focuses primarily on the elements and principles present in an artwork and how they work to make an artwork successful. It does not take into account the motivations of the artist, the historical context, the emotions that the artwork evokes, or other considerations including style. In this example, the trompe l'oeil does not factor into the success of the elements and principles present in this artwork. The critique would focus more on the colors, values, and textures, among other elements and principles.

73. B: Rose windows, like mandalas, have radial symmetry. Rose windows are commonly found in Gothic cathedrals, and they can also be called wheel windows. They are divided into segments by spokes from a central point, much like a bicycle wheel. A rose window might have decorative stained glass, and it is often found in the nave or end of the transepts of a cathedral. Examples of these windows can be found all throughout Europe.

74. D: Thomas Cole, Albert Bierstadt, and Frederic Edwin Church were all painters of the Hudson River School, an American art movement in the mid-19th century. Hans Fredrik Gude was a painter in the Düsseldorf school of painting, which was a group of painters who studied at the Düsseldorf Academy in the 1830s and 1840s and inspired some of the Hudson River School painters. The Hudson River School focused on Romantic landscape paintings.

75. A: Still-life objects are usually grouped in odd amounts for visual interest; therefore, including three objects creates more visual interest than just two. Flattening the perspective of the table so that the objects do not look like they will slide off will ease some tension from this painting. It would also help if the bottoms of the rounded objects were more consistently rounded. Objects that are close together should either overlap, or not touch at all, rather than having "kissing" edges that barely touch.

76. B: Keith Haring was an American artist whose work focused on graffiti-styled chalk outlines. His subjects included babies, spaceships, dogs, as well as many political and social themes. Although he did use bright colors on often black or white backgrounds, his signature style was to use line to create his subjects and express his ideas. His drawings were flat and did not include texture, and they did not focus on using multiple values either.

77. A: Pattern and rhythm are both principles of design, but they differ in that pattern will repeat elements in the exact same order, whereas rhythm can repeat elements in a different order. The pattern can be of shapes, colors, lines, or other elements of art, and it can be in a line, a grid, or

238

another arrangement. Either of these principles can be used to order and arrange elements within an artwork.

78. C: Philip Pearlstein is best known for creating photorealistic representations by painting from live models. He chooses to work from life rather than using photographs to capture accurate lighting and space for his artwork and paint what he sees in front of him rather than what is captured by a camera. His process is different than that of Chuck Close, who creates his photorealistic paintings using photographs and a grid system.

79. D: One of the themes that Cindy Sherman focused on in her photographic series was the various roles of women in society. She used photography to portray herself in various roles, including housewife, mother, and actress. By doing this, she was both herself and those characters, calling into question the concept of identity and how one woman could occupy various roles in society. She encourages society to examine the identities and roles of women.

80. C: If an artist is said to be a contemporary of another artist, it means that they lived at the same time as each other. People working during the same time are considered contemporaries. Artists working in the same style at the same time within the same group are contemporaries, but artists working in different styles in different groups at the same time are also considered contemporaries.

81. B: Appropriation involves taking an original idea or image and using it in a new or different context while it is still recognizable as the original image or object. Appropriation recontextualizes an image for a different purpose or different audience. Marcel Duchamp used the concept of appropriation when he took a premade urinal and presented it as artwork, signed "R. Mutt." Pop artists also often used appropriation to incorporate images from pop culture into their artwork.

82. A: The domes shown in this image are onion domes. These domes are larger around than the base on which they sit, and they taper to a point at the top. The height is usually greater than the width. They are often found on Eastern Slavic churches, especially in Russia. It can also be found in Indo-Islamic architecture and in the Middle East and Central Asia. The onion domes on some cathedrals are brightly colored.

83. A: Surrealist artists were attempting to bypass reason and unlock ideas from the unconscious mind. Artists such as Salvador Dali and Rene Magritte sought to put these ideas down as artwork. Impressionist artists were trying to capture the effect of lighting on a scene. Cubist artists showed simultaneously interlocking planes used to construct a scene, and Dada artists were reacting against the bourgeois and departing from the traditional values of art.

84. D: Fine art is art that has no purpose other than being aesthetically pleasing. This can include paintings, drawings, and sculptures. Applied art is art that serves a purpose and might include graphic design, interior design, and architecture. Applied art can also include jewelry, ceramics, textiles, and other forms of art that are both decorative and serve a useful purpose. The line between fine art and applied art can be blurred depending on the intent of the creator.

85. D: A subtractive sculpture technique is one that starts with a large piece of material and the artist removes pieces to create the finished work. This is also known as carving, and it is commonly done with stone or wood. Michelangelo's *David,* carved from marble, is an example of the subtractive technique. An additive technique is any in which materials are added together to create the finished work, and this can be done with any number of materials.

86. C: Tempera paint, along with ink and gold foil, was used in illuminated manuscripts during the Middle Ages. Many different natural materials were used in creative ways to make the pigments and surfaces for these manuscripts. Parchments were crafted from animal skins, and colors were made from ultramarine, insects, nuts, and other materials that would lend their natural dyes to this artistry.

87. B: A tortillon is a tightly rolled piece of paper, tapered at one end, that is used for blending with pencil or charcoal. A blending stump is similar, but it is longer and is pointed at both ends. Using a tortillon can help the artist keep their fingers clean when blending their drawing materials, and it can also help them achieve more control over blending because the tortillon has a finer point at the end.

88. A: Egg tempera was a popular medium until the 1500s when oil paints became more widely used. Although oil paint was used prior to the 1500s, it became more popular at this time and became the primary means of creating artwork, first on panels and then on canvas as canvas became more affordable and more readily available. Slow-drying oils helped Renaissance artists achieve the naturalism they sought.

89. B: It is recommended to remove all combustible materials from the kiln area before operating a kiln. Always unplug a kiln before working on the electrical components, and turn off the circuit breaker if it is hard wired. Use protective glasses if looking into the kiln for long periods of time. Do not unload the kiln before the temperature has dropped to at least 125°F. It is safer to allow the materials to cool slowly and unload them when they are cooler.

90. D: Repoussé is a metalworking technique that involves hammering a design into a malleable metal to create a low-relief design on the reverse side. The technique of chasing is used to refine this design on the front of the metal. Chasing is the opposite of repoussé, and when used together these two techniques are known as embossing. These techniques use the elasticity of the metal, and no metal is lost in the process.

91. A: A representation of the Virgin Mary holding the dead body of Christ is called a pietà. Michelangelo sculpted several pietàs throughout his life, including this example titled *Pietà,* which was carved from marble in 1498–1499. A predella is the lowest section of an altarpiece. A cassone is a traditional Italian marriage or hope chest. A campanile is a freestanding bell tower in Italian architecture.

92. C: Local color is the term for the true color of an object without the effect of light or shadow altering its appearance. When considering how to portray colors in artwork, an artist must understand the difference between local color and how light, shadow, atmosphere, and other factors can affect that color and then make decisions about how to portray the color in their artwork. They will also decide whether to portray the color faithfully or alter the color scheme.

93. C: A figurative artwork is one that contains a recognizable subject, such as a landscape, people, animals, or still life. This is also called representational artwork, and it is clearly derived from real sources. This is in contrast to abstract art, which does not have a recognizable subject and which might focus instead on color, shapes, form, and space rather than expressing the artist's ideas through the subject of the artwork.

94. D: Repoussoir is the deliberate framing of a two-dimensional work along a side so that the viewer's eye is directed toward the center. This is a compositional choice made by the artist, and in a landscape painting it might include branches or other landscape elements framing the artwork. In an artwork involving architecture, the framing could include columns or arches. In an interior, it could consist of a wall, archway, or curtain.

95. B: A registration mark is used in graphic design so that the printer can line up multiple printing plates. When a graphic is printed using CMYK, for example, each color will need to be aligned so that the colors overlap precisely for the final image. The registration mark is a check to see that all colors are aligned correctly. The registration mark is printed outside of the area of the final work and will be trimmed away from the final piece.

96. A: The artists of the Pointillism movement relied heavily on optical color mixing. They would place small dots of colors next to each other and allow the brain to involuntarily mix the colors rather than mixing the colors on their palette. The Pointillism movement was pioneered by Georges Seurat, who experimented with juxtaposition of colors. Other prominent artists of this movement included Paul Signac and Camille Pissarro.

97. C: A siccative is an agent that is added to an oil or varnish to shorten its drying time. Sinopia is a reddish-brown underpainting created prior to a fresco, some of which have been found to be quite different from the final fresco. Retardataire describes an artwork created with a seeming lack of awareness of other styles of that time. Trucage is the forgery of a painting, and a person who forges a painting is a truqueur.

98. B: Cerography, also called glyphography, is a printmaking method in which an image is carved into a layer of wax that has been applied to a metal surface. A positive plate is then created through a method of electrotyping or stereotyping, and the plate can then be used for printing. This method was developed in the 1830s and was intended mainly to reproduce line drawings and maps because it was not able to recreate shading.

99. D: The Aesthetic movement rebelled against Victorian ideals and sought to create "art for art's sake." Artists emphasized quality craftsmanship and art as a part of everyday life. The artists of this movement embraced all forms of art, including fine arts and crafts. They pursued beauty in form and color, independent of any message or agenda. Prominent artists of this movement included James Abbott McNeill Whistler and Dante Gabriel Rossetti.

100. A: The four stages of art criticism are description, analysis, interpretation, and judgment. Description involves noticing what we see within the artwork. Analysis involves scrutinizing the formal qualities, or elements and principles, within an artwork. Interpretation involves trying to understand what the artist is attempting to communicate through their artwork. Judgment involves deciding whether the artwork is successful.

Praxis Practice Test #3

1. Which of the following best describes a fugitive pigment?

    a. A pigment that tends to run or drip off of a canvas
    b. A pigment that changes qualities when exposed to environmental conditions
    c. A pigment that has lasted throughout many centuries without change
    d. A pigment that is difficult to locate sources for its creation

2. Which of the following color systems is considered a subtractive color system?

    a. CMYK
    b. RGB
    c. RYB
    d. ROYGBIV

3. Which of the following best describes putti in Renaissance artwork?

    a. Groupings of fruit shown in still life paintings
    b. Depictions of naked, chubby male children, sometimes with wings
    c. A hazy quality created by gradually blending tones together
    d. A perspective effect created by shortening lines

4. Which of the following art movements was the Der Blaue Reiter movement most closely related to?

    a. Neo-Expressionism
    b. Les Nabis
    c. German Expressionism
    d. Dada

5. This statue is an example of which period of Greek sculpture?

   a. Archaic
   b. Classical
   c. Hellenistic
   d. Geometric

6. An artist creates a sculpture from found objects, similar to a three-dimensional collage. Which of the following is the correct term for this sculpture method?

   a. Construction
   b. Arrangement
   c. Fabrication
   d. Assemblage

7. Which of the following art movements does this work exemplify?

    a. Romanticism
    b. Neoclassicism
    c. Rococo
    d. Baroque

8. Which of the following is the correct term for a brownish-red porous earthenware clay?

    a. Terra cotta
    b. Porcelain
    c. Raku
    d. Kaolin

9. Which of the following describes a computer graphics term for smoothing the edges of images to minimize distortion?

    a. Planing
    b. Antialiasing
    c. Leveling
    d. Trimming

10. Which of the following is the correct term for these dots that are placed at various sizes to create a gradient effect?

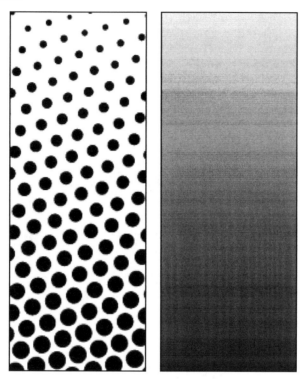

a. Dither
b. Rasterization
c. Halftone
d. Ben-Day dots

11. Which of the following would NOT be a part of an entablature in Classical Greek architecture?

a. Architrave
b. Frieze
c. Cornice
d. Pediment

12. Which of the following was the first type of photograph invented by Niépce around 1824?

a. Heliograph
b. Calotype
c. Cyanotype
d. Daguerreotype

13. Which of the following is NOT a reason for using an underpainting technique in a painting?

a. To build up textures for an artwork
b. To lay out the highlights and shadows for an artwork
c. To establish the tones for an artwork
d. To build the foundation for the colors of the artwork

245

14. Which of the following best describe the Ancient Egyptians' attitude toward art?

    a. Art emphasized the idea that all people were equal in the afterlife, regardless of their role on earth.

    b. Art highlighted the youth and vitality of warriors in their culture.

    c. Art expressed emotion, and it was meant to show the beauty of the world.

    d. Art was functional, provided an idealized view of the world, and maintained order.

15. An art critic analyzes this artwork's repetition of color, shapes, and lines, as well as the unity created throughout the piece by these elements. The critic is using which of the following aesthetic theories of art criticism?

    a. Emotionalism

    b. Formalism

    c. Socialism

    d. Imitationalism

16. Which of the following colors can the phthalocyanine pigment be found in?

    a. Red and yellow

    b. Blue and green

    c. Yellow and green

    d. Blue and violet

17. The dots that Roy Lichtenstein used in his comic-style artwork were named after which of the following people?

    a. Shepard Fairey
    b. Benjamin Henry Day Jr.
    c. Milton Glaser
    d. Saul Bass

18. Which of the following best describes the motivation of the Deconstructivism architectural movement?

    a. To undermine preconceived notions of meaning and symbols
    b. To incorporate natural materials within the creation of a structure
    c. To recall the styles and traditions of the classical era
    d. To break down elements into their most basic geometric parts

19. Which of the following best describes Le Corbusier's attitude toward designing living spaces?

    a. People should be allowed easy contact with the nature around them.
    b. People should have a tightly regimented living space that provides only for their basic needs.
    c. People should have an open, unencumbered living space to decorate and design as they desire.
    d. People should have a functional living space, providing for all their physical and psychosomatic needs.

20. Which of the following describes the point of view used by the artist in this artwork?

   a. Bird's-eye view
   b. Eye level view
   c. Worm's-eye view
   d. Open view

21. Which of the following best describes iconography in regard to an artwork?
   a. What a work is about
   b. The style of the work
   c. The artist's intention
   d. The context of the work

22. Which of the following situations would NOT fall under fair use provisions of U.S. copyright law when using an image?
   a. Using an image for educational purposes
   b. Using another artist's entire image for resale purposes
   c. Repurposing and recontextualizing an image to create new meaning
   d. Using a small part of an image openly available for reuse

23. Which of the following would be the correct method of making a shade of the color blue?
   a. Adding white to blue
   b. Adding black to blue
   c. Adding red to blue
   d. Adding green to blue

24. Which of the following best describes the fiber art technique of macramé?

   a. Looping material with a hooked needle
   b. Interlacing long threads on a loom to create a large piece of fabric
   c. Combining fibers to make a thread or a yarn
   d. Tying knots in a thread or cord in a geometric pattern

25. Which of the following best describes the goal of East Asian sumi-e brush painting?

   a. To faithfully reproduce the details of a subject
   b. To recreate the colors of a subject
   c. To capture the spirit of a subject
   d. To replicate the contours of a subject

26. Which of the following is true about photographs such as this one taken by Civil War photographer Matthew Brady?

   a. The subjects of the photograph were often moved and staged for a better composition.
   b. Brady did not acquire permission to take these photographs on the battlefield.
   c. The dead shown in these photos were often live subjects pretending to be dead for the photographs.
   d. Brady took all of the photographs himself, without the help of an assistant.

27. Which of the following groups of colors could be classified as warm colors?

   a. Red, yellow, and orange
   b. Red, yellow and blue
   c. Blue, green, and violet
   d. Orange, green and violet

28. Which of the following best describes representation in artwork?

   a. Combining different styles in one image
   b. Using colors creatively
   c. Depicting objects in a faithful manner
   d. Using signs that stand for something else

29. Which of the following elements does artist Helen Frankenthaler most focus on in her artwork?

    a. Line
    b. Color
    c. Texture
    d. Form

30. Which of the following is NOT known to be a highly toxic pigment?

    a. Manganese violet
    b. Cobalt yellow
    c. Cadmium red hue
    d. Chrome orange

31. Which of the following best describes the deckle as it relates to the papermaking process?

    a. A screen used to drain the water away from the paper slurry
    b. The fiber that is combined to create the paper pulp for the papermaking process
    c. A wooden frame used to control the size of the sheet of paper
    d. The lines made by the screen when the paper dries

32. Which of the following best describes the motivation behind the artwork of the Guerrilla Girls?

    a. To gain acceptance for women's right to vote
    b. To include more images of women in artwork in museums
    c. To create separate spaces for women's artwork
    d. To speak out against racism and sexism in the art world

33. Which of the following best describes the term icon as it relates to artwork?

    a. A religious painting, usually of one or two subjects
    b. An artwork of an arrangement of objects, usually fruit or flowers
    c. A painting of a person, usually just of the head and shoulders
    d. An artwork of an outdoor scene

34. If viewing this artwork as foreground, middle ground, and background, which of the following elements would be considered the middle ground?

a. The reclining man
b. The mountains
c. The tree
d. The man herding two cows

35. This image is an example of which of the following artistic rendering techniques?

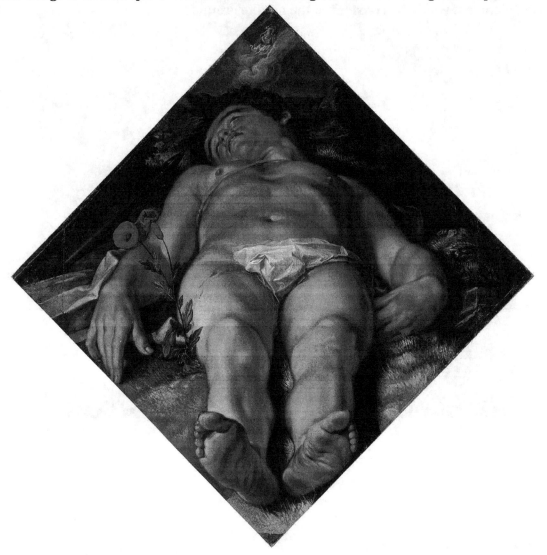

    a. Foreshortening
    b. Vanishing point
    c. Golden mean
    d. Chiaroscuro

36. A graphic designer needs to send files to a printer for a high-resolution brochure project. Which of the following file formats should the graphic designer NOT send?

    a. .psd
    b. .pdf
    c. .tif
    d. .png

37. Which of the following best describes a kylix?

a. A wine drinking cup that is wide and shallow
b. A statue of a young boy, standing tall and symmetrically
c. A large vase used to water down wine
d. A tall jar with a narrow neck and two handles

38. Which of the following art movements would be more likely to include figurative subjects?

a. De Stijl
b. Op art
c. Mannerism
d. Color field

39. Which of the following best describes the metalworking technique of brazing?

a. Using high heat to melt two or more adjoining metal items together
b. Heating two or more metal items to a high heat and then hammering them together
c. Joining two or more metal items by melting and flowing a filler metal with a lower melting point than the adjoining metal
d. Joining two or more metal items by melting and flowing a filler metal with a higher melting point than the adjoining metal

40. Which of the following best describes azulejos used in architecture?

a. Roughly textured, hand-applied mix of cement, water, sand, or lime
b. Painted, tin-glazed ceramic tiles used to embellish walls, floors, and ceilings
c. Red clay roof tiles
d. Functional tower-like chimneys

41. Which of the following is NOT a type of representation of an emanation of light around a sacred person in an artwork?

a. Nimbus
b. Mandorla
c. Aureole
d. Gisant

42. Which of the following drawing techniques, used in the 15th and 16th centuries on a specially coated paper, is shown here?

a. Silver point
b. Conté crayon
c. Charcoal
d. Graphite

43. A building is being returned as nearly as possible to its original condition. Which of the following terms most closely applies to this process?

a. Renovation
b. Conservation
c. Preservation
d. Restoration

44. Which of the following pigments was NOT available to Paleolithic artists?

a. Yellow
b. Blue
c. Brown
d. Black

45. Which of the following best describes a pagoda?

a. A tall, four-sided stone pillar with a pyramidal top
b. A small, dome-like structure on the top of a building
c. A multistory tower with multiple eaves, found in South or East Asia
d. A rectangular, terraced temple in ancient Mesopotamia

46. Which of the following periods of Greek sculpture was known for perfecting naturalism in portraying the human figure?

a. Geometric
b. Archaic
c. Hellenistic
d. Classical

47. Which of the following best describes outsider art?

a. Art created by self-taught artists outside of the mainstream art world
b. Art created with natural materials in the outdoor environment
c. Art created by artists who have not been allowed to join an art movement
d. Art created en plein air, or in the natural light

48. Which of the following art movements did NOT fight against the commodification of art?

a. Pop Art
b. Performance art
c. Conceptual art
d. Earth art

49. A member of which of the following groups of artists created this artwork?

a. Cobra Group
b. Ashcan School
c. Les Fauves
d. Hudson River School

50. Which of the following best describes the fiber arts practice of tatting?

a. Making interlocking loops of yarn with a hook
b. Decorative sewing using a needle
c. Using a needle or shuttle to create lace with knots and loops
d. Using needles to create multiple stitches of yarn in a line

51. If an artist creates a pastiche, which of the following best describes what they are creating?

    a. A decorative motif based on a palm leaf
    b. A small model as a trial sketch for a larger sculpture
    c. An artwork created in three panels
    d. A work of art in the style of another artist

52. Which of the following best describes the focus of the Fluxus art movement?

    a. Cynicism and antirational artwork, with appropriation and a rethinking of the concept of art
    b. Idealizing the working class and making artwork accessible to everyone
    c. Conceptual performances and emphasis on the process rather than on the product
    d. Juxtaposing dots of pure color for optical color mixing

53. Which of the following best describes gesso?

    a. A stick of colored material bound with gum arabic and used for drawing
    b. A paint containing gypsum, pigment, or chalk that is used for preparing a surface for painting
    c. An inexpensive opaque form of watercolor containing fugitive pigments
    d. A sizing that also acts as a glue, created from refined collagen

54. Which of the following is the correct term for a distorted drawing such as this that only looks optically correct when viewed with a mirror or lens?

    a. Algraphy
    b. Antiphonary
    c. Anamorphosis
    d. Antependium

55. Which of the following theories of art criticism is the most straightforward for critiquing modern artwork, by analyzing the visual aspects of the artwork?

    a. Formalism
    b. Expressionism
    c. Deconstructivism
    d. Representationalism

56. Which of the following critical responses was directed at the Minimalist art movement?

    a. It undervalued art by blurring the line between art and everyday objects.
    b. It did not contain enough color to qualify as artwork.
    c. Artwork without representational subjects does not count as art.
    d. Critics were not able to critique it with any of the art criticism theories.

57. Which of the following best describes the architectural element spandrel?

    a. The middle part of an entablature, between the cornice and architrave
    b. An ornamental molding common on facades
    c. A stylized leaf used as a decorative motif
    d. The triangular area between the outer curve of an arch and the framework

58. Which of the following is the term for the method shown of portraying heads in an artwork all at the same height, regardless of posture?

    a. Gisant
    b. Isocephaly
    c. Chinoiserie
    d. Squaring

59. Which of the following refers to the Christian art of the Eastern Roman Empire beginning in the 5th century?

    a. Carolingian art
    b. Byzantine art
    c. Etruscan art
    d. Ottonian art

60. Which of the following compositional techniques is being used in this painting?

   a. Baroque composition
   b. Golden mean
   c. Pyramidal composition
   d. Rule of thirds

61. An artist wants to use a white oil paint for glazing. Which of the following pigments would be best suited for this?

   a. Zinc white
   b. Flake white
   c. Titanium white
   d. Cremnitz white

62. Which of the following best describes the sculpture technique of casting?

   a. A material is built up, sometimes over an armature.
   b. Different materials are gathered and put together.
   c. Pieces of a material are carved or chipped away.
   d. A material is melted down, and then it is poured into a mold.

63. Which of the following best describes the oil painting technique of scumbling?

a. Applying a glaze over a light area to create a shadow
b. Using a tool to scratch through a layer of paint while it is still damp
c. Applying a thin layer of an opaque color over an area to produce a softened effect
d. Creating very gradual transitions between dark and light for a smoky effect

64. Which of the following is another term for a watercolor painting?

a. Aquarelle
b. Aquatint
c. Aquamanile
d. Aquagraph

65. Which of the following best describes how the realism movement rejected the ideas of Romanticism?

a. Realism preferred to portray people heroically and sentimentally, rather than in unpleasant scenes.
b. Realism rejected heightened emotions and exaggerated scenes, preferring to portray accuracy and truth.
c. Realism showed the monarchy in the best possible light, rejecting the portrayal of everyday scenes.
d. Realism depicted the rich and poor living on the same level, rejecting the idea of social hierarchy.

66. Which of the following best describes characteristics of Bauhaus architecture?

a. Enclosed courtyards, arches, domes, and arcades
b. Steel frames, open floor plans, and primary colors
c. Columns, grandeur of scale, and clean lines
d. Horseshoe arches, perforated screens, and geometric designs

67. Which of the following principles of design is most evident in this painting?

a. Balance
b. Contrast
c. Emphasis
d. Rhythm

68. Which of the following is the correct term for art that moves, driven by forces of nature, magnets, motors, or other outside forces?

a. Kinetic
b. Dynamic
c. Magnetic
d. Agile

69. Which of the following best describes the tintype process?

a. A direct positive image is made on a thin plate of metal.
b. An image is created on a silvered copper plate.
c. An image is created on paper coated in silver iodide.
d. An image is created on a piece of glass.

70. Which of the following best describes the greenware stage of clay?

a. Clay that is partially dry but not completely dry
b. Clay that has been fired once but is still porous
c. Clay that has been shaped and dried but not fired yet
d. Clay that is still soft and easily worked

71. Which of the following describes a benefit of dry mounting artwork?

a. It is easily removable if needing to remove the artwork from the backing.
b. It uses a uniform coat of adhesive to keep the artwork from slumping in the frame.
c. Dry mounting is considered archival.
d. It is an inexpensive way to mount artwork.

72. An artist wants to create a loose, sketchy gesture drawing. Which of the following would NOT be the best choice for this type of drawing?

a. Conté crayon
b. 4H pencil
c. Vine charcoal
d. Soft pastel

73. In this landscape by Thomas Cole, which of the following best describes the term sublime as it applies to the mood of the painting?

a. Drama and emotion
b. Awe in the face of greatness and beauty
c. Love and absolute power
d. Sadness and a sense of despair

74. Which of the following best describes the term transformation as it relates to artwork?

a. Placing an object next to a contrasting object to emphasize it
b. Using unusual proportion to call attention to an object
c. Using preexisting images or objects with little or no changes
d. Changing an object and presenting it in a new way

75. Which of the following types of perspective is used to portray buildings shown from above or below?

a. One-point perspective
b. Two-point perspective
c. Three-point perspective
d. Four-point perspective

76. Which of the following describes the printmaking process of manière criblée?

a. The design is punched into a metal plate, creating a white spotted background.
b. The artist draws or paints on a smooth, nonabsorbent surface.
c. Material is cut off of a sheet of linoleum or wood to create a design.
d. Lines are cut into a sheet of metal to create a design.

77. Which of the following best describes the form of this sculpture?

a. An open, dynamic form, composed of organic shapes
b. A closed, dynamic form, composed of geometric shapes
c. An open, static form, with no interior contours
d. A closed, static form with exterior contours

78. Which of the following is the correct term for the rigid frame that a sculptor might use within a sculpture?

a. Maquette
b. Armature
c. Minaret
d. Iconoclast

79. Which of the following best describes the concept of composition in an artwork?

    a. The presentation of shapes in a work of art
    b. The subject matter of a work of art
    c. How form is organized in a work of art
    d. The range of colors used in a work of art

80. Which of the following is the tool used to draw lines in hot wax when using a batik technique?

    a. Cassone
    b. Cornice
    c. Colonette
    d. Canting

81. How did the creator of this mask use a principle of design to organize an element of art?

    a. Rhythm to organize value
    b. Pattern to organize line
    c. Emphasis to organize space
    d. Movement to organize shape

82. Which of the following best describes the function of an image sensor on a digital camera?

   a. Converting the information of the image into an electronic signal
   b. Changing the size of the lens opening
   c. Storing the image information
   d. Where light enters the camera

83. Which of the following does NOT describe a way that the advent of oil paints affected the use of egg tempera as a medium?

   a. Artists used egg tempera as an underpainting for oil paintings.
   b. Artists combined an egg yolk and oil emulsion called tempera grassa.
   c. Artists' use of egg tempera versus oils was well documented.
   d. Artists switched back and forth between both media.

84. Which of the following describes an advantage of lossy file compression for images?

   a. The size of the file is reduced, but the file is still recognizable.
   b. Unnecessary metadata are removed but the file can still be used.
   c. The file can be emailed and is now pixelated.
   d. Quality is lost, and the file is visibly smaller.

85. During which of the following time periods would panel paintings have been most prevalent?

   a. Baroque
   b. Mannerism
   c. Neoclassical
   d. Middle Ages

86. Which of the following best describes this example of photo retouching?

    a. The man was removed from this photo for aesthetic purposes.
    b. The man was removed from this photo for political purposes.
    c. The man was removed from this photo for ethical purposes.
    d. The man was removed from this photo for historical purposes.

87. An art critic describes an artwork based solely on its context within the art world. Which theory is this critic using?

    a. Formalism
    b. Institutional
    c. Expressionism
    d. Deconstructivism

88. Which of the following best describes the term tessellation?

    a. A continuous landscape painting around the walls of a room
    b. Decorative painting used to replicate the look of marble or other finishings
    c. The tiling of a shape potentially infinitely with no overlaps or gaps
    d. A network of hairline cracks found in aged paintings and ceramics

89. Which of the following best describes a triadic color scheme?

    a. Three colors evenly spaced on the color wheel
    b. One color plus the two adjacent to its complement
    c. Three adjacent colors on the color wheel
    d. Three colors within the same color family (warm or cool)

90. Which of the following is the LEAST likely way to display a stone sculpture?

a. On a pedestal
b. In a glass display case
c. On the ground
d. Hung on the wall

91. Which of the following is the correct term for this device that projects an image through a small hole as an inverted image?

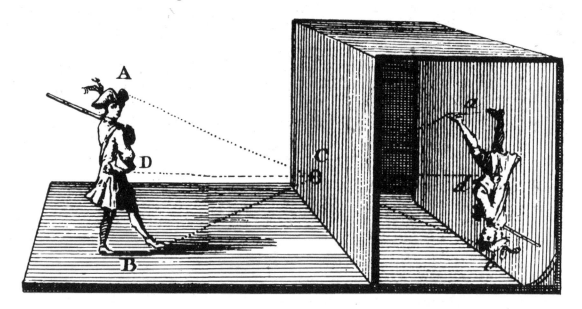

a. Daguerreotype
b. Stereoscope
c. Camera obscura
d. Calotype

92. Which of the following is NOT a common safety concern when using a spray can?

a. Inhalation of the solvent in sprayed paint
b. Dust creating chronic lung problems
c. Inhalation of pigments in sprayed paint
d. Flammable propane and propellants contained in aerosol spray paints

93. Which of the following best describes the medium encaustic?

a. Paint made from pigment mixed with gum arabic
b. Paint made from pigment mixed with a drying oil, usually linseed
c. Paint made from pigment added to heated beeswax
d. Paint made from pigment added to acrylic polymer emulsion

94. Which of the following is NOT a standard frame size for presenting artwork for display?

a. $10'' \times 20''$
b. $11'' \times 14''$
c. $8'' \times 10''$
d. $16'' \times 20''$

95. Which of the following best describes a periodic, or intermittent, kiln?

    a. The ware is loaded into cars and slowly brought through the kiln on rails while the kiln is kept at a constant temperature.

    b. The kiln is opened, loaded, and unloaded while already at its desired temperature.

    c. The ware is loaded into cars and slowly brought through the kiln on rails and the kiln is brought up to the desired temperature.

    d. The kiln is loaded, brought up to its desired temperature, cooled, then unloaded.

96. Which of the following categories would this artwork best fit under?

    a. Color field art

    b. Op art

    c. Minimalist art

    d. Pop Art

97. Which of the following best describes the reason for applying sizing to a canvas prior to painting?

    a. To create a blank white surface to begin a painting on

    b. To protect the canvas from the acids within the paints

    c. To stiffen the canvas so that it is easier to paint on

    d. To shrink the canvas slightly to tighten the wooden stretchers

98. Which of the following would be considered a modern sculpture material?

    a. Stainless steel

    b. Bronze

    c. Marble

    d. Stoneware

99. Which of the following best describes the difference between form in two- and three-dimensional artwork?

    a. In two-dimensional artwork, form consists of geometric shapes, but in three-dimensional artwork, it can include organic shapes.

    b. In two-dimensional artwork, form can be repeated, but in three-dimensional artwork, it is not.

    c. In two-dimensional artwork, form consists of the dimensions of the paper or canvas, but in three-dimensional artwork, it is the size of the sculpture.

    d. In two-dimensional artwork, form has width and height, but in three-dimensional artwork, it also has depth.

100. Which of the following terms describes the relationship of the size of the central figure to the surrounding figures in this image?

    a. Golden proportion

    b. Inaccurate proportion

    c. Hierarchical proportion

    d. Compositional proportion

Answer Key and Explanations

1. B: A fugitive pigment is an impermanent pigment that changes over time with exposure to environmental conditions such as light, heat, cold, pollution, and humidity. Fugitive pigments can be found in markers, paints, inks, and other art media, and they may be used purposely for temporary applications. Paints that are more likely to have longevity have permanence and lightfastness ratings to tell the artist how durable the pigment will be over time.

2. A: CMYK is a subtractive color system because the pigments absorb some wavelengths of light, but not others, and they "subtract" the colors green, red, and blue from white light. White minus green, red, and blue gives us cyan, magenta, and yellow. The additive system includes red, green, and blue (RGB), and it works by adding red, green, and blue in various ways to create a wide array of colors through light, such as on television screens or computers.

3. B: Putti are chubby, naked male children depicted in Renaissance artwork, sometimes shown with wings. The singular of putti is putto. Although these were often found in Renaissance artwork, they originally came from sarcophagi in the 2nd century, and they were also depicted in the Baroque and Mannerist periods as well. Cupid was often depicted as a putto, and putti were depicted along with humans in many artworks.

4. C: The Der Blaue Reiter movement was one of the two pioneering movements of German Expressionism, along with Die Brücke. Der Blaue Reiter was a group of German artists who created abstract art and promoted the expression of spirituality in artwork. This group created work from 1911–1914, and it included artists such as Wassily Kandinsky, August Macke, Franz Marc, and Paul Klee.

5. A: This sculpture is an example of the Archaic period of Greek sculpture, which lasted from 650–500 BC. The Archaic period is characterized by a stiff and formal pose, similar to Egyptian statues. The standing nude male youth, a common subject, was called kouros. They were broad shouldered and narrow waisted, had their hands clenched at their sides, and had a slight, closed-mouth smile.

6. D: An assemblage is a sculpture method that involves putting together, or assembling, various pieces that might include found objects. This method originated with Pablo Picasso, and it has been used by artists including Robert Rauschenberg and Louise Nevelson. The origin of the term dates back to Jean Dubuffet's collages of butterfly wings from the 1950s, which he titled *assemblages d'empreintes.*

7. A: Eugene Delacroix's *Liberty Leading the People* (1830) is one of the best-known examples of Romantic history painting. Romanticism also calls to mind vast and awe-inspiring landscapes, such as those painted by the Hudson River School. Romanticism was a movement not only in art, but also in literature and music from about 1800 to 1850. It glorified nature and the past, and it emphasized feelings and emotion, causing artists to create awe-inspiring and grand artworks.

8. A: Terra cotta is a brownish-red earthenware clay. It is used for sculptural purposes as well as utilitarian purposes including tiles, pots, bricks, and pipes. It is porous after being fired, and it can be glazed or can be left unglazed. In ancient times, terra cotta sculptures and other wares were left in the sun to dry. When kilns were used later, this clay was fired to 600–1000°C, and the iron content of the clay would give the piece its reddish color.

270

9. B: Antialiasing is a term for techniques used to smooth the edges of graphics to minimize the distortion. This might be used when presenting a graphic at a lower resolution, and it smooths the jagged edges to appear less abrupt. In addition to images, antialiasing can also be used in the graphics of games, to diminish jagged edges and make graphics look more realistic. At higher resolutions, the amount of antialiasing that is needed decreases.

10. C: Halftone is a graphic technique in which dots are created in various sizes to create a gradient effect. This can be done with black-and-white images by using black dots only, or it can be done with color images by overlaying CMYK dots and using them in combination. The transparency of the inks creates an optical effect that allows the colors to blend when printed together, allowing the finished image to look realistic.

11. D: The pediment is the triangular element that is situated atop the horizontal entablature in Classical Greek architecture. The entablature consists of the cornice, directly below the pediment, then the frieze, and the architrave, which is above the columns. In the Doric order, the frieze may be divided into triglyphs and metopes. The frieze can be omitted completely in the Corinthian order.

12. A: Nicéphore Niépce developed the first photographic technique, called heliography. This technique took anywhere from 8 hours to several days of exposure, and the initial results were coarse. After this, Louis Daguerre developed the daguerreotype, which became the first commercially available photographic process. This was a great advancement: It required a much shorter exposure and produced better results than the heliograph.

13. A: Underpainting is a technique used to create a thin layer that is a base for a finished painting, and it can be used to establish tone, darks and lights, and colors as a base for the final artwork. It is not used to build up textures. The underpainting layer is done in a thin layer to dry quickly and to serve as a base for the painting, almost as a sketch underneath the painting to establish where everything will go.

14. D: For Ancient Egyptians, art was functional, provided an idealized view of the world, and maintained order. Portraying an object in artwork gave it permanence, and the Ancient Egyptians used this concept to portray their own idealistic view of the world. They stylized people, used hierarchical proportion to designate importance, and they used colors and symbols to establish their own symbolism throughout their artwork, leaving a legacy of what was important to them.

15. B: If a critic uses an artwork's elements and principles to analyze it, they are using the formalism aesthetic theory. When using this theory, the critic would be looking to see how successfully the artist used the elements and principles within their artwork. They would not be looking at the subject, the emotions, the message, or other parts of the artwork. The emotion behind the work would be analyzed in the emotionalism theory, and imitationalism focuses on whether the representation is realistic.

16. B: Phthalocyanine is a pigment that is found in blue and green paints. It is a bright synthetic pigment with a brilliant coloring in paints and dyes, and It has a high lightfastness rating, high tinting strength, and superior covering power. Phthalocyanine is a strong dye that is insoluble in water. In paints, this color makes a strong glaze when diluted, while keeping its color intensity. Phthalo blue paint can be found in a red shade or a green shade.

17. B: Ben-Day dots are named after Benjamin Henry Day Jr., who was an illustrator and printer. He was the son of a 19th-century publisher, and he developed this process that distributes dots of an equal size throughout an area in the four process colors: cyan, magenta, yellow, and black. These dots could be purchased in sheets, and they are cut and applied by the graphic artist to create tonal shading for an area.

18. A: The Deconstructivism architectural movement was a postmodern movement in the 1980s, and it sought to question the preconceived ideas of meanings and symbols. The meanings of things exist in context and change over time, so Deconstructivists sought to challenge these preconceived meanings and challenge the idea of what a building or a structure should look like. Deconstructivist architecture deforms and dislocates what one would normally expect to see.

19. D: Charles-Édouard Jeanneret, who designed architecture under the name Le Corbusier, decided that people should have a functional living space, providing for all their physical and psychosomatic needs. He designed the Dom-ino House project, his design for an ideal dwelling, which he described as a "machine for living." It provided sun, space, vegetation, controlled temperature, ventilation, and insulation, as well as protection against noise. The design was eventually dubbed the International Style.

20. C: In this artwork, *St. James Led to Martyrdom* by Andrea Mantegna (c. 1455), a worm's-eye view is being used to provide an unusual perspective on the subjects in the artwork. The people and arch are being viewed from below, rather than at eye level, which gives a different view than usual. Mantegna experimented with different views and perspectives in his work, including extreme foreshortening and bird's-eye view.

21. A: The iconography of an artwork shows what the artwork is about. The images used in an artwork convey what it represents. The meaning, however, depends on how the representation was made (the style of the artwork) and the artist's reason, purpose, or intentions of making these representations. Different works of art can have the same subjects but differ in style and purpose, and they can differ in intentions and meaning.

22. B: Fair use involves using images for educational or nonprofit uses, using a small part of an image instead of the entire work, or using images that have been designated as openly available for reuse. Fair use also can include using artwork that is repurposed or recontextualized in such a way that the image is given a new meaning, or when only a small part of a whole image is used. Several factors are considered when judging fair use.

23. B: To make a shade of a color, an artist would add black to that color and make it darker. A tint, on the other hand, would be made by adding white to that color. A variety of shades of blue can be made by adding various amounts of black to blue. A variety of tints of blue can be made by adding various amounts of white to blue. Just by using blue, white, and black, a wide range of tones could be created.

24. D: Macramé is a fabric art technique that involves tying knots in a thread or cord in a geometric pattern. This art form was most popular in the Victorian era, and it is usually done with various types of cord or thicker yarn. Looping material with a hooked needle is crochet. Interlacing long threads on a loom to create a large piece of fabric is weaving, and combining fibers to make a thread or a yarn is spinning.

25. C: The goal of East Asian sumi-e brush painting, or ink wash painting, is to capture the essence or spirit of a subject. The artist is not attempting to reproduce the appearance of the subject or capture the details. Because the painting is done with black ink, the artist is not reproducing the colors, either. This technique emphasizes brushwork and the permanence of each stroke, while capturing the essence or temperament rather than the representation.

26. A: In early war photography, the subjects of photographs were often moved and staged to create a better and more moving composition. Brady acquired permission to take these photographs on the battlefield from Lincoln himself, as long as Brady financed the project. Brady had assistants throughout his career, and as his eyesight deteriorated, it is thought that many of his later photographs were the work of his assistants, and not of Brady himself.

27. A: Red, yellow, and orange are classified as warm colors, whereas blue, green, and violet are classified as cool colors. Warm colors are associated with daylight, intensity, and happiness, and cool colors are associated with nighttime, cold, and sadness. Warm colors tend to advance in an artwork, but cool colors tend to recede. Artists take these qualities into consideration when using these colors within an artwork.

28. D: Representation is the use of signs that stand for something else in an artwork. Throughout history, artists have represented not what they see as much as what they know or mean. They decide how to represent what they see rather than rendering it faithfully as a camera would. This can be seen in the representation of humans in the artwork of Ancient Egypt, in which people are represented in a culturally agreed-upon way that does not indicate that they were too unskilled to represent them in another way.

29. B: Color is the element that artist Helen Frankenthaler focused most on in her artwork. She worked within the Abstract Expressionism movement, and she was known for her poured paint technique. Frankenthaler poured turpentine-thinned paint onto canvas, creating color wash stains on the canvas. These areas of color were luminous and focused her artwork on the color, not texture, line, or form.

30. C: Many artists' materials are created with pigments that are known to be highly toxic if ingested, inhaled, or even contacted with skin. Manganese violet is manganese ammonium pyrophosphate. Cobalt yellow contains cobalt, which is toxic. Chrome orange is basic lead carbonate, which contains lead. The cadmium red hue is created to emulate the color of cadmium red, without the toxicity of the cadmium-based pigment.

31. C: The deckle is the removable frame that controls the size of the paper in the papermaking process. This keeps the paper slurry within a certain size on the screen to control the size of the paper that is created. This is also where the term deckle edge comes from, when a sheet of paper has an irregular edge that is created from the manual papermaking process. The edge appears rough and feathered.

32. D: In 1985, the Guerrilla Girls formed as an anonymous art group to fight racism and sexism within the art world. Rather than drawing attention to their identities, they wanted to focus on their cause. They wanted to expose corruption within the art world and begin including more women and people of color within the art community, by creating shocking protest art that was seen by a wide audience.

33. A: An icon is a religious painting, usually of one or two subjects, and commonly of saints, angels, Mary, or Jesus Christ. These are common in Eastern Orthodox religions, and they date back to early days of Christianity. An artwork that is of an arrangement of objects, usually fruit or flowers, would be a still life. A painting of a person, usually just the head and shoulders, is a portrait, and an outdoor scene is a landscape.

34. D: In this scene, the group of five people, which would include the man reclining and the tree, would be considered the foreground. The middle ground of this scene would include the man to the left herding two cows. In the background would be the mountains and other shapes obscured by atmospheric perspective.

35. A: This artwork is an example of foreshortening, which compresses and exaggerates the illusion of depth. This is a method of showing perspective and dramatically shortening the subject, and it is a departure from the frontal view of a subject. Foreshortening showed the distortion that the eye would see from the view at this angle as artists experimented with their subjects in new ways.

36. D: A graphic designer should send a high-quality CMYK file format to a printer, and a .png file will be RGB, not CMYK. The file should be at least 300 dpi, and it should be in the CMYK color mode. A .psd file is the Photoshop file format with the layers still separated and fonts included. A .pdf is also acceptable if the fonts are included and it is saved at a high resolution. A .tif file is also a lossless file format that can be of high enough resolution to print.

37. A: A kylix is a wine drinking cup that is wide and shallow. It may or may not have a slender stem, and the inside was used for painting. A krater is a vessel with a broad body used for watering down wine, and it was often decorated. An amphora is a tall jar with a narrow neck and two handles. A kouros is a type of statue of a young boy, standing, shown facing front and symmetrically posed.

38. C: The Mannerism movement occurred during the late Renaissance, from about 1520 until the end of the 16th century when it was replaced by the Baroque style. Mannerism is characterized by an exaggeration of ideas of beauty and proportion. Figurative artwork is artwork that contains recognizable subjects, such as portraits and landscapes, so this would not apply to the De Stijl, op art, or color field movement artworks.

39. C: The metalworking technique of brazing involves joining two or more metal items by melting and flowing a filler metal with a lower melting point than the adjoining metal. Using high heat to melt two or more adjoining metal items together is welding, and heating them to a high heat and hammering them together is a process called forge welding. Different metal joining techniques are used depending on the metals that are used and the end results that are desired.

40. B: Azulejos are painted, tin-glazed ceramic tiles that are used to decorate and embellish walls, floors, and ceilings in architecture in Spain and Portugal. These were used not only for ornamental purposes, but also for temperature control. These tiles have a Persian influence in their design, with their geometric and floral designs and interlocking patterns. These can be found in churches, homes, restaurants, and palaces.

41. D: A gisant, French for recumbent, is a reclining sculptured form that lies on the lid of a deceased person's tomb. A glory is the general term for the representation of light around a sacred person, and this could be around the whole person or just around their head. Some names for it are aureole, halo, nimbus, and mandorla. These are often depicted in religious artworks, specifically, with saints and holy persons.

42. A: Silver point is a drawing method that involves using a silver-tipped drawing instrument, or a rod of fine silver in a wooden holder, on a specially coated paper. This method was first used on manuscripts by medieval scribes. The paper or surface could be coated by rabbit-skin glue, chalk, or lead white. Modern supports could be coated by gesso or gouache. The coating gives the support more tooth and helps give the drawing a darker value than on unprepared paper.

43. D: Restoration describes the return of a building to its original condition, or as close to original as possible. Renovation is the upgrading of a building with restoring its original features, while also including some contemporary needs. Preservation describes the prevention of the destruction or deterioration of a building, and conservation is a term applied to restoring artwork to its original condition, or as closely as possible.

44. B: Paleolithic artists had a few colors available to them, including brown, black, red, yellow, and white. These colors were created from pigments using earth and charcoal mixed with animal fat and saliva. The colors could depend on the mineral content of the rocks and soil nearby. Blue was made in later times out of lapis lazuli, ultramarine, and cobalt, and then later it was made synthetically.

45. C: A pagoda is a multistory tower with multiple eaves, found in South or East Asia. It is usually related to a Buddhist temple. The structure is derived from the stupa of India, which symbolized a sacred mountain. A tall, four-sided stone pillar with a pyramidal top is an obelisk. A small, dome-like structure on top of a building is a cupola. A rectangular terraced temple in ancient Mesopotamia is a ziggurat.

46. C: Although the Classical period of Greek sculpture showed more realistic anatomy, the poses were still stiff and unnatural, as shown with the *Venus de Milo*'s asymmetrical stance. The Hellenistic period of Greek sculpture was the pinnacle of naturalism and expressive movement, as shown in many examples including *Laocoön and His Sons*.

47. A: Outsider art is art created by artists who are self-taught and who work outside of the mainstream art world. Their work may be discovered after their death. Outsider art might be created by people who are mentally ill or by those who are untrained and aspire to create art. Other terms for outsider art include art brut, raw art, naive art, folk art, and marginal art. Folk art can be associated with peasant communities.

48. A: The commodification of art is the creation of artwork into marketable works that can be bought and sold. In the 20th century, art had become a product that involved auction houses, museums, collectors, and galleries. Some art movements began to fight against art becoming a commodity, including performance art, conceptual art, and earth art, which were each time and location specific in their own ways, and they were not able to be bought and sold like paintings and sculptures.

49. D: Thomas Cole, a member of the Hudson River School, painted this landscape titled *Destruction* from *The Course of Empire.* The Hudson River School was a group of American realist artists who painted landscapes from 1820 to 1880. The Cobra Group was a group of Dutch, Danish, and Belgian Expressionists. The Ashcan School were American realist painters who depicted urban life beginning in 1908, and Les Fauves were the artists who created Fauvism.

50. C: Tatting involves using a needle or shuttle to create lace with knots and loops. Tatting can be used to make edging, collars, doilies, and other lace accessories. The technique dates back to the 17th century. Crochet is the technique of making interlocking loops of yarn with a hook. Needlework is any decorative sewing using a needle. Knitting uses needles to create multiple stitches of yarn in a line.

51. D: A pastiche is a work of art created in the style of another artist. It is not a copy of the artist's work, but one with a similar style or motifs. This is different than a fake, in that a fake is attempting to deceive a viewer. A decorative motif based on a palm leaf is a palmette. An artwork created in three panels is a triptych. A small model that is created as a trial sketch before creating it as a larger sculpture is called a bozzetto or a maquette.

52. C: The Fluxus art movement during the 1960s and 1970s focused on conceptual performances and an emphasis on the process rather than the end result. The Fluxus movement contributed new media including intermedia, conceptual art, and video art. Some artists included Nam June Paik and Yoko Ono, and participants in the movement included architects, poets, musicians, designers, writers, and more.

53. B: Gesso is a paint ground that is traditionally white and has pigment, chalk, or gypsum as an ingredient, and it is used to coat a painting surface prior to starting a painting. Gesso can be used to smooth a painting surface because it can be applied in coats and sanded in between coats. It can also be used as a barrier to protect the paint from breaking down the support because oil paints will break down canvas fabric over time.

54. C: An anamorphosis can be a drawing that is viewed with a mirror or lens to change the distorted drawing optically into the normal view. This is often seen as a stretched drawing around a cylindrical vertical mirror, as shown. The artwork has to be laid out in such a way that when reflected in the mirror, the viewer sees it changed back into the normal view. This can also be accomplished with a sculpture that has to be viewed from a certain angle to see the recognizable image.

55. A: The formalism aesthetic theory is the most straightforward for critiquing modern artwork by analyzing the elements and principles, rather than looking for meaning, emotions, or representation within nonrepresentational artwork. By using the formalism aesthetic theory to critique modern artwork, including color field, minimalist, and other movements, the artwork can be assessed by its success at using the elements and principles.

56. A: One of the criticisms of the Minimalist art movement was that it undervalued art in general by blurring the line between art and everyday objects. Minimalist sculpture was too pared down, according to this criticism, and it was too far removed from what was previously considered as art. Another criticism was that it lacked the qualities that people normally expected to see in artwork, lessening the viewer's experience.

57. D: A spandrel is the triangular area between the outer curve of an arch and the framework. The middle part of an entablature, between the cornice and the architrave, is called the frieze. The ornamental molding commonly found on facades is the cornice. This can also be the molding between a ceiling and a wall. A stylized leaf used as a decorative motif in Renaissance, Greek, and Roman architecture and art is an acanthus.

58. B: Isocephaly is a method of portraying the main figures' heads at the same heights in an artwork or sculptural relief, regardless of their posture or action in the scene. This was popular in Classical Greek artwork, and it comes from a Greek word meaning "like-headed." Gisant is a reclined effigy on a tomb. Chinoiserie is a French term for decoration based on Chinese motifs. Squaring is a technique for transferring a smaller drawing to a larger drawing.

59. B: The Christian art from the Eastern Roman Empire beginning in the 5th century is Byzantine art. This style grew out of classical Roman art, and it was mostly concerned with religious expression. Byzantine art showed religious ideas in sculptural, mosaic, and painting forms. The icons, or small portrayals of religious figures including saints, are the best-known form of Byzantine art.

60. C: This painting, *Virgin of the Rocks* by Leonardo da Vinci, uses pyramidal composition, also called triangular composition, which is a method of grouping the figures so they form the outline of a pyramid. This was a popular compositional technique in Renaissance artwork, especially with

Madonna and Child subject artworks, with the Madonna forming the apex of the pyramid or triangle.

61. A: Glazing is a technique that consists of placing thin layers of transparent paint on top of each other. For this to work, the paint must be transparent, not opaque. Of the white pigments listed, the only pigment that is transparent is zinc white. Titanium white, flake white, and Cremnitz white are all opaque pigments with strong covering power, but they would not be suited for the glazing technique.

62. D: The four basic sculpture techniques are carving, assembling, modeling, and casting. Carving involves chipping or cutting away pieces of a larger material, such as stone or marble. Assembling is an additive technique that involves gathering materials and putting them together to form the sculpture. Modeling is another additive technique, involving building up a soft material, sometimes on an armature. Casting involves melting down a material and pouring it into a mold.

63. C: Scumbling is an oil painting technique of applying a thin layer of an opaque color over an area to produce a softened effect. Applying a glaze over a light area to create a shadow is called sfregazzi. Using a tool, such as a paintbrush handle or palette knife, to scratch through a layer of paint while it is still damp, is called sgraffito. Sfumato is creating gradual transitions between dark and light for a smoky effect.

64. A: An aquarelle is another term for a watercolor painting. Aquatint is an etching process that involves using acid to bite into lines and tonal areas on a metal plate, to give the effect of watercolor in the print. An aquamanile is a medieval vessel that is usually made of bronze or brass, and it is in the shape of an animal. An aquagraph is a monoprint technique that uses a water-based medium.

65. B: Realism rejected heightened emotions and exaggerated scenes, preferring to portray accuracy and truth. The realism movement started in the 1850s in France, and it rejected the idea of portraying subjects heroically or sentimentally. Rather, they sought to portray subjects realistically and seriously, bringing attention to all walks of society. Realism rejected the traditions of art and expanded the definition of what was considered art.

66. B: Bauhaus architecture is characterized by, among other things, steel frames, open floor plans, and primary colors. This style developed in 1927 and sought unadorned functionality, focusing on function over form. Enclosed courtyards, arches, domes, and arcades are characteristic of Renaissance architecture. Columns, grandeur of scale, and clean lines are seen in Neoclassical architecture. Horseshoe arches, perforated screens, and geometric designs are common in Islamic architectural designs.

67. D: This artwork, *The Shoots of Autumn Crops* by Zinaida Serebriakova, focuses on rhythm with the repeated element of the rows of crops leading to the horizon. Because the repetition is not uniform, this is not considered a pattern. Balance is the visual weight of parts of in a composition. Contrast is how parts of a composition differ, and emphasis is how an artist brings attention to a certain part of the composition by making it stand out.

68. A: Kinetic art is art that moves, driven by outside forces including the atmosphere, magnets, motors, or other forces. This category includes Alexander Calder's mobiles, which were suspended and moved by the flow of air around them. He also created kinetic sculptures that would move by cranks and motors. His kinetic art was one of the earliest examples of art that departed from the standard idea of static artwork.

69. A: For a tintype, a direct positive image is made on a thin plate of metal, or tin. For the daguerreotype process, an image is created on a silvered copper plate. To create a calotype, an image is created on paper coated in silver iodide. An ambrotype is an image created on a piece of glass. These are all photographic processes that were used prior to film cameras being invented.

70. C: The greenware stage of clay, also called bone dry, is when clay is in its most fragile state. This is when clay has been shaped and dried, but not fired yet. When clay is partially but not completely dried, it is considered leather hard. When clay has been fired once but it is still porous, it is called bisque. This is when glaze would be added. Clay that is still soft and easily worked is considered plastic.

71. B: Dry mounting involves using a uniform coat of adhesive to affix an artwork, photograph, or print to a backing. Once this is done, it is considered permanent and it is not easily removable from the backing. Unless one is using special materials, dry mounting is not considered archival, although it will usually last long enough for most purposes. The materials used for dry mounting can be pricey, and unless someone prefers its specific results, one might prefer to use photo corners or other methods instead.

72. B: If an artist wants to create a loose, sketchy drawing, with sweeping gestures, a soft drawing media would be ideal for this. A Conté crayon, vine charcoal, or soft pastels would all be good choices for this type of drawing because they are all soft media and could be blended easily. A 4H pencil is a hard pencil with a sharp point, which would be better suited for fine-detail work. This hardness of the 4H pencil will make a light mark.

73. B: Sublime in artwork refers to a greatness and magnitude that is difficult for a person to comprehend. Seeing the sublime can make a person feel overwhelmed and feel small in comparison to their surroundings. The sublime brings attention to the beauty of the landscape and the vastness of what surrounds us. It can generate strong feelings inside the viewer, which is what the painters of Romantic landscapes are attempting to evoke.

74. D: Transformation in artwork involves changing an object and presenting it in a new way. Andy Warhol used transformation when he changed everyday objects into artwork by changing the scale, colors, and materials, presenting them as artwork. Juxtaposition is placing an object next to a contrasting object to emphasize it. Using preexisting objects or images with little or no changes is appropriation. Using unusual proportion to call attention to an object is hierarchical proportion.

75. C: Three-point perspective is used to show buildings from above or below. It uses two points along the horizon line, plus a third point above or below depending on how the buildings are being depicted. One-point perspective uses one point along the horizon line. This is often used for roads or railways. Two-point perspective uses two points along the horizon line, and it can have a building directly in front of the viewer.

76. A: For the printmaking process of manière criblée, practiced in the 15th and 16th centuries, the design is punched into a metal plate, creating a white spotted background. A monoprint is made by the artist drawing or painting on a smooth, nonabsorbent surface. For a linocut or woodcut print, material is cut off a sheet of linoleum or wood to create a design. For an etching, lines are cut into a sheet of metal to create the design.

77. A: This sculpture is best described as an open, dynamic form composed of organic shapes. An open form means that this sculpture has inward recesses that the viewer can see through. The dynamic form describes the sense of movement in this sculpture, as opposed to a heavy, static sculpture such as a pyramid or obelisk-type form. The organic shapes are natural, free-flowing shapes, which differ from geometric shapes. This also has interior and exterior contours.

78. B: An armature is the rigid frame that a sculptor might use within a sculpture. This is used for an additive sculpture process, which is when a sculptor adds pieces of material to create a sculpture. This differs from a subtractive method, in which material is removed from a larger piece, such as marble or wood. An armature is used as a foundation around which a malleable material, such as clay, is formed and allowed to dry. The armature is usually made out of metal.

79. C: Composition describes how the artist organizes form in a work of art. This includes where they place shapes, areas of light and dark, the subjects, and more. Composition describes how the artist arranges the elements in their artwork and generally how the artwork is arranged and put together. The presentation of shapes in a work of art is the form. Form can also refer to the three-dimensional shape of a sculptural artwork.

80. D: The canting, also spelled tjanting, is a tool used to draw lines in hot wax on fabric for the batik technique. The word batik is Javanese in origin, and it refers to a technique of wax-resist dyeing. Lines are drawn on fabric in hot wax, and then the wax cools and dries. The fabric is dyed, and the wax is scraped or boiled off. This technique is also used in many other cultures. The canting is a small pen-like instrument with a small reservoir and spout for the wax to flow through.

81. B: The creator of this African mask used the principle of design, pattern, to organize the element of art, line. Pattern is a principle of design that describes the uniform repetition of an element of art. If the repetition was not uniform, it could be described as rhythm instead. The principles of design can be used by the artist to organize the elements of art in an artwork. These lines were carved and painted by the artist to be repeated in a uniform way.

82. A: The image sensor on a digital camera is responsible for converting the information of the image detected by the camera into an electronic signal. The aperture changes the size of the lens opening, which changes the amount of light that can reach the image sensor. The memory card in a digital camera stores the image information, and the size of the memory card can vary. The lens is where light enters a camera.

83. C: When oil paints became the new, popular medium, artists began to find new ways to use their old medium, egg tempera. Some used egg tempera as an underpainting for oil paintings. Others combined an egg yolk and oil emulsion called tempera grassa. Others switched back and forth between both media, and oil paints eventually won out due to their slow-drying qualities and ease of use. Unfortunately, many paintings are now mislabeled and only documented as tempera, with no way to tell for sure whether they are egg tempera or what binder was used.

84. A: An advantage of lossy file compression is that the size of the file is reduced buts the file is still recognizable. This makes the file easier to be emailed or published online. If a file needs to be printed, it must be kept as a high-resolution file and will likely be saved as a lossless file format. It would not be pixelated, and quality would not be lost. The file would still be the same size as when it was created.

85. D: Panel paintings, which consisted of artwork created on either a flat single piece of wood, or pieces of wood joined together, was popular throughout parts of history, including the Middle Ages and the early Renaissance. It fell out of popularity as canvas became a more popular medium. Panels were used to create small icon paintings and larger altarpiece works. They were used for miniatures and illuminated manuscripts. By the first half of the 16th century, canvas took over as a preferred support for painting in Italy.

86. B: In this example of photo retouching, the man was removed from the photograph for political purposes. Early photo retouching was accomplished not with the help of software, but through manipulation of the negative while creating the print. In this example, the man who disappeared had fallen out of favor and was made to "disappear" by the Soviet press. This photograph shows Stalin, in 1920, to the left in the photograph.

87. B: If a critic describes and analyzes art based solely on its context within the art world, they are using the institutional theory of art. This theory is based on art only having value within the context of the art world or the value that museums and galleries give it. The formalism aesthetic theory is based on how an artwork is analyzed just by the elements and principles. The expressionism aesthetic theory looks at the emotions within an artwork, and the deconstruction criticism theory involves finding hidden meanings and implied messages within an artwork.

88. C: Tessellation is a method of tiling a shape with no gaps or cracks in every direction, potentially infinitely. This is a method used often by M.C. Escher, and it is also seen in Islamic tiles on architecture. The unending tile patterns contain geometry and symbolism, as well as botanical themes, and their ability to be repeated in this way suggests infinity. Tessellation can also be seen in quilting, math, wallpaper, and many other patterns.

89. A: A triadic color scheme consists of three colors spaced evenly on a color wheel, forming a triangle. This is a good choice for beginners because it is easy to balance in an artwork. One color plus the two adjacent to its complement makes a split complementary scheme. Three adjacent colors on the color wheel can make an analogous color scheme. Using colors from within the same color family, either warm or cool, can make a warm or a cool color scheme.

90. D: Depending on the size of the sculpture, and the intention of the artist of how it is displayed and viewed, it could be displayed on a pedestal at eye level, on the ground outside or the floor of a museum, or in a glass display case inside a museum or gallery. It is least likely that a stone sculpture would be hung on the wall due to the heaviness of the material and the potential size of the artwork.

91. C: The camera obscura, also known as a pinhole camera, projects an image through a hole in a wall to the other side, but in reverse and inverted. For the image to be clear, the surroundings must be dark. This is sometimes used nowadays to safely get a clear image of an eclipse, without looking directly at the sun. The camera obscura is a predecessor of the camera, and it came before the daguerreotype and the calotype.

92. B: Sprayed paint poses several hazards to the artist, including the inhalation of the solvent and pigments in the sprayed paint and the flammable propane and propellants contained in aerosol spray paints. Different types of sprayed paints can be used depending on the type of artwork that is being created. An artist can use a water-based paint through an airbrush rather than a can of flammable spray paint. Dust is not an issue from a sprayed paint.

93. C: Paint made from pigment added to heated beeswax is called encaustic. This medium was used by the Egyptians, Romans, and Greeks to paint on walls. Some encaustic mixtures also included linseed oil, damar resin, and other types of waxes. Paint made from pigment mixed with gum arabic as a binder is called watercolor. Paint made by mixing pigment with a drying oil, usually linseed oil, is oil paint. Paint made from adding pigment to an acrylic polymer emulsion is called acrylic paint.

94. A: In this list of sizes presented, 10″ × 20″ is not a standard frame size. Using a standard frame size allows an artist to use standard premade sizes of paper that will fit easily into a premade frame without cutting. These can also be used with precut mats, which will also fit into a premade frame. If an artist chooses to work with different sizes of paper or stretch their own canvases, they will have to make their own frames or get their work custom framed, which will increase the cost.

95. D: In an intermittent, or periodic, kiln, the kiln is loaded while it is cool, closed and brought up to its desired temperature, and the ware is fired. Then the kiln is cooled, and the door can be opened and the ware unloaded. There are several types of periodic kilns. In a continuous or tunnel kiln, the kiln is kept at a constant temperature while the ware is loaded into cars and slowly brought through the kiln on rails to be fired.

96. B: This would be considered op art, or optical art, which is a style that relies on optical illusions. Op art manages to use lines and colors on flat planes in such a way that it deceives the eye into thinking that the plane is advancing and receding. In this example, the center of the image appears to recede into the distance, although the artist used only black and white in the artwork. Famous artists who used this style include Victor Vasarely, Bridget Riley, and Wen-Ying Tsai.

97. B: The purpose of applying sizing to a canvas is to protect the fabric canvas from the acidic qualities of the paint. Rabbit-skin glue, created with boiled-down animal collagen, was a traditional sizing used for canvas, but there are store-bought alternatives now. After the sizing has been applied, the canvas is primed by applying gesso or another primer, which is traditionally white and provides the surface upon which the artist will paint.

98. A: Stainless steel was invented in 1913. Bronze has been used as a metal for casting, including the lost wax casting method, for centuries. The oldest known example is 6,000 years old. Other metals have been used in various ways for sculptural techniques and for jewelry making since ancient times. Marble has been used for centuries for sculpture, and stoneware is one of the oldest forms of sculpture.

99. D: Form is the presentation of shapes in an artwork, or its shape in three dimensions. In two-dimensional artwork, form has width and height, but in three-dimensional artwork, it also has depth. In two-dimensional artwork, form can create the illusion of space. Shapes can be geometric or organic, and this applies to either two- or three-dimensional artwork. Form should not be confused with size or shape.

100. C: Hierarchical proportion is a type of proportion that shows the hierarchy that the artist intended in the artwork. In this case, the artist is showing the importance of the central figures over the surrounding figures by portraying them proportionally larger. This method was often used in Egyptian artwork, showing the rulers as being larger than those of lower status. It was also used in Renaissance artwork, showing perceived importance as the artist intended.

Praxis Practice Test #4

1. The artists Man Ray, Marcel Duchamp, and Max Ernst are all associated with which art movement?

    a. Constructivism
    b. Dada
    c. De Stijl
    d. Bauhaus

2. Which of these techniques involves the application of small dots of paint or ink to create patterns or areas of value?

    a. Stippling
    b. Sgraffito
    c. Glazing
    d. Impasto

3. Which of the following best describes one of Ai Weiwei's motivations for creating his *Sunflower Seeds* artwork?

    a. To expose the benefits of the nutrients of sunflower seeds
    b. To create jobs for metalsmiths throughout China who fabricated the seed replicas
    c. To provide a large-scale exhibit for an exhibit hall at the Tate Modern
    d. To comment on China's mass production techniques that process items for the West

4. Which of the following best describes a change from the Classical period to the Hellenistic period of Greek sculpture?

    a. Sculptures were created with a less natural pose.
    b. Sculptures showed a more religious purpose.
    c. Sculptures showed more emotion, energy, and suffering.
    d. Sculptures mainly adorned temples.

5. Which of the following best describes the color scheme of this artwork?

    a. Tetradic
    b. Monochromatic
    c. Analogous
    d. Triadic

6. How did a major medical event affect Chuck Close's subsequent painting career?

    a. Close modified his techniques to accommodate his restrictions.
    b. Close stopped painting and continued to publicize his artwork.
    c. Close turned to other forms of artwork instead of large-format painting.
    d. Close stopped painting and turned to teaching.

7. Which of the following is an ingredient traditionally used by Renaissance painters to seal a canvas?

    a. Tempera
    b. Rabbit-skin glue
    c. Linseed oil
    d. Acrylic

8. Which of the following is NOT a method that is used to create a successful composition in a photograph?

    a. The rule of thirds
    b. Frame within a frame
    c. Boxing it in
    d. The rule of odds

9. Which of the following color schemes was used to create this painting?

    a. Split complementary
    b. Triadic
    c. Complementary
    d. Tetradic

10. Which of the following best describes raku pottery?

    a. A medium-fire clay, often reddish brown in color
    b. A high-fire clay, often thrown on the wheel
    c. A low-fire clay, usually white and impermeable
    d. A low-fire clay, usually hand shaped and porous

11. Which of the following best describes the artist Jean-Michel Basquiat?

    a. He was part of a graffiti duo called SAMO in the 1970s.
    b. He created elaborate collages that depicted Harlem.
    c. He portrayed slavery in the form of life-sized silhouette artwork.
    d. He led a group of artists that began the Minimalist movement.

12. Which of the following color schemes did Vincent van Gogh use to create contrast in this painting?

    a. Analogous
    b. Complementary
    c. Triadic
    d. Tetradic

13. Which of the following was a tenet of Bauhaus design and architecture?

    a. Agility and flexibility.
    b. Form follows function.
    c. Structure should appear married to the ground.
    d. Visual weightlessness.

14. Which one of the following pigments is considered toxic?

    a. Yellow ochre
    b. Burnt umber
    c. Chrome yellow
    d. Cadmium red hue

15. Which of the following best describes a salon-style exhibition?

    a. Artwork is shown in a line at eye level to give each piece equal importance.

    b. Artwork is hung slightly above eye level to prevent the line of sight from being obstructed.

    c. Artwork is hung at and above eye level to show the artists' reputations.

    d. Artwork is hung at, below, and above eye level to maximize the number of artworks shown on a wall.

16. Which of the following is the correct way to write an aspect ratio of a height of 9 and width of 16?

    a. 9:16

    b. 9x16

    c. 16:9

    d. 16x9

17. Which of the following is a term for a preliminary small-scale model created prior to a finished sculpture?

    a. Maquette

    b. Armature

    c. Crucible

    d. Majolica

18. Which of the following describes a characteristic that Egyptian and Mayan pyramids have in common?

    a. A tiered structure

    b. A square base with four sides

    c. An exterior of white limestone

    d. A temple at the top

19. Which of the following describes an advantage of using gouache instead of acrylic paint?

    a. It can be rewet and reworked.

    b. It dries to a gloss finish.

    c. It dries very slowly and can be worked with for long periods of time.

    d. It stays the same color when it dries.

20. What is the difference between PPI and DPI when referring to resolution?

    a. PPI refers to parts per inch on a digital screen, whereas DPI refers to dots per inch on a digital screen.

    b. PPI refers to pixels per inch on a digital screen, whereas DPI refers to dimensions per inch on a printed material.

    c. PPI refers to parts per inch on a digital screen, whereas DPI refers to dimensions per inch on a digital screen.

    d. PPI refers to pixels per inch on a digital screen, whereas DPI refers to dots per inch on a printed material.

21. Which photo editing software filter can be used to achieve the effect in this image?

    a. Emboss
    b. Extrude
    c. Glowing edges
    d. Trace contour

22. Which of the following does NOT describe warp and weft in weaving?

    a. The warp is stretched into place on a loom.
    b. The weft is woven through the warp.
    c. The weft is longitudinal and is held in high tension.
    d. The warp threads must be stronger than the weft threads.

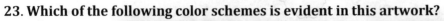
23. Which of the following color schemes is evident in this artwork?

    a. Triadic
    b. Tetradic
    c. Analogous
    d. Complementary

24. In which art period did the artist's status begin to change from that of a skilled laborer to a more respected and admired profession?

    a. Medieval
    b. Baroque
    c. Rococo
    d. Renaissance

25. **Which of the following principles of design does this artwork most focus on?**

a. Balance
b. Pattern
c. Rhythm
d. Unity

26. **How many megabytes are in 1 gigabyte?**

a. 1,000 megabytes
b. 10,000 megabytes
c. 100 megabytes
d. 10 megabytes

27. **Which of the following is the best use of glassine paper?**

a. To create an egg tempera painting
b. To create a detailed pen and ink drawing
c. To place between prints for protection and conservation
d. To cut and glue for collage artwork and assemblages

28. Which of the following describes an analysis of this artwork using the formalism aesthetic theory?

    a. The artist loosely represented a horse as the subject of this artwork.
    b. The artist expressed his feelings through the varied use of lines.
    c. The artist used both primary and secondary colors in this artwork.
    d. The artist used the subject to express his experience with equestrianism.

29. A color harmony that forms a rectangle on a color wheel, with the four corners on two complementary pairs, forms which of the following color harmonies?

    a. Split complementary
    b. Tetradic
    c. Triadic
    d. Analogous

30. Due to an emphasis in African culture on health and strength, many African sculptures portray

    a. Youthfulness
    b. Geometry
    c. Luxury
    d. Magnificence

31. Which of the following art movements was the Art Deco movement influenced by?

    a. Impressionism
    b. Expressionism
    c. Cubism
    d. Realism

32. Which of the following sculptural methods are considered to be additive processes?

    a. Casting, assembling, and carving
    b. Carving, modeling, and assembling
    c. Casting, modeling, and carving
    d. Casting, modeling, and assembling

33. Frida Kahlo was known for using symbolism throughout her many self-portraits. Which of the following themes were common throughout her self-portraits?

    a. Pain and suffering
    b. Freedom and social change
    c. Immigration and migration
    d. Industry and progress

34. Which of the following describes the appeal of automatism to surrealist artists?

    a. It made drawings much quicker to produce.
    b. It brought subconscious thoughts to the surface.
    c. It made use of a newly created type of machine.
    d. It helped artists use materials in a different way.

35. If an artist wanted to cover a background evenly with watercolor, the best method to use would be

    a. Wet on dry
    b. Glazing
    c. Wash
    d. Dry brush

36. Why are some precious metals often mixed with alloys or plated with rhodium?

    a. To improve their appearance
    b. To improve their value
    c. To make them softer
    d. To strengthen the base metal

37. Which of the following is an example of post-and-lintel construction?

    a. Colosseum
    b. Stonehenge
    c. Washington Monument
    d. Taj Mahal

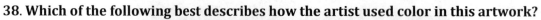
38. Which of the following best describes how the artist used color in this artwork?

a. The monochromatic color scheme simplifies the artwork and helps the viewer focus on the subject.
b. The warmth of the greens and blues creates an inviting and happy scene.
c. The analogous colors help the viewer's eye flow through the scene.
d. The warm colors advance and draw the viewer's eye, whereas the cool colors recede.

39. Which of the following methods were used to create this photograph?

a. Macro
b. Dodge and burn
c. Long exposure
d. Short depth of field

40. Which of the following graphic file formats is an example of lossy compression?

a. .tif
b. .bmp
c. .gif
d. .jpg

41. Which of the following is a reason that canvas needs to be primed prior to being used for oil painting?

a. Without primer, the oil will eventually cause the canvas to deteriorate.
b. Without primer, oil paints cannot be layered as effectively.
c. Oil paints will dry too quickly if the canvas is not primed first.
d. The impasto technique will not work as well without primer.

42. Which of the following color harmonies could consist of green, orange, and purple?

a. Split complementary
b. Triadic
c. Tetradic
d. Analogous

43. Which of the following terms describes a decorative artistic repeating pattern used in Islamic art, which includes rhythmic lines and foliage?

    a. Damask
    b. Paisley
    c. Arabesque
    d. Toile

44. An artist wants to capture a ballet performance while it is in progress. Which of the following methods would work best?

    a. Oil painting
    b. Egg tempera
    c. Gesture drawing
    d. Pointillism

45. Which of the following architectural styles is characterized by tall spires, stained glass, and flying buttresses?

    a. Neoclassical
    b. Baroque
    c. Italianate
    d. Gothic

46. Which of the following is NOT a name for a type of photographic positive created on a thin sheet of metal?

    a. Ambrotype
    b. Tintype
    c. Melainotype
    d. Ferrotype

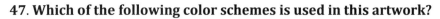

47. Which of the following color schemes is used in this artwork?

    a. Complementary
    b. Triadic
    c. Analogous
    d. Tetradic

48. Which of the following describes the placing of two visual elements next to each other to create the effect of contrast?

    a. Juxtaposition
    b. Appropriation
    c. Transformation
    d. Extrudation

49. If an artist wants to engrave a metal plate for printmaking, which of the following tools would they use?

    a. Brayer
    b. Intaglio
    c. Burin
    d. Gouge

50. With which of the following media would this image have been created on a wood panel, in 1546?

a. Acrylic paint
b. Watercolor
c. Oil pastel
d. Egg tempera

51. Which of the following best describes the purpose of a patron for a Renaissance artist?

a. Patrons purchased artwork that had been created by artists.
b. Patrons encouraged artists to explore new media.
c. Patrons commissioned artists to create artworks.
d. Patrons helped artists find sites to create their sculptures.

52. Which of the following binders is used in watercolor paints?

a. Gum arabic
b. Linseed oil
c. Acrylic polymer
d. Turpentine

53. Which of the following is NOT a name for the printing method in which ink is pressed through a fabric with a squeegee onto a substrate below?

　　a. Silkscreen printing
　　b. Monoprinting
　　c. Screen printing
　　d. Serigraph printing

54. Which of the following stone carving tools would be used for the first "roughing out" step of creating a sculpture?

　　a. A rasp
　　b. A hammer and chisel
　　c. Sandpaper
　　d. A riffler

55. This painting by Vincent van Gogh uses which of the following color schemes?

　　a. Complementary
　　b. Triadic
　　c. Warm
　　d. Analogous

56. Which of the following describes the purpose of photography by Farm Security Administration (FSA) photographers during the Dust Bowl?

a. To create artistic photographs for gallery shows
b. To create propaganda photographs of bread lines
c. To document the need for government assistance for the farmers
d. To discourage families from moving to rural areas

57. Which of the following correctly describes the relationship between an element of art and a principle of design?

a. Movement could be created with wavy lines leading the viewer's eye throughout the piece.
b. Shapes could be created with the use of different lines.
c. Texture could be created by the use of different colors.
d. Unity could be created with a similar pattern used through an artwork.

58. Which of the following gave rise to the portrayal of secular figures in Renaissance era artwork?

a. A lack of funding for artists
b. A surge of humanism
c. The death of the Medici family
d. A stronger devotion to the Catholic Church

59. An artwork is analyzed by the recognition of the subject as being important to the viewer's perception. This artwork is being analyzed using which of the following aesthetic theories of art criticism?

   a. Emotionalism
   b. Formalism
   c. Deconstructivism
   d. Representationalism

60. Which of the following fibers used in fiber arts is NOT a man-made fiber?

   a. Polyester
   b. Rayon
   c. Acrylic
   d. Jute

61. Which of the following is a characteristic that acrylic and oil paints have in common?

   a. Acrylic and oil paint can be applied either thickly or thinly to the canvas.
   b. Acrylic and oil paint both dry slowly and allow time for the artist to continue to work.
   c. Acrylic and oil paint both need turpentine or solvent to clean the brushes.
   d. Acrylic and oil paint can both be thinned with water.

62. In this image, which of the following techniques was used in which the lines intersect as close sets of parallel lines, especially in the darker areas including the underbelly of the horse and the ground on which it stands?

    a. Stippling
    b. Lining
    c. Crosshatching
    d. Contouring

63. Which of the following is the best reason to float-mount a piece of artwork when preparing artwork for hanging?

    a. The artwork goes all the way to the edge of the paper.
    b. The artwork is too big to fit into a frame.
    c. The artwork is too delicate for framing.
    d. The artwork is the wrong size for the frame.

64. How did the advent of acrylic paints help to facilitate the Surrealist technique of grattage?

    a. Artists were able to repaint over acrylic more quickly after it had dried.
    b. Artists were able to scrape and peel acrylic paints from the surface of canvas more easily.
    c. Artists were able to mix more water-based media into acrylic paints.
    d. Artists were able to mix oil-based media with acrylics to get more interesting effects.

65. Which of the following best describes the balance, emphasis, and movement of the *Red Wire Sculpture*?

a. Symmetrically balanced, with movement following the red wire element clockwise, and emphasis on the red wire.
b. Asymmetrically balanced, with movement following the red wire element counterclockwise, and emphasis on the red wire.
c. Symmetrically balanced, with movement following the red wire element clockwise, and emphasis on the black sphere at the bottom.
d. Asymmetrically balanced, with movement following the red wire element counterclockwise, and emphasis on the black sphere at the bottom.

66. Which of the following drawing media was created in response to a shortage of graphite and was created in a range of neutral and sanguine tones?

a. Chalk pastels
b. Charcoal
c. Conté crayons
d. Oil pastels

67. Which of the following types of artwork would have been created by aboriginal artists in Australia?

a. Wooden masks, dot paintings, and obelisks
b. Petroglyphs, dot paintings, and stone arrangements
c. Petroglyphs, stone arrangements, and wooden masks
d. Dot paintings, wooden masks, and temples

68. Which type of symmetry is being used in this mandala?

    a. Radial
    b. Circular
    c. Round
    d. Diverging

69. Which of the following best describes why hinging tissue or mounting corners are used to hold artwork in place when framing, rather than taping the image on all four sides to the mat?

    a. Conservation-grade tape is expensive, and this method uses less tape.
    b. Using hinging tissue or mounting corners allows the framer to reposition the image in case of errors.
    c. The photo corners can be reused on another image, whereas the tape cannot.
    d. When the image, mat, and mat board expand and contract with fluctuations in temperature and moisture, it will not damage the image.

70. Which of the following accurately describes the control of depth of field?

    a. A higher iso setting results in a shallow depth of field.
    b. A wide aperture results in a shallow depth of field.
    c. A higher shutter speed results in a shallow depth of field.
    d. Being closer to the subject results in a large depth of field.

71. Which of the following is NOT a video file format?

    a. .avi
    b. MP4
    c. .wmv
    d. .png

72. Which of the following describes how the artist used the elements and to create emphasis in this artwork?

a. The artist used primary colors to contrast against the neutral colors throughout.
b. The artist used the contrast of warm and cool colors to help the orange buildings stand out against the green.
c. The artist used a wide variety of textures to create emphasis in the artwork.
d. The artist used different values and shapes throughout the artwork to create emphasis in the artwork.

73. Which of the following artists is NOT associated with land art, earthworks, or earth art?

a. Robert Smithson
b. Joseph Beuys
c. Walter De Maria
d. Andy Goldsworthy

74. Which of the following best describes Roy Lichtenstein's motivation for using comic book styling in his artwork?

a. He wanted to close the gap between fine art and commercial art.
b. He was attempting to draw attention to growth in the comic book industry.
c. He hoped to practice creating comic art on a larger scale.
d. He wanted to push the boundaries of copyright by using previously created comic panels.

75. Which of the following scenarios correctly describes the "fat over lean" oil painting principle?

    a. Each layer of paint added needs to have less oil and more solvent than the paint underneath.

    b. The layers of paint closest to the canvas need to be the most flexible.

    c. Each layer of paint added on top needs to be subsequently more flexible than the one underneath.

    d. Each layer of paint should have exactly the same oil-to-medium ratio to prevent cracking.

76. Which of the following describes the biggest risk of dealing with clay dust?

    a. Clay dust is toxic to the touch, and gloves should be worn.

    b. Many types of clay dust can be toxic and can cause respiratory problems if inhaled.

    c. Clay dust can irritate the eyes and skin.

    d. Clay dust can cause the floors to be slick, so nonslip boots should be worn.

77. Which of the following types of printers will produce the best-quality photo prints?

    a. Solid ink

    b. Dot matrix

    c. Laser

    d. Inkjet

78. Which of the following best describes the artist's use of elements to convey space in this painting?

    a. The shapes of the buildings make them appear farther in the distance.

    b. The lines of the trees make them appear closer in space.

    c. The texture of the trees and bushes makes them appear closer in space.

    d. The lighter colors and values recede, whereas the darker colors and values advance in space.

79. If an artist wanted to draw on a lithographic printing plate or stone to create a print, which of the following materials would he or she use?

a. Tusche
b. Gouache
c. Charcoal
d. Conté crayon

80. Which of the following correctly describes the difference between resizing a raster image versus a vector image?

a. Both a raster and a vector image will lose quality if resized.
b. Neither a raster nor a vector image will lose quality if resized.
c. A vector image can be scaled larger indefinitely without loss of quality, whereas a raster image cannot.
d. A raster image can be scaled larger indefinitely without loss of quality, whereas a vector image cannot.

81. Which of the following terms is NOT associated with crochet?

a. Turning chain
b. Purl
c. Slip stitch
d. Front post

82. This sculpture by Michelangelo from 1513 to 1515 was made out of which of the following materials?

a. Marble
b. Wood
c. Bronze
d. Ivory

83. Which of the following correctly describes the purpose of a baren in printmaking?

a. To cut V-shaped grooves into a block of wood or linoleum before inking for printing.
b. To align the paper onto a plate before running the paper and plate through a press.
c. To etch lines into a plate before rubbing ink into the plate for printing.
d. To transfer the ink onto the paper by rubbing the back of the paper against the ink on the plate.

84. Which of the following types of perspective is being shown in this image?

   a. One-point perspective
   b. Two-point perspective
   c. Three-point perspective
   d. Four-point perspective

85. Which of the following describes a strategy for using the golden ratio for creating a pleasing composition?

   a. Divide the image into even rectangles.
   b. Use the "eye of the rectangle" method to position the subject.
   c. Place the subject in the center of the artwork.
   d. Use the background of the image to create a spiral.

86. Which of the following media would an artist use to leave small highlights of white in a watercolor painting?

   a. Burin
   b. Tempera
   c. Liquid frisket
   d. Mahlstick

87. Which of the following does SDS stand for when relating to potentially hazardous art supplies?

   a. Safety Data Summary
   b. Summary of Data Safety
   c. Safety Data Sheet
   d. Safety Data Synopsis

88. Which of the following is the best of example of using appropriation in artwork?

    a. Marcel Duchamp's use of a urinal in his artwork *Fountain*
    b. Kara Walker's use of silhouettes in *Insurrection!*
    c. Yayoi Kusama's use of dots in *Infinity Dots Mirrored Room*
    d. David Smith's use of steel in *CUBI VI*

89. Which of the following types of stone is softer than the others and is therefore often used by beginning sculptors?

    a. Limestone
    b. Soapstone
    c. Alabaster
    d. Marble

90. Which of the following types of paintbrush bristles would be the least likely to be recommended for watercolor painting?

    a. Sable
    b. Squirrel
    c. Synthetic
    d. Hog bristle

91. An artist wants to complete a painting in one sitting, without allowing the paint layers to dry before applying more layers on top. Which of the following techniques would the artist use?

    a. Alla prima
    b. Trompe l'oeil
    c. Sgraffito
    d. Sfumato

92. Which of the following best describes the issue that oiling out is used to repair in an oil painting?

    a. The oil reacts to a medium used in the painting, causing it to crystallize.
    b. The oil runs when the painting is upright, causing the colors to shift.
    c. The oil pools in certain parts of the canvas, giving it an oily appearance.
    d. The oil soaks into the canvas, leaving the painting looking dull in spots.

93. Which of the elements of art would best direct the viewer's eye when representing this road in an artwork?

a. Color
b. Line
c. Texture
d. Value

94. Which of the following best describes the lightfastness of a pigment?

a. The pigment's ability to retain a light value against factors such as heat or water
b. The pigment's color value in relation to other colors
c. The pigment's stability against exposure to light
d. The pigment's resistance to an acidic environment

95. Which of the following best describes the purpose of pyrometric cones in ceramics?

a. To hold ceramic works in place while in the kiln
b. To provide a visual of the level of heat in the kiln
c. To mold ceramic pieces into consistent cone shapes
d. To pierce ceramic works to prevent explosions within the kiln

96. Which of the following fiber art techniques is shown in this image?

a. Knitting
b. Crochet
c. Embroidery
d. Weaving

97. Which of the following materials is NOT comprised of or colored mainly with carbon?

a. Black ink
b. Charcoal
c. Graphite
d. Soft pastels

98. Which of the following terms refers to a quick sketch of a person, which is often used in fashion illustration?

a. Croquis
b. Pochade
c. Plein air
d. Grisaille

99. An artist wants to send in clear, high-resolution images of an artwork to a virtual gallery show. Which of the following file formats should the artist NOT use?

a. .tif
b. .jpg
c. .png
d. .bmp

100. Which of the following accurately reflects what DSLR stands for in camera terminology?

a. Default shield lens recorder
b. Diameter size-lens remake
c. Dynamic screen lens render
d. Digital single-lens reflex

Answer Key and Explanations

1. B: Duchamp, Ray, and Ernst were all associated with the Dada art movement. Dada artists rejected traditional aesthetics and embraced the irrational and absurd. They sought to challenge traditional artwork and protest war and violence. Duchamp's well-known Dada work is called *Fountain*, and it is a urinal signed "R. Mutt." Man Ray was best known for his photography, and Ernst was an innovator in collage and a pioneer of Dada art.

2. A: Stippling is a technique that involves applying small dots of paint or ink to create a pattern or area of value. Stippling balances the negative space between the dots with the positive space of the dots as the artist places them at varying distances. A higher concentration of dots placed close together can create a darker value, whereas dots placed farther apart can create a lighter value. Stippling can also create a texture in artwork.

3. D: Weiwei had many motivations behind creating his *Sunflower Seeds* artwork, but one of these was to comment on China's mass production that benefits Western countries. *Sunflower Seeds* was made of porcelain, not metal, and it was created by many porcelain artists in China. It also represented the small snacks that even the poorest families were able to share when he was growing up in China.

4. C: The Hellenistic period of Greek sculpture showed a departure from the Classical period and a change in aesthetics as sculptors created an increase in emotion and realism. Figures showed more energy, intensity, and suffering. Figures no longer were made for mainly religious reasons, but they became tools to promote politicians. Rather than decorating mainly temples, sculpture was used in public places as well.

5. D: This painting shows a triadic color scheme with the main colors of red, blue, and yellow. A triadic color scheme is evenly spaced around the color wheel. Analogous colors are next to each other on the color wheel. A tetradic color scheme includes two complementary pairs, for example red and green plus blue and orange or yellow and purple plus red and green. Monochromatic would consist of shades and tints of one color.

6. A: In 1988, Chuck Close suffered a spinal artery collapse. He continued his painting career from a wheelchair, and he used modified techniques to continue to create large-format paintings. Rather than his detailed, photorealistic portraits, his new artwork used small abstract elements that visually combined to create a cohesive large portrait. Close overcame his disability and continued his career successfully.

7. B: Rabbit-skin glue was used to coat a canvas to prevent linseed oil from soaking into the fibers and destroying the canvas. This was used in traditional oil painting, and it was created by boiling connective tissue. This was also used as an adhesive. The rabbit-skin glue also helps to tighten the canvas prior to painting on it. Modern painters will usually now use gesso instead of rabbit-skin glue to prepare a canvas.

8. C: Boxing it in is not a compositional technique for photography. The rule of thirds is when a photographer divides an image into three parts both horizontally and vertically, and he or she then places the focal point at one of those places where the lines intersect. A frame within a frame is when the photographer uses an element such as an arch or window to frame the shot and to show depth. The rule of odds is when the photographer uses an odd number of subjects to create a more appealing image.

9. C: This painting by Agnolo Bronzino uses a complementary color scheme, meaning that the main colors in the painting are directly across from each other on the color wheel. The woman's dress is green, whereas the background is red. Red and green are complementary colors, and they help each other stand out and appear vibrant in an artwork. Other complementary combinations are blue and orange or yellow and violet.

10. D: Raku is a Japanese clay that is low fire and usually hand shaped rather than wheel thrown. It is porous when fired, and it is cooled in the open air or in a bin of combustible material after being removed from the hot kiln. Raku is porous after it is fired. The clay has to deal with the significant stress of temperature change. Glazes are suited to low-fire temperatures. Raku pieces are better suited to decorative purposes due to their porous and fragile nature.

11. A: Jean-Michel Basquiat was an artist who first achieved fame as part of a duo called SAMO, who created graffiti in New York City in the 1970s. They used the tag SAMO and wrote short phrases and poems throughout Manhattan. Basquiat collaborated with Al Diaz, and the cryptic messages slowly became noticed throughout the city. Basquiat and Diaz gained notoriety as the work was discovered, and Basquiat delved into other forms of art, continuing his success.

12. B: In this painting, *Café Terrace at Night* (1888), van Gogh used complementary colors to create contrast and make the colors stand out from each other. The bright orange and various blues used throughout this artwork are complementary, lying directly across from each other on a color wheel. Complementary colors create contrast and work to make each other stand out further, adding more visual depth to the artwork. They also make each other appear to glow.

13. B: Walter Gropius and his Bauhaus school are known for the tenet "form follows function," meaning that the shape, or form, of a building should be decided by the purpose it is created for. The phrase is attributed to architect Louis Sullivan, and the idea was later applied not only in architecture but also in product design, furniture design, and software engineering. Bauhaus provided design education that applied to architecture, advertising, typography, and more.

14. C: Chrome yellow is considered toxic because it contains lead, which is a toxic heavy metal. The pigment chrome yellow darkens over time when exposed to air. It is thought that this is why Van Gogh's *Sunflowers* have turned almost an olive green rather than bright yellow. Although cadmium is also toxic, cadmium red hue is a pigment created to mimic the color of cadmium red, without the toxicity.

15. D: In a salon-style exhibition, artwork is hung at, above, and below eye level, sometimes from floor to ceiling, to maximize the number of artworks that can be shown on a wall and to include more artists or artworks. This style was originally established at the Paris Salon in the 1700s. Larger artworks would be hung higher toward the ceiling, and canvases would be tilted slightly toward the floor for better viewing.

16. C: The aspect ratio refers to the proportion of an image or video. An aspect ratio for an image or video is written in a ratio of width to height, or W:H. In this example, the width is 16 and the height is 9, so the correct aspect ratio is 16:9. This is a common aspect ratio for an HDTV display. This ratio means that if the width is divided into 16 parts equally, then the height would be 9 of these parts.

17. A: A Maquette is a small-scale rough draft of a sculpture, which is used so the sculptor can work out issues with materials and see the sculpture from different angles prior to creating the full-scale version. An armature is a support used inside a structure, usually made of metal. A crucible is a container that holds molten metal for some casting methods. Majolica is a type of earthenware glazed in opaque white, which is then painted and fired.

18. B: Egyptian and Mayan pyramids have a square base and four sides. Mayan pyramids are tiered and have steps leading to a temple at the top. Egyptian pyramids are smoother and were covered in white limestone with gold at the top. Egyptian pyramids were much larger than Mayan pyramids, and the Mayan pyramids were built much later. Both were used for tombs.

19. A: Gouache, unlike acrylic paint, can be rewet and reworked once it is dry. It dries to a matte finish, which makes it easier to photograph, and it dries quickly, much like acrylics. Gouache, like acrylics, will dry to a darker shade because the medium in the paint is white and dries to clear, which ends up darkening the paint. Gouache and acrylic have similarities but also several differences.

20. D: Although PPI and DPI both refer to resolution, PPI refers to pixels per inch on a digital screen, whereas DPI refers to dots per inch on a printed material. A pixel is the smallest element of a digital display, and it is used to measure digital resolution. Dots are created on printed material by printers putting tiny dots of cyan, magenta, yellow, and black on the surface. DPI measures the resolution or density of these dots.

21. A: The emboss filter in the Stylize menu of photo editing software will make the image seem stamped or raised, and it will change the color to gray. The glowing edges filter finds the edges in an image and applies a neon glow to them. The edge brightness, width, and smoothness can be adjusted. Extrude will give a three-dimensional feel to the image. Trace contour finds the edges within the image and traces them with outlines, like in a contour map.

22. C: The warp threads are longitudinal and are held in high tension; thus, the warp threads must be stronger than the weft threads to hold up to this tension. The warp threads are stretched into place in a loom, and the weft thread is woven in and out between these warp threads. The weft threads are vertical. A tool called a shuttle can be used to carry the weft thread through the warp threads for weaving.

23. D: This image, *Paul Gachet* by Vincent van Gogh uses a complementary color pattern by using colors on opposing sides of the color wheel. By using cold blues as the predominant color in this work with oranges as a warm contrast, it brings balance and contrast to the image, which serves to reduce tension, while adding to the intensity of the artwork.

24. D: Renaissance artists saw a change in their status from a skilled laborer, much like a carpenter or seamstress, to a more respected and admired profession. Artists in the Renaissance period underwent more formal training than before, first working under an established artist. They were educated and achieved success under the patronage of wealthy families, or patrons, who commissioned their artwork.

25. C: Rhythm is most present throughout this artwork because it consists of repeated elements without a specific order. In this artwork, *Rythme, Joie de vivre* by Robert Delaunay (1930), rhythm is created by repeating the concentric circles throughout the painting in different sizes and different colors. For this to be a pattern, the elements would have to be repeated the same way and in the same order.

26. A: There are 1,000 megabytes (MB) in 1 gigabyte (GB). The storage space on a computer or thumb drive might be measured in GB. A kilobyte is 1,000 bytes, and 1 MB is 1,000,000 bytes or 1,000 kilobytes. 1,000 GB equal 1 terabyte (TB), which might be the size of a hard drive now. These are all standard measures of size for information stored on a computer or other electronic device.

27. C: Glassine is a paper that is used for conservation and preservation. It is thin and glossy, and it is used to interleave between prints or other artwork that is already dry, to protect the artwork from outside elements and each other. It is not very good for drawing or painting due to the slick surface. Glassine is acid free and archival, and it can be found in large sheets that can be used with large works of art.

28. C: To analyze artwork using the formalism aesthetic theory, one would consider the formal elements of the artwork, including the artist's use of elements and principles throughout the work. Analyzing the use of colors would be included in this analysis. This method does not consider the artist's background, emotions, or the narrative behind the work. This method would also not be concerned with the subject of the artwork.

29. B: A tetradic color harmony forms a rectangle on the color wheel, with the corners on two complementary pairs. When using this color harmony, it is best to focus on one color and let the others support it. A split complementary harmony uses one color with two on each side of the one opposite on the color wheel. Triadic uses three evenly spaced colors on the color wheel, and analogous uses colors next to each on the color wheel.

30. A: Because African cultures value fortitude and vitality, they often portray youthfulness in their statues. These values can be traced back to the times when people lived off the land and had to be strong to hunt and survive. Ousmane Sow's contemporary sculptures are a good example of this portrayal of strength, youthfulness, and endurance in the bodies of strong warriors because he builds these structures from a wire frame.

31. C: Art Deco's style was partially derived from the geometry of Cubism, and the colors were influenced by Fauvism. Art Deco also had elements of Constructivism and Futurism. This popular international decorative style spanned the 1920s to the 1940s, and it affected various arts including fashion, architecture, furniture, and graphics. The structure of architecture was based on geometric shapes and incorporated new materials including aluminum, stainless steel, and lacquer.

32. D: Casting, modeling, and assembling are considered to be additive sculptural processes, whereas carving is a subtractive process. Additive processes consist of adding materials to the sculpture to create the final product, whereas subtractive processes consist of subtracting materials. When carving, the sculptor carves or chips away stone or wood to remove pieces of material and arrive at the desired product.

33. A: Frida Kahlo expressed pain and suffering throughout her art career in symbolism in her paintings. She was in an accident when she was young, and she had lifelong medical issues. She had a volatile relationship with artist Diego Rivera and was unable to have children. Many of her paintings dealt with the pain and suffering relating to her medical issues and her relationship with Rivera, as well as her miscarriages.

34. B: Automatism helped artists tap into the subconscious, which appealed to surrealist artists. In theory, artists would let their subconscious dictate the artwork by creating spontaneous artwork directly from the mind. In reality, the artist would still use some degree of intervention to create work that was aesthetically pleasing. This artwork was not representational and was thought to represent underlying dreams and the psyche.

35. C: A wash involves painting a large area in one or two colors, usually for a background or sky area. This can be achieved by using a broad, flat brush and laying wide strokes of color. If using two colors, this can be done as a gradient. A wash can also be done with ink or acrylics, and it will involve using watered-down paint or ink and painting flat areas of this watered-down pigment or ink.

36. D: In jewelry making, base metals are often mixed with alloys or coated with rhodium (such as with white gold) to strengthen the base metal and make it more durable. Gold and silver on their own are soft and malleable, so they are mixed with metals such as nickel, copper, and zinc to improve their strength and durability and improve their ability to hold gemstones. This also makes them easier to work with.

37. B: Stonehenge is an example of post-and-lintel construction. Post-and-lintel is a building system in which a vertical element is supported by horizontal elements. This is also seen in Ancient Greek architecture and in other examples throughout history. Stonehenge is an example of Neolithic architecture from roughly 3000 to 2000 BC. The later development of the arch allowed for larger structures to be supported.

38. D: In this artwork by Paul Gauguin, color is used effectively to help the viewer navigate the scene. Gauguin used warm colors and cool colors strategically to draw the viewer's eye throughout the artwork. The cool colors recede in the background, whereas the warm colors advance and attract the viewer's eye. The main figure in the foreground is wearing red, which becomes the focal point of the artwork due to the color focus.

39. C: Long exposure is a useful technique for night photography. When using this technique, it is best to use a tripod and a wide-angle lens. The aperture should be set small to keep the elements sharp. The photographer can experiment with the times of exposure to capture light trails of stars, traffic lights, and other lights. The resulting effect will show a sharp image of the still elements and longer trails of lights.

40. D: A .jpg file is an example of lossy compression in a graphic file. Lossy compression will result in a significantly reduced file size, but once information is lost from a graphic file, it cannot be retrieved. Lossless compression refers to when files are compressed without losing any quality. Examples of this type of compression include .tif, .gif, .bmp, and .raw. This will result in larger files than lossy compression.

41. A: Without the primer as a buffer between the oil paint and the canvas, the oil will soak into the canvas and eventually eat away at the fibers of the canvas. Acrylic paints, on the other hand, will benefit from a smoother surface that is created by primer, but they do not necessarily need primer in the same way that oils do and will not affect canvas in the same way. Gesso or rabbit-skin glue is often used as a primer on canvas.

42. B: A triadic color harmony consists of three colors spaced evenly apart on the color wheel. One example of this could be orange, green, and purple, the complementary colors. This could also consist of the primary colors, blue, red, and yellow. A triadic color harmony is best used by allowing one color to dominate, and using the other two colors to support or accent the dominating color.

43. C: An arabesque pattern is used often in Islamic art, and it consists of a floral pattern, often with lines and leaves that can be repeated seamlessly. The pattern can be extended infinitely, which starkly contrasts man's finite existence on earth. Islamic art uses these patterns because depicting human and animal forms is discouraged. The word arabesque derives from an Italian word meaning Arabic style.

44. C: Gesture drawing would work best to quickly capture the action of a ballet performance. Oil painting, egg tempera, and Pointillism would all take more time and attention to materials than gesture drawing would. Gesture drawing is meant to capture a figure in motion. The artist can use sweeping motions of the arm to capture the action and direction of the figure, and to make quick studies of figures. These can later be used for more detailed artwork.

45. D: Gothic architecture was a style used in Europe during the 12th to 16th centuries. It was characterized by stained glass windows, vaulted ceilings, flying buttresses, and spires reaching toward the heavens. Gothic architecture was heavily used for churches and cathedrals, and it was used to create some of the most distinctive buildings throughout Europe. This style abandoned the thick walls of Romanesque architecture.

46. A: An ambrotype is a photographic process created on a piece of glass. This process was introduced in the 1850s, and it was followed in the 1860s by the tintype, which is also called a melainotype or ferrotype. A tintype is a direct photographic positive created on a thin sheet of metal, coated with collodion-nitrocellulose. Tintypes were popular in the 1860s and 1870s and are still used as a fine-art medium today.

47. A: This artwork, *Plum Garden at Kamata* by Hiroshige, uses a complementary color scheme. The main colors used are red and green, which are directly across from each other on the color wheel. A triadic color scheme consists of three colors that are spaced evenly around the color wheel. An analogous color scheme uses colors that are next to each other on the color wheel, and tetradic uses colors that form two complementary pairs.

48. A: Juxtaposition describes a method of placing two visual elements next to each other to create a contrasting effect. This can help draw attention to the elements, or it can help one stand out more. Juxtaposing two complementary colors can make the colors stand out and can create a jarring effect. Juxtaposing light and dark values, different textures, and other visually opposing elements can draw the viewer's eye and help the artist create a focal point.

49. C: A burin is an engraving tool used to create lines in a metal plate for printmaking. This type of chisel will often have a mushroom-shaped handle to grip and a steel shaft with a sharp cutting point. It can be used to create a V-shaped groove in a copper plate. Burrs are left behind with the lines, which are then removed with scrapers and burnishers to make a smoother surface.

50. D: This image was created with egg tempera in 1546, and it was painted on wood panel so that the egg tempera would be less likely to crack over time. This was the main painting medium for panels up until the 1500s when oil painting became more popular and began to replace tempera paint. Egg tempera uses the yolk and pigment, and it must be prepared right before using.

51. C: During the Renaissance, patrons would commission artists to create artwork and tell the artists exactly what they wanted created. The wealthy Medici family were responsible for a majority of arts patronage in Florence during this time, supporting artists including Michelangelo, Donatello, and Raphael. They were one of the richest families in Europe, and their patronage allowed artists to work without being concerned about money.

52. A: Gum arabic is the binder that is used to hold watercolor paint together with the pigment. It is also often used in gouache paint and soft pastels. These would all be paints and artists' media that could be water soluble and reworked with water. Linseed oil is more commonly used as an oil painting medium, and acrylic polymers are used in acrylic paints. Oil and acrylic media cannot be rewet or reworked.

53. B: Screen printing is also called serigraph printing, serigraphy, or silkscreen printing. This is a method in which the artist presses ink through a fine mesh screen with a squeegee onto a substrate below, and this can be done onto many surfaces including fabric, walls, and electronics. Monoprinting involves creating a single print, unlike other printmaking methods which can make multiple copies of prints.

54. B: A sculptor will begin "roughing out" their sculpture with some sort of hammer and chisel, which could include a point chisel or a pitching tool combined with a driving hammer. These will be used to break off larger chunks of stone and begin to shape the sculpture. As the sculpture takes shape, the sculptor will take off smaller pieces and refine it, then finally polish it with sandpaper to finish the sculpture.

55. D: This painting uses an analogous color scheme. Analogous colors are next to each other on the color wheel. This helps to create a sense of unity in the artwork. Complementary colors would be across from each other, while a triadic color scheme consists of three colors evenly spaced on the color wheel. Warm colors would include red, yellow, or orange.

56. C: The Farm Security Administration sought to capture the raw emotion of how the Great Depression and the Dust Bowl were affecting the farmers on the Great Plains. This also helped to document the need for government assistance and show the realities of farm life to the city dwellers. While the photographers helped to justify the government assistance, they also showed the strength and determination of those living through the tough times on those farms and rural areas.

57. A: This example is the only one that uses an element of art and a principle of design. In this example, movement is a principle of design, and lines are an element of art. Lines can be used to create movement in the artwork. Shape, texture, and color are elements of art, whereas unity and pattern are principles of design. The principles of design are used to organize the elements of art in an artwork.

58. B: Secular figures were portrayed more in Renaissance art as the artists moved away from sacred figures and humanism was on the rise. This caused a shift away from a focus on the church and more toward classical antiquity and other subjects. Artists began portraying other subjects rather than focusing only on sacred church-based artwork. Humanism focused more on education and the freedom to create.

59. D: The representationalism aesthetic theory states the importance of the viewer understanding and recognizing the subject of an artwork. For example, if an artist wishes to show the subject of a landscape or a person sitting in a chair, he or she will clearly express this subject, and the viewer will be able to clearly receive this message from the artist. The artist will be able to represent the message to the viewer.

60. D: Jute is not a man-made fiber. It is considered a bast fiber, which is a plant fiber collected from the inner bark or skin of a plant. Other examples of bast fibers include hemp, nettle, and ramie. Jute is used to make burlap or gunny cloth; it is a long vegetable fiber that can be spun into strong, coarse threads. The fibers are tan to brown, and it is one of the most affordable fibers used.

61. A: Acrylic and oil paints can be applied thinly, as a glaze, or thickly, in an impasto style. Oil paint will dry very slowly and allow more time for the artist to work with the painting, whereas acrylic will dry more quickly, usually within 24 hours. Oil paints require turpentine or another solvent for cleaning, whereas acrylics can be thinned and cleaned up with water. Oil paint can be thinned with oils including linseed oil if the artist wants to achieve other effects.

62. C: Crosshatching involves creating sets of parallel lines that cross each other at perpendicular angles. Because these lines are created as closer sets, the illusion of a darker value is created. Lines created farther apart can create a lighter value. The artist can control the value throughout their piece by using hatching and crosshatching throughout a drawing or etching and by varying their techniques as well.

63. A: When float-mounting an artwork, the edges of the artwork are not covered by the frame. The artwork is fixed to a piece of matboard, and then the matboard is put into the frame with the edges of the artwork still showing. This is done when the artwork goes all the way to the edge of the paper and the artist does not want to obscure these edges by the frame, which will always hide a little on each edge.

64. B: Grattage is a Surrealist technique used by Max Ernst and Joan Miro, and it involves laying a canvas over a textured object, then scraping and scratching wet paint off of the canvas, which was made easier by using acrylic paints. This would reveal interesting patterns and textures underneath. After using this technique, Ernst would often work further on the canvas, taking cues from the textures and responding to these marks and shapes.

65. D: In this example sculpture titled *Red Wire Sculpture,* the balance is asymmetrical because it is not the same or a mirror image on both sides. The movement is following the red wire counterclockwise, as it tapers off on the left side and points down to the focal point. The emphasis of this sculpture, where the movement leads and which draws the viewer's eye, is on the black sphere at the bottom.

66. C: Conté crayons were created in 1795 by Nicolas-Jacques Conté because of a shortage of graphite. They were comprised of a combination of graphite and clay and were made in a range of neutral colors and sanguine tones. They have been used for sketches, studies, and finished drawings, and they can be used on a middle-value paper, with a white Conté crayon providing the lighter values in the drawing. They are frequently used on rough paper and with a painterly style.

67. B: Aboriginal artists in Australia were known for creating petroglyphs, dot paintings, and stone arrangements, among other types of artwork. They were not known for creating wooden masks or pyramids. Aboriginal or indigenous artists in Australia also created rock paintings, weavings, ceremonial clothing, sand painting, and string art. They often depicted animals and humans in their rock engravings and paintings. Dot paintings are also called papunya art and can depict patterns or representational subjects. They also relied on symbols to relay meaning.

68. A: Radial symmetry is a type of symmetry in which elements are arranged to radiate from the center of the artwork. This falls under the principle of balance and is a type of symmetrical balance. A starfish and a bicycle wheel each have radial symmetry. Mandalas are a common type of artwork that contain radial symmetry. Mandala is a word in Sanskrit that means "circle," and mandalas are often composed of many geometric forms.

69. D: With fluctuations in temperature and humidity, the mat, mounting board, and image will all expand and contract at different rates. If the image is attached securely to the board by means of tape, it can damage the artwork as the different materials expand and contract. If hinging paper tissue or photo corners are used, the image will be safe and will not be damaged by these temperature and humidity fluctuations.

70. B: A camera's aperture, or f-stop setting, is the primary means to determine the depth of field in the photograph. The depth of field shows the range over which the objects appear in focus from the foreground to the background. A wide aperture, which is a lower f-stop value, will create a shallow depth of field in a photograph, whereas a narrow aperture, which is a higher f-stop value, will create a large depth of field, meaning more of the picture will be in focus. The camera's aperture changes the size of the lens opening, which controls the amount of light that passes through the lens and reaches the image sensor. A secondary means of changing depth of field is by moving toward or away from the subject. Moving toward a subject results in a shallower depth of field and moving away from a subject will increase the depth of field.

71. D: Of the listed formats, .png (Portable Network Graphics) is not a video format. The .avi extension stands for Audio Video Interleave. It is an old format that contains audio and video for playback together. The MP4 extension is of high quality and nearly lossless, and it is a popular format for sharing videos across many platforms. The .wmv extension uses Windows Media Video compression and is of lower quality than an MP4 video.

72. B: In this painting by Gustav Klimt, a limited color palette of oranges, greens, and neutrals was used to create contrasts and emphasis throughout the artwork. There is repetition of shapes and values throughout, as well as a repetition of textures in the buildings and trees. The majority of green helps the white and orange to stand out further, and this arrangement leads the viewer's eye around the painting in a circle.

73. B: Robert Smithson, Walter De Maria, and Andy Goldsworthy are all prominent artists in the land art, earthworks, or earth art movements. These movements focus on combining artwork with the landscape and using natural materials from the surrounding area to create the artwork. Other outside materials can also be introduced, although this is not necessary. These works might bring environmental issues to the attention of the viewer, and they are often time sensitive, meaning that time and weather will wear the artwork away. The best-known artist of this genre, Robert Smithson, is known for his work *Spiral Jetty.*

74. A: Roy Lichtenstein spearheaded the Pop Art movement and began to close the gap between commercial art and fine art. He worked as a draftsman prior to his career in art. Lichtenstein used this comic style on a large scale, including the bold lines and colors and the Ben-Day dots, to create a new kind of artwork that was highly criticized for its simplicity and coldness. At the same time, his style is recognized as helping to usher in a new style of artwork.

75. C: The fat over lean principle in oil painting states that the layers of paint with the most fat, or oil, should be on top of the leanest, or those thinned with a medium. The amount of medium, or fat, can be increased as the layers are built up. This causes each subsequent layer to dry more slowly. If a fast-drying layer is placed over a slower drying layer, that fast drying layer will crack when it dries on top of that slow drying layer, which is an undesirable result.

76. B: Although clay dust can be a hazard on the floor and can irritate the eyes and skin, the main issue is that many types of clay dust can be toxic and can cause respiratory problems if inhaled. Silica powder can cause silicosis over time. Inhalation of kaolin powder can cause kaolinosis. Some other materials can contain asbestos, which is also dangerous to inhale. A proper respirator should be used at all times when dealing with clay dust, and the filter cartridges should be changed regularly.

77. D: Although laser printers have come a long way, inkjet printers are still known for producing the best-quality photo images on glossy photo paper. The ink cartridges can be expensive, and the paper trays do not hold a lot of paper. They are also much slower than laser printers. Laser printers are great for printing sharp text in black and white and can print quickly at high volumes. They cannot use a wide variety of paper like inkjet printers can, though.

78. D: This painting is *Les Cyprès à Cagnes* by Claude Monet. He used lighter colors and values to make the background recede, whereas the darker colors and values appear to advance in space. This is referred to as atmospheric or aerial perspective, in which colors and values decrease as objects recede into the distance. Mountains and trees farthest in the distance will appear whitish and hazy in scenes. Here, the sky farthest away behind the building appears the whitest.

79. A: Tusche is a medium created by mixing ink with grease for creating lithographic prints. It can be made into the form of a stick for drawing or into a liquid form. Lithography is a form of printing in which parts of the surface are treated to repel the ink. The process is based on the fact that water and oil do not mix. Offset lithography involves an intermediate sheet, so that the image is reversed twice before it is printed onto a surface.

80. C: A raster image is made of pixels, and scaling it larger will cause it to look pixelated or blurry. More pixels cannot be created to fill it in and make it look clearer. Photographs will be raster images. A vector image, on the other hand, is made up of points and lines that keep track of their positions in relation to each other. These are infinitely scalable up or down without any loss of quality. Fonts and logos will usually be vector graphics.

81. B: Purl is a knitting term, and it is one of the types of knitting stitches made with knitting needles. A turning chain in crochet is a chain stitch used at the beginning of the row to bring the yarn to the correct height to work the rest of the row. A slip stitch is a short stitch used as a technique usually to join two pieces or the end of one part to another. The term front post is used for when stitches are worked into the front of a double or triple crochet stitch instead of into the top.

82. A: Although Michelangelo did occasionally work in other materials, the overwhelming majority of his works were carved from marble, including his most famous works of *David, Pieta, Moses, Bacchus,* and this example, *Dying Slave.* Michelangelo's father owned a marble quarry, and it was here that he began to enjoy working with the medium. He became a master of the medium and created many exquisite, lifelike figures out of this cold, hard substance.

83. D: To use a baren for printmaking, first the plate is inked and a piece of paper is placed on top of the plate. Then the baren is rubbed onto the back of the paper to transfer the ink onto the paper. The baren is usually disc-shaped and flat with a handle. If a baren is not available, a wooden spoon can be used or the bottom of a flat, smooth jar or mug. The print could also be run through a press instead of being printed by hand.

84. A: One-point perspective is when there is only one vanishing point at the horizon line and all lines can be drawn back to this point. In this image, the vanishing point would be in the center of the opposite end of the tunnel. All of the lines of the bricks, columns, and tunnel could be drawn back to that one point. This is often the first type of perspective that is learned to show the illusion of depth for roads and train tracks.

85. B: One way to position a subject in a pleasing way is to use the eye of the rectangle method. First divide the rectangle into four even triangles, and then find the midpoint of these four lines. Each of these four points will be an eye of the rectangle. Many artists have positioned their subjects in this way to create visual interest. Subjects are not usually positioned in the center of an artwork, and artworks are not usually divided into even rectangles unless one is creating a triptych.

86. C: Liquid frisket can be used to leave highlights on a watercolor painting without having to carefully paint around these small highlights. The artist can first paint the liquid frisket onto the white paper and let it dry. He or she can then paint the watercolor painting over the frisket and allow the watercolor to dry as well. The frisket is like a layer of dried rubber, and it can be rubbed off of the paper, revealing the white paper underneath which has been masked off from and protected from the paint.

87. C: SDS stands for Safety Data Sheet (formerly Material Safety Data Sheet [MSDS]), and it contains information on the potentially harmful effects of exposure to materials as well as the proper safety procedures for handling these materials. Not all materials require this information, but when this information is provided in the form of an SDS, it is important to read and understand it so that the risks and procedures for using the materials are fully understood.

88. A: Appropriation involves taking an object or an existing artwork and using it in an artwork after changing the original object very little, if at all. When Marcel Duchamp created *Fountain,* he took an already created urinal and signed "R. Mutt" on the bottom, then he called it his artwork. This is an example of appropriation, and it is also an example of rejecting the traditional ideas of what art is and should be. Duchamp called this concept a readymade.

89. B: Soapstone has a hardness of 2 on the Mohs scale, and it is often used for beginning sculpting. This type of stone is easily worked, but it is not as durable as other stones.

Limestone has a hardness of 4 on the Mohs scale, and along with sandstone, it is categorized as a sedimentary stone. These are both used for sculptures. Alabaster has a hardness of 3 on the Mohs scale, and it can be translucent when carved. Marble is harder, at a 6 on the Mohs scale. Marble has been used frequently since the time of the Classical Period of Greek sculptors.

90. D: Hog bristle brushes are coarse and stiff and are best suited for painting with oils and acrylics. Watercolor paints are usually used with softer bristles, such as those from sable, squirrel, ox, or goat. Kolinsky sable is the most expensive, and it actually comes from the mink. It has the ability to hold a fine point, which is a sought-after characteristic for round watercolor brushes. Synthetic brushes come in a wide range of sizes and prices and can be a good choice for any type of paint.

91. A: Alla prima, which is Italian for "at first," is also known as a wet-on-wet technique or direct painting. This technique is used to complete a painting in a short time, and it lends a freshness and spontaneity to the artwork. This could be useful for a portrait study, so the subject does not have to pose for long periods of time. The technique was pioneered by Frans Hals in the early 1600s. Prior to his new technique, visible brushstrokes were rarely seen in paintings.

92. D: Oiling out involves fixing the issue of the oil soaking into the canvas and giving the painting a dull appearance. This is also known as sinking, when the oil sinks to layers underneath. This can be caused by a surface that is too absorbent, using too much solvent, or not using enough medium in the painting. To use this oiling out technique, the artist can paint a thin coat of medium over the painting to restore the sheen and colors.

93. B: The element of art, line, would best direct the viewer's eye when representing this road in an artwork. A line can be curvy, straight, wavy, broken, or even implied, so the road would not have to be outlined with a border, the lines could be implied. A line can be used to indicate movement in an artwork, and to lead a viewer's eye into the artwork, bringing them toward a focal point.

94. C: Lightfastness is a pigment's chemical permanence against long exposure to light. This is not the same as a pigment's permanence, which is its ability to hold up to other environmental factors such as water, heat, acid, or mold. Different pigments will have different lightfastness ratings, which can be taken into account by the artist and can affect the artist's choice of media. This also affects how the artwork should be displayed and exposed to outside elements.

95. B: Pyrometric cones are devices used when firing ceramic works within a kiln. They are used to visually gauge the heat within the kiln. These cones have a triangular base and are often used in pairs or groups of three depending on the intent of the artist. The cones are made of materials that will bend when they reach a certain temperature, indicating that the kiln has reached that temperature for firing the ceramics.

96. A: This image shows the knitting technique. Knitting involves using knitting needles, usually two, but this can vary depending on the technique. Knitting creates loops of yarn in a tube or a line, and it is often used for textile work. Each new row creates new loops through the prior row of loops. A wide variety of yarn can be used, as well as several different techniques and stitch types. The basic stitches in knitting are called knit and purl.

97. D: Black ink is carbon black suspended in water or a media, and graphite and charcoal are both composed of carbon. Carbon is a nonmetallic chemical element that has been used in many art materials. Soft pastels, however, are made of many different materials including a powdered pigment and a binder. One binder often used is gum arabic, which is also used in watercolors. Gypsum or chalk is also often found in soft pastels.

98. A: Croquis is a term for a quick sketch of a live model. This is a French word that means "sketch." In fashion design, croquis follow specific proportions, usually making the figure nine heads tall to make them appear tall and elongated. Pochade is a term for a quick landscape sketch to capture the fleeting effects of light on the land, and this sketch can be used for a more finished piece later. Plein air refers to painting outdoors, and grisaille is a monochromatic oil painting often used as an underpainting.

99. B: Of the file formats listed, .jpg is a lossy format, meaning that when it is saved and compressed, information in the image is lost. These files are well suited for keeping files small and easy to manage and can look good on the web, but once the information is gone, it cannot be retrieved. The other formats, .tif, .png, and .bmp, are lossless, meaning that they will not lose information when saved. When submitting artwork to be judged, it is best to send the clearest image possible.

100. D: In camera terminology, DSLR stands for digital single-lens reflex. A DSLR camera combines the single-lens reflex camera mechanisms with a digital image sensor. The camera is able to capture images directly as a digital format, rather than onto film. DSLR cameras allow the photographer to see their photographs instantly, and the camera memory is able to hold more images than film cameras could.

Image Credits

Licensed Under CC SA 1.0 (CREATIVECOMMONS.ORG/LICENSES/SA/1.0/)

The San Francisco Opera House (1932) as an example of Beaux Arts Architecture : "San Francisco's War Memorial Opera House, morning October 31, 2005" by Leonard G. (https://commons.wikimedia.org/wiki/File:SFOperaHouse.jpg)

Licensed Under CC BY 2.0 (CREATIVECOMMONS.ORG/LICENSES/BY/2.0/)

An African mask: "African mask" by Peter Rivera (https://commons.wikimedia.org/wiki/File:Africanmask(3146098034).jpg)

Discus Thrower by Myron: "Discus Thrower by Myron" by Erik Drost (https://commons.wikimedia.org/wiki/File:DiscusThrower_by_Myron(5987202412).jpg)

Open Cubes (1991) by Solomon "Sol" LeWitt: "Sculpture White Cubes by Sol LeWitt" by laurenatclemson (https://commons.wikimedia.org/wiki/File:Open_Cubes.jpg)

St. Peter's Basilica: "Saint Peters Basilica" by mtsrs (https://commons.wikimedia.org/wiki/File:St_Peters_Basilica.jpg)

Chinese Porcelain Vase: "Schloss Oranienburg" by Thomas Quine (https://commons.wikimedia.org/wiki/File:LargeMing_vase(22697703003).jpg)

van der Rohe's Seagram Building in New York (1958) as an example of International Style of Architecture: "Seagram Building - NewYork - architects: Mies van der Rohe and Philip Johnson" by Tom Ravenscroft (https://commons.wikimedia.org/wiki/File:Seagram_Building-NewYork-1.jpg)

Licensed Under CC BY 3.0 (CREATIVECOMMONS.ORG/LICENSES/BY/3.0/)

Composition with Red, Yellow, and Blue (1927) by Piet Mondrian: "Piet mondrian, composizione con rosso, giallo e blu, 1927" by Sailko (https://commons.wikimedia.org/wiki/File:Piet_mondrian,_composizione_con_rosso,_giallo_e_blu,_1927.jpg)

Monsieur Fourcade (1889) by Henri de Toulouse-Lautrec: "Monsieur Fourcade" by São Paulo Museum of Art (https://commons.wikimedia.org/wiki/File:Toulouse-Lautrec_-_Monsieur_Fourcade.jpg)

Licensed Under CC BY 4.0 (CREATIVECOMMONS.ORG/LICENSES/BY/4.0/)

A Street art artist: "Keith Haring at work in the Stedelijk Museum in Amsterdam" by Nationaal Archief (https://commons.wikimedia.org/wiki/File:KeithHaring(1986)_original.jpg)

Licensed Under CC BY-SA 2.0 (CREATIVECOMMONS.ORG/LICENSES/BY-SA/2.0/)

An example of Street Art by Banksy: "graffiti by Banksy, Clerkenwell, London" by Justin Cormack (https://commons.wikimedia.org/wiki/File:Banksy_people_Clerkenwell.jpg)

Rock Painting as an example of Aboriginal Art: "Bradshaw rock paintings in the Kimberley region of Western Australia" by TimJN1 (https://commons.wikimedia.org/wiki/File:Bradshaw_rock_paintings2.jpg)

An example of Romanticism art: "Liberty Leading the People by Eugène Delacroix" by Dennis Jarvis (https://commons.wikimedia.org/wiki/File:France-003348-_Liberty_Leading_the_People_(16238458795).jpg)

Amiens Cathedral in France as an example Gothic Architecture: "Cathedral of Amiens front" by cavorite (https://www.flickr.com/photos/cavorite/91687866/)

Example of Haut-Relief sculpture: "Middlesex Guildhall (Westminster)" by Jaume Meneses (https://commons.wikimedia.org/wiki/File:Middlesex_Guildhall_relief_sculpture_(02).jpg)

Spiral Jetty by Robert Smithson: "Spiral Jetty from atop Rozel Point, in mid-April 2005" by Soren Harward (https://commons.wikimedia.org/wiki/File:Spiral-jetty-from-rozel-point.png)

LICENSED UNDER CC BY-SA 2.5 (CREATIVECOMMONS.ORG/LICENSES/BY-SA/2.5/)

Lincoln Memorial in Washington, D.C as an example of Neoclassical Architecture: "The Lincoln Memorial" by David Bjorgen (https://commons.wikimedia.org/wiki/File:Lincoln_Memorial_Close-Up.jpg)

Casa Batlló in Barcelona Spain as an example of Art Nouveau Architecture: "Casa Batlló - Barcellona by Antoni Gaudí" by tato grasso (https://commons.wikimedia.org/wiki/File:CasaBatllo_0056.JPG)

Wright's Frederick C. Robie House in Chicago, Illinois as an example of Prairie School Architecture: "Frank Lloyd Wright's Robie House" by Dan Smith (https://commons.wikimedia.org/wiki/File:Robie_House.jpg)

Process of Screen Printing or Silk Screening : "Screenprinting-example-obin" by Garabombo (https://commons.wikimedia.org/wiki/File:Screenprinting-example-obin.jpg)

LICENSED UNDER CC BY-SA 3.0 (CREATIVECOMMONS.ORG/LICENSES/BY-SA/3.0/)

Color Wheel: "BYR color wheel" by Sakurambo (https://commons.wikimedia.org/wiki/File:BYR_color_wheel.svg)

Embrace IV by Emilia Bayer: "Embrace IV, glased ceramic" by Emilia Bayer (https://commons.wikimedia.org/wiki/File:Embrace_IV,_glased_ceramic.jpg)

Venus of Willendorf as an example of Prehistoric Art: "Venus of Willendorf" by User: MatthiasKabel (https://commons.wikimedia.org/wiki/File:Venus_of_Willendorf_frontview_retouched.jpg)

Lascaux Cave Art in France: "Lascaux 4, Montignac, Dordogne, France." by Traumrune (https://commons.wikimedia.org/wiki/File:Lascaux-IV_26.jpg)

Belief + Doubt (2012) by Barbara Kruger: "Belief+Doubt (2012)" by BettyLondon (https://commons.wikimedia.org/wiki/File:Belief%2BDoubt_(2012).jpg)

Academy of Athens as an example of Classical Architecture: "The upper part of the Greek National Academy building in Athens" by User: Adam Carr (https://commons.wikimedia.org/wiki/File:Pediment.jpg)

Hagia Sophia in Constantinople as an example of Byzantine architecture: "Hagia Sophia" by Arild Vågen (https://commons.wikimedia.org/wiki/File:Hagia_Sophia_Mars_2013.jpg)

An example of Romanesque Architecture: "Romanesque church in Ócsa, Hungary" by Dr. Péter Kaboldy (https://commons.wikimedia.org/wiki/File:Ocsai_templom.JPG)

St. Andrew's Church in Kiev, Ukraine as an example of Rococo Architecture: "St. Andrew's Church in Kyiv in 2012" by Kaiser matias (https://commons.wikimedia.org/wiki/File:St_Andrews_Church_Kyiv_20120620.jpg)

Salt Lake Temple in Utah as an example of Neo-Gothic Architecture: "The Salt Lake Temple of The Church of Jesus Christ of Latter-day Saints in Salt Lake City, Utah, USA" by David Iliff (https://commons.wikimedia.org/wiki/File:Salt_Lake_Temple,_Utah-_Sept_2004.jpg)

The Chrysler Building in New York City (1928) as an example of Art Deco Architecture : "Chrysler Building, New York" by Leena Hietanen (https://commons.wikimedia.org/wiki/File:Chrysler_building-_top.jpg)

Bauhaus Building in Dessau, Germany (1926) as an example of Bauhaus Architecture: "Bauhaus Dessau main building from the south" by Cethegus (https://commons.wikimedia.org/wiki/File:Bauhaus-Dessau_main_building.jpg)

The Rule of Thirds: A compositional technique used in photography: "Site um Bois de Cazier w" by Cornischong (https://commons.wikimedia.org/wiki/File:Site_um_Bois_de_Cazier_w.jpg)

LICENSED UNDER CC BY-SA 4.0 (CREATIVECOMMONS.ORG/LICENSES/BY-SA/4.0/)

An African Mask: "Masque africain" by Roman Bonnefoy (https://commons.wikimedia.org/wiki/File:African_mask2-romanceor.jpg)

Pablo Picasso (1937) by Guernica: "Picasso, Guernica 1937" by Laura Estefania Lopez (https://commons.wikimedia.org/wiki/File:GUERNICA.jpg)

Ka Statue as an example of Egyptian Art: "Ancient Egyptian work in LACMA" by Amr (https://commons.wikimedia.org/wiki/File:Ancient_Egyptian_in_LACMA_05.jpg)

The Trevi Fountain in Rome (1732): "Rome Italy" by Eastcoast20 (https://commons.wikimedia.org/wiki/File:Trevi_Fountain_closeup.jpg)

An example of Greek red figure pottery: "Red-figure pottery drinking vessel" by Zde (https://commons.wikimedia.org/wiki/File:Artisan,_red-figure_pottery,_480_BC,_AshmoleanM,_142566.jpg)

A pilaster as an upright architectural element: "Sydney Town Hall" by Sardaka (https://commons.wikimedia.org/wiki/File:(1)Sydney_Town_Hall_037.jpg)

The Church of the Society of Jesus as an example of Baroque Architecture : "Main altar of the Church of the Society of Jesus (La Iglesia de la Compañía de Jesús)" by Diego Delso (https://commons.wikimedia.org/wiki/File:Iglesia_de_La_Compa%C3%B1%C3%ADa,_Quito,_Ecuador,_2015-07-22,_DD_116-118_HDR.JPG)

Michelangelo's David: "Michelangelo's David" by Livioandronico2013 (https://commons.wikimedia.org/wiki/File:Michelangelo%27s_David_(Foreground).jpg)

The Dinner Party by Judy Chicago: "The Dinner Party" by Donald Woodman (https://commons.wikimedia.org/wiki/File:Judy_Chicago_The_Dinner_Party.jpg)

A DSLR Camera: "Sony DSLR-A700" by Jacek Halicki (https://commons.wikimedia.org/wiki/File:2016_Sony_DSLR-A700.jpg)

Praxis Practice Tests #2, #3, and #4

To take these additional Praxis practice tests, visit our bonus page:
mometrix.com/bonus948/priiartck0134

How to Overcome Test Anxiety

Just the thought of taking a test is enough to make most people a little nervous. A test is an important event that can have a long-term impact on your future, so it's important to take it seriously and it's natural to feel anxious about performing well. But just because anxiety is normal, that doesn't mean that it's helpful in test taking, or that you should simply accept it as part of your life. Anxiety can have a variety of effects. These effects can be mild, like making you feel slightly nervous, or severe, like blocking your ability to focus or remember even a simple detail.

If you experience test anxiety—whether severe or mild—it's important to know how to beat it. To discover this, first you need to understand what causes test anxiety.

Causes of Test Anxiety

While we often think of anxiety as an uncontrollable emotional state, it can actually be caused by simple, practical things. One of the most common causes of test anxiety is that a person does not feel adequately prepared for their test. This feeling can be the result of many different issues such as poor study habits or lack of organization, but the most common culprit is time management. Starting to study too late, failing to organize your study time to cover all of the material, or being distracted while you study will mean that you're not well prepared for the test. This may lead to cramming the night before, which will cause you to be physically and mentally exhausted for the test. Poor time management also contributes to feelings of stress, fear, and hopelessness as you realize you are not well prepared but don't know what to do about it.

Other times, test anxiety is not related to your preparation for the test but comes from unresolved fear. This may be a past failure on a test, or poor performance on tests in general. It may come from comparing yourself to others who seem to be performing better or from the stress of living up to expectations. Anxiety may be driven by fears of the future—how failure on this test would affect your educational and career goals. These fears are often completely irrational, but they can still negatively impact your test performance.

Elements of Test Anxiety

As mentioned earlier, test anxiety is considered to be an emotional state, but it has physical and mental components as well. Sometimes you may not even realize that you are suffering from test anxiety until you notice the physical symptoms. These can include trembling hands, rapid heartbeat, sweating, nausea, and tense muscles. Extreme anxiety may lead to fainting or vomiting. Obviously, any of these symptoms can have a negative impact on testing. It is important to recognize them as soon as they begin to occur so that you can address the problem before it damages your performance.

The mental components of test anxiety include trouble focusing and inability to remember learned information. During a test, your mind is on high alert, which can help you recall information and stay focused for an extended period of time. However, anxiety interferes with your mind's natural processes, causing you to blank out, even on the questions you know well. The strain of testing during anxiety makes it difficult to stay focused, especially on a test that may take several hours. Extreme anxiety can take a huge mental toll, making it difficult not only to recall test information but even to understand the test questions or pull your thoughts together.

Effects of Test Anxiety

Test anxiety is like a disease—if left untreated, it will get progressively worse. Anxiety leads to poor performance, and this reinforces the feelings of fear and failure, which in turn lead to poor performances on subsequent tests. It can grow from a mild nervousness to a crippling condition. If allowed to progress, test anxiety can have a big impact on your schooling, and consequently on your future.

Test anxiety can spread to other parts of your life. Anxiety on tests can become anxiety in any stressful situation, and blanking on a test can turn into panicking in a job situation. But fortunately, you don't have to let anxiety rule your testing and determine your grades. There are a number of relatively simple steps you can take to move past anxiety and function normally on a test and in the rest of life.

Physical Steps for Beating Test Anxiety

While test anxiety is a serious problem, the good news is that it can be overcome. It doesn't have to control your ability to think and remember information. While it may take time, you can begin taking steps today to beat anxiety.

Just as your first hint that you may be struggling with anxiety comes from the physical symptoms, the first step to treating it is also physical. Rest is crucial for having a clear, strong mind. If you are tired, it is much easier to give in to anxiety. But if you establish good sleep habits, your body and mind will be ready to perform optimally, without the strain of exhaustion. Additionally, sleeping well helps you to retain information better, so you're more likely to recall the answers when you see the test questions.

Getting good sleep means more than going to bed on time. It's important to allow your brain time to relax. Take study breaks from time to time so it doesn't get overworked, and don't study right before bed. Take time to rest your mind before trying to rest your body, or you may find it difficult to fall asleep.

Along with sleep, other aspects of physical health are important in preparing for a test. Good nutrition is vital for good brain function. Sugary foods and drinks may give a burst of energy but this burst is followed by a crash, both physically and emotionally. Instead, fuel your body with protein and vitamin-rich foods.

Also, drink plenty of water. Dehydration can lead to headaches and exhaustion, especially if your brain is already under stress from the rigors of the test. Particularly if your test is a long one, drink water during the breaks. And if possible, take an energy-boosting snack to eat between sections.

Along with sleep and diet, a third important part of physical health is exercise. Maintaining a steady workout schedule is helpful, but even taking 5-minute study breaks to walk can help get your blood pumping faster and clear your head. Exercise also releases endorphins, which contribute to a positive feeling and can help combat test anxiety.

When you nurture your physical health, you are also contributing to your mental health. If your body is healthy, your mind is much more likely to be healthy as well. So take time to rest, nourish your body with healthy food and water, and get moving as much as possible. Taking these physical steps will make you stronger and more able to take the mental steps necessary to overcome test anxiety.

Mental Steps for Beating Test Anxiety

Working on the mental side of test anxiety can be more challenging, but as with the physical side, there are clear steps you can take to overcome it. As mentioned earlier, test anxiety often stems from lack of preparation, so the obvious solution is to prepare for the test. Effective studying may be the most important weapon you have for beating test anxiety, but you can and should employ several other mental tools to combat fear.

First, boost your confidence by reminding yourself of past success—tests or projects that you aced. If you're putting as much effort into preparing for this test as you did for those, there's no reason you should expect to fail here. Work hard to prepare; then trust your preparation.

Second, surround yourself with encouraging people. It can be helpful to find a study group, but be sure that the people you're around will encourage a positive attitude. If you spend time with others who are anxious or cynical, this will only contribute to your own anxiety. Look for others who are motivated to study hard from a desire to succeed, not from a fear of failure.

Third, reward yourself. A test is physically and mentally tiring, even without anxiety, and it can be helpful to have something to look forward to. Plan an activity following the test, regardless of the outcome, such as going to a movie or getting ice cream.

When you are taking the test, if you find yourself beginning to feel anxious, remind yourself that you know the material. Visualize successfully completing the test. Then take a few deep, relaxing breaths and return to it. Work through the questions carefully but with confidence, knowing that you are capable of succeeding.

Developing a healthy mental approach to test taking will also aid in other areas of life. Test anxiety affects more than just the actual test—it can be damaging to your mental health and even contribute to depression. It's important to beat test anxiety before it becomes a problem for more than testing.

Study Strategy

Being prepared for the test is necessary to combat anxiety, but what does being prepared look like? You may study for hours on end and still not feel prepared. What you need is a strategy for test prep. The next few pages outline our recommended steps to help you plan out and conquer the challenge of preparation.

STEP 1: SCOPE OUT THE TEST

Learn everything you can about the format (multiple choice, essay, etc.) and what will be on the test. Gather any study materials, course outlines, or sample exams that may be available. Not only will this help you to prepare, but knowing what to expect can help to alleviate test anxiety.

STEP 2: MAP OUT THE MATERIAL

Look through the textbook or study guide and make note of how many chapters or sections it has. Then divide these over the time you have. For example, if a book has 15 chapters and you have five days to study, you need to cover three chapters each day. Even better, if you have the time, leave an extra day at the end for overall review after you have gone through the material in depth.

If time is limited, you may need to prioritize the material. Look through it and make note of which sections you think you already have a good grasp on, and which need review. While you are studying, skim quickly through the familiar sections and take more time on the challenging parts.

Write out your plan so you don't get lost as you go. Having a written plan also helps you feel more in control of the study, so anxiety is less likely to arise from feeling overwhelmed at the amount to cover.

STEP 3: GATHER YOUR TOOLS

Decide what study method works best for you. Do you prefer to highlight in the book as you study and then go back over the highlighted portions? Or do you type out notes of the important information? Or is it helpful to make flashcards that you can carry with you? Assemble the pens, index cards, highlighters, post-it notes, and any other materials you may need so you won't be distracted by getting up to find things while you study.

If you're having a hard time retaining the information or organizing your notes, experiment with different methods. For example, try color-coding by subject with colored pens, highlighters, or post-it notes. If you learn better by hearing, try recording yourself reading your notes so you can listen while in the car, working out, or simply sitting at your desk. Ask a friend to quiz you from your flashcards, or try teaching someone the material to solidify it in your mind.

STEP 4: CREATE YOUR ENVIRONMENT

It's important to avoid distractions while you study. This includes both the obvious distractions like visitors and the subtle distractions like an uncomfortable chair (or a too-comfortable couch that makes you want to fall asleep). Set up the best study environment possible: good lighting and a comfortable work area. If background music helps you focus, you may want to turn it on, but otherwise keep the room quiet. If you are using a computer to take notes, be sure you don't have any other windows open, especially applications like social media, games, or anything else that could distract you. Silence your phone and turn off notifications. Be sure to keep water close by so you stay hydrated while you study (but avoid unhealthy drinks and snacks).

Also, take into account the best time of day to study. Are you freshest first thing in the morning? Try to set aside some time then to work through the material. Is your mind clearer in the afternoon or evening? Schedule your study session then. Another method is to study at the same time of day that you will take the test, so that your brain gets used to working on the material at that time and will be ready to focus at test time.

STEP 5: STUDY!

Once you have done all the study preparation, it's time to settle into the actual studying. Sit down, take a few moments to settle your mind so you can focus, and begin to follow your study plan. Don't give in to distractions or let yourself procrastinate. This is your time to prepare so you'll be ready to fearlessly approach the test. Make the most of the time and stay focused.

Of course, you don't want to burn out. If you study too long you may find that you're not retaining the information very well. Take regular study breaks. For example, taking five minutes out of every hour to walk briskly, breathing deeply and swinging your arms, can help your mind stay fresh.

As you get to the end of each chapter or section, it's a good idea to do a quick review. Remind yourself of what you learned and work on any difficult parts. When you feel that you've mastered the material, move on to the next part. At the end of your study session, briefly skim through your notes again.

But while review is helpful, cramming last minute is NOT. If at all possible, work ahead so that you won't need to fit all your study into the last day. Cramming overloads your brain with more information than it can process and retain, and your tired mind may struggle to recall even previously learned information when it is overwhelmed with last-minute study. Also, the urgent nature of cramming and the stress placed on your brain contribute to anxiety. You'll be more likely to go to the test feeling unprepared and having trouble thinking clearly.

So don't cram, and don't stay up late before the test, even just to review your notes at a leisurely pace. Your brain needs rest more than it needs to go over the information again. In fact, plan to finish your studies by noon or early afternoon the day before the test. Give your brain the rest of the day to relax or focus on other things, and get a good night's sleep. Then you will be fresh for the test and better able to recall what you've studied.

STEP 6: TAKE A PRACTICE TEST

Many courses offer sample tests, either online or in the study materials. This is an excellent resource to check whether you have mastered the material, as well as to prepare for the test format and environment.

Check the test format ahead of time: the number of questions, the type (multiple choice, free response, etc.), and the time limit. Then create a plan for working through them. For example, if you have 30 minutes to take a 60-question test, your limit is 30 seconds per question. Spend less time on the questions you know well so that you can take more time on the difficult ones.

If you have time to take several practice tests, take the first one open book, with no time limit. Work through the questions at your own pace and make sure you fully understand them. Gradually work up to taking a test under test conditions: sit at a desk with all study materials put away and set a timer. Pace yourself to make sure you finish the test with time to spare and go back to check your answers if you have time.

After each test, check your answers. On the questions you missed, be sure you understand why you missed them. Did you misread the question (tests can use tricky wording)? Did you forget the information? Or was it something you hadn't learned? Go back and study any shaky areas that the practice tests reveal.

Taking these tests not only helps with your grade, but also aids in combating test anxiety. If you're already used to the test conditions, you're less likely to worry about it, and working through tests until you're scoring well gives you a confidence boost. Go through the practice tests until you feel comfortable, and then you can go into the test knowing that you're ready for it.

Test Tips

On test day, you should be confident, knowing that you've prepared well and are ready to answer the questions. But aside from preparation, there are several test day strategies you can employ to maximize your performance.

First, as stated before, get a good night's sleep the night before the test (and for several nights before that, if possible). Go into the test with a fresh, alert mind rather than staying up late to study.

Try not to change too much about your normal routine on the day of the test. It's important to eat a nutritious breakfast, but if you normally don't eat breakfast at all, consider eating just a protein bar. If you're a coffee drinker, go ahead and have your normal coffee. Just make sure you time it so that the caffeine doesn't wear off right in the middle of your test. Avoid sugary beverages, and drink enough water to stay hydrated but not so much that you need a restroom break 10 minutes into the test. If your test isn't first thing in the morning, consider going for a walk or doing a light workout before the test to get your blood flowing.

Allow yourself enough time to get ready, and leave for the test with plenty of time to spare so you won't have the anxiety of scrambling to arrive in time. Another reason to be early is to select a good seat. It's helpful to sit away from doors and windows, which can be distracting. Find a good seat, get out your supplies, and settle your mind before the test begins.

When the test begins, start by going over the instructions carefully, even if you already know what to expect. Make sure you avoid any careless mistakes by following the directions.

Then begin working through the questions, pacing yourself as you've practiced. If you're not sure on an answer, don't spend too much time on it, and don't let it shake your confidence. Either skip it and come back later, or eliminate as many wrong answers as possible and guess among the remaining ones. Don't dwell on these questions as you continue—put them out of your mind and focus on what lies ahead.

Be sure to read all of the answer choices, even if you're sure the first one is the right answer. Sometimes you'll find a better one if you keep reading. But don't second-guess yourself if you do immediately know the answer. Your gut instinct is usually right. Don't let test anxiety rob you of the information you know.

If you have time at the end of the test (and if the test format allows), go back and review your answers. Be cautious about changing any, since your first instinct tends to be correct, but make sure you didn't misread any of the questions or accidentally mark the wrong answer choice. Look over any you skipped and make an educated guess.

At the end, leave the test feeling confident. You've done your best, so don't waste time worrying about your performance or wishing you could change anything. Instead, celebrate the successful completion of this test. And finally, use this test to learn how to deal with anxiety even better next time.

> **Review Video: Test Anxiety**
> Visit mometrix.com/academy and enter code: 100340

Important Qualification

Not all anxiety is created equal. If your test anxiety is causing major issues in your life beyond the classroom or testing center, or if you are experiencing troubling physical symptoms related to your anxiety, it may be a sign of a serious physiological or psychological condition. If this sounds like your situation, we strongly encourage you to seek professional help.

Tell Us Your Story

We at Mometrix would like to extend our heartfelt thanks to you for letting us be a part of your journey. It is an honor to serve people from all walks of life, people like you, who are committed to building the best future they can for themselves.

We know that each person's situation is unique. But we also know that, whether you are a young student or a mother of four, you care about working to make your own life and the lives of those around you better.

That's why we want to hear your story.

We want to know why you're taking this test. We want to know about the trials you've gone through to get here. And we want to know about the successes you've experienced after taking and passing your test.

In addition to your story, which can be an inspiration both to us and to others, we value your feedback. We want to know both what you loved about our book and what you think we can improve on.

The team at Mometrix would be absolutely thrilled to hear from you! So please, send us an email at tellusyourstory@mometrix.com or visit us at mometrix.com/tellusyourstory.php and let's stay in touch.

Additional Bonus Material

Due to our efforts to try to keep this book to a manageable length, we've created a link that will give you access to all of your additional bonus material:

mometrix.com/bonus948/priiartck0134